101
German
Verbs

The Art of Conjugation

Rory Ryder

Illustrated by Francisco Garnica

New York   Chicago   San Francisco   Lisbon   London   Madrid   Mexico City
Milan   New Delhi   San Juan   Seoul   Singapore   Sydney   Toronto

Library of Congress Cataloging-in-Publication Data

Ryder, Rory.
    101 German verbs : the art of conjugation / Rory Ryder, Francisco Garnica. —1st ed.
       p.   cm. — (101 verbs)
    Includes indexes.
    ISBN 0-07-149907-5 (alk. paper)
      1. German language—Verb.   2. German language—Textbooks for foreign
speakers.   I. Garnica, Francisco.   II. Title.   III. Title: One hundred and one German
verbs.   IV. Title: One hundred one German verbs.

    PF3271.R93   2008
    438.2'421—dc22
                                    2007031831

1 2 3 4 5 6 7 8 9 10 11 12 13 14 15 16 17 18 19 20 21 22 23   CTP/CTP   0 9 8 7

ISBN 978-0-07-149907-1
MHID   0-07-149907-5

McGraw-Hill books are available at special quantity discounts to use as premiums and sales
promotions, or for use in corporate training programs. For more information, please write to the
Director of Special Sales, Professional Publishing, McGraw-Hill, Two Penn Plaza, New York, NY
10121-2298. Or contact your local bookstore.

Also in this series:
101 English Verbs: The Art of Conjugation
101 French Verbs: The Art of Conjugation
101 Italian Verbs: The Art of Conjugation
101 Spanish Verbs: The Art of Conjugation

This book is printed on acid-free paper.

Contents

How to Use this Book

When learning a language, it is often difficult to remember the words. This does not mean we have totally forgotten them. It just means that we can't recall them at that particular moment. This book is designed to help language learners recall verbs and their conjugations instantly.

Research

Research has shown that one of the most effective ways to remember something is by association. The way the verb (keyword) has been hidden in each illustration to act as a retrieval cue in this book stimulates long-term memory. This method is shown to be seven times more effective than passively reading and responding to a list of verbs and their meanings.

New Approach

Most grammar and verb books relegate the vital task of learning verbs to a black-and-white world of bewildering tables, leaving the student bored and frustrated. *101 German Verbs* is committed to clarifying the importance of this process through stimulating the senses, not by dulling them.

Beautiful Illustrations

The illustrations throughout this book come together to form a story—an approach beyond conventional verb books. To make the most of this book, spend time with each picture to become familiar with everything that is happening. The pictures construct a story involving characters, plots, and subplots, with clues that add meaning to other pictures. Some pictures are more challenging than others, adding to the fun, but more importantly, aiding the memory process.

Keywords

Throughout the book, an infinitive will be referred to as a "keyword" to highlight its central importance in remembering the multiple ways it can be used. Once the keyword is located and a connection with the illustration is made, it is time to learn the colo(u)red tenses.

Colo(u)r-Coded Verb Tables

The verb tables are designed to save learners valuable time by focusing their attention and allowing them to make immediate connections between the subject and the verb. Making this association clear and simple from the beginning gives learners more confidence to start speaking the language.

This book selects the six most commonly used tenses for beginning language learners.

Example Sentences

Each of the 101 conjugation pages contains two example sentences in German, accompanied by their English equivalents. These sentences, loosely inspired by the illustration on the page, show the art of conjugation in practice. The key verb form is colo(u)r-coded to help learners understand the correct selection of tense and subject on the grid.

Verb Indexes

The 101 verb conjugations in this book follow a story line, so are not ordered alphabetically by German infinitive. To look up the page number of a specific verb, use the German Verb Index at the back of the book. In addition to the 101 verbs featured (which appear in blue), a further 150 common German verbs are also listed; these are cross-referenced to verbs that follow the same pattern. To locate a German verb conjugation by English meaning, use the English Verb Index.

Independent Learning

101 German Verbs can be used for self-study or it can be used as a supplement as part of a teacher-led course. Pronunciation of all the verbs and their conjugations (spoken by a native speaker) are available online at: **www.learnverbs.com**.

Master the Verbs

Once you are confident with each tense, congratulate yourself because you have learned over 3,600 verb forms—an achievement that can take years to master!

Meet the Characters

Guten Tag! Ich heiße Paul.

Ich bin zweiundzwanzig Jahre alt. Ich studiere und nebenbei jobbe ich. Ich male gern; ich interessiere mich auch für Physik. Eines Tages werde ich mit einer Erfindung berühmt werden.

Meine Freundin heißt Mimi. Sie feiert gern und mag Abenteuer. Sie ist die schönste Frau der Welt.

Hello, my name is Paul.

I am twenty-two years old. I'm a student and I do odd jobs on the side. I like to paint; I also enjoy physics. One of these days, I will invent something that will make me famous.

My girlfriend's name is Mimi. She likes to party and she likes adventure. She is the most beautiful woman in the world!

Wau, wau! Ich heiße Toby.

Ich bin der einzige blaue Hund der ganzen Welt. Ich renne gern hinter Katzen und Autos her. Aber ich brauche ein liebes Herrchen oder Frauchen.

Woof, Woof! My name is Toby.

I'm the only blue dog in the world. I love to run after cats and cars. But I need a friendly master or mistress.

Hallo! Ich heiße Mimi. Ich sag' Ihnen nicht, wie alt ich bin—das ist ein Geheimnis! Ich bin Modedesignerin. Ich liebe Tiere aber ich besitze keins. Ich gehe gern am Strand spazieren; ich jogge auch gern.

Mein Freund, Paul, ist lieb und witzig und kocht gern!

Hi, my name is Mimi. I won't tell you how old I am—it's a secret! I'm a fashion designer. I love animals, but I don't have a pet. I like walking on the beach; I also like jogging.

My boyfriend, Paul, is kind, funny, and likes to cook!

Grüß Gott! Ich heiße Max, bin erfolgreicher Filmregisseur und passionierter Sammler. Mein Lieblingsort in der Welt ist Las Vegas.

Hello, My name is Max. I'm a successful director, and I like to collect things. My favo(u)rite place in the world is Las Vegas!

The Art of Conjugation

Conjugating a verb requires the ability to first select the correct verb form needed in a sentence. This book makes it as simple as locating a square on a grid. Simply follow these steps:

- Select the appropriate verb (use the Indexes at the back of the book to find the page).
- Select the correct person (see the following list of personal pronouns to help you choose the correct row on the grid).
- Select the correct tense (see the explanations on pages x to xviii to guide you in choosing the correct column).

Select the correct tense ↓

Sub.	Präsens	Plusquam-perfekt	Präteritum	Futur	Konditional	Perfekt
ich	male	hatte gemalt	malte	werde malen	würde malen	habe gemalt
du	malst	hattest gemalt	maltest	wirst malen	würdest malen	hast gemalt
er sie es	malt	hatte gemalt	malte	wird malen	würde malen	hat gemalt
wir	malen	hatten gemalt	malten	werden malen	würden malen	haben gemalt
ihr	malt	hattet gemalt	maltet	werdet malen	würdet malen	habt gemalt
Sie sie	malen	hatten gemalt	malten	werden malen	würden malen	haben gemalt

Select the correct person →

. . . to locate the correct verb form!

The Person of the Verb

To select the correct person, you must know the subject of the verb: who is doing the action. In each conjugation panel throughout the book, there are six rows. Each row corresponds to a *person*. The first column in the panel represents each person by using the following personal pronouns:

Personal Pronouns

ich	*I* (the speaker)
du	*you* (informal singular; used when talking to a friend, a child, a relative, a pet)
er	*he, it* (male person, masculine noun)
sie	*she, it* (female person, feminine noun)
es	*it* (thing, neuter noun)
wir	*we* (includes the speaker)
ihr	*you* (plural informal; used when talking to friends, children, relatives, pets)
Sie	*you* (singular or plural formal; used when talking to stranger[s], superior[s], elder[s])
sie	*they*

Note the following pronoun rules:

- Pronouns can be grouped by person. For example:

    first person: **ich, wir** (includes the speaker or writer)
    second person: **du, ihr** (the person or persons being addressed)
    third person: **er, sie, es** (the person or persons talked about). The third person is also used for nouns or names of people or animals that are subjects of the sentence.

- Pronouns can also be grouped by number:

    singular: **ich, du, er, sie, es** (one single person, animal, or object)
    plural: **wir, ihr, Sie, sie** (more than one person, animal, or object)

Note that the **Sie** form is third person (formal) in German (whereas *you* is second person [whether formal or informal] in English), and is used for both singular as well as plural, though the ending always appears plural.

Verb Tenses and Forms

In addition to knowing the appropriate verb in German (the keyword or infinitive) and the correct person, you also need to select the correct tense. Tenses relate to *time*: when the action or state takes place. And, though there are only three basic time states (past, present, future), there are at least fourteen different tenses in German! But don't worry—many are not frequently used, and this book has selected just six of the most common tenses that you will need.

All six tenses are colo(u)r-coded to help you recognize and learn them. The following pages explain each tense and when it is used, as well as how each of the tenses is formed. While using the conjugation charts in this book to find the correct verb-tense forms, you will notice your knowledge of German grows as you begin to recognize and learn verb patterns—particularly with the conjugations of regular German verbs.

In German, there are two main groups of verbs:

- **weak** verbs
- **strong** verbs

Most weak verbs are regular; they follow predictable patterns. The indicator of a weak verb is that it forms its past tense by adding **-te** to the root (infinitive less **-en**).

Strong verbs are much more complicated. There are seven main classes, in addition to numerous irregular verbs! In the past tenses, strong verbs usually change the vowel in the infinitive stem, as English does in the verb *to give, I gave.*

Note: These types of spelling changes commonly apply in conjugations; in particular, **-e-** is added or omitted to help pronunciation.

Präsens (*Present*)

Equivalent English tenses: Present, present continuous, or present progressive

The present tense of regular verbs is formed by adding the present tense endings to the verb stem. For weak verbs, the verb stem is the infinitive less -en; for strong verbs, there is usually a vowel change.

		Trinken
Präsens	**Ich**	trink e
	Du	trink st
	Er/Sie/Es	trink t
	Wir	trink en
	Ihr	trink t
	Sie/sie	trink en

The present tense is used in German in the following situations:

- for actions going on at the current or present time. In English, the present continuous/progressive is often used (*to be* _____ *ing*).

  *Max **dirigiert** einen Film über deutsche Verbformen.*

  Max is directing a movie about German verb forms.

- for habitual actions; actions that happen regularly, usually, or always.

  *Wenn Toby Durst hat, **trinkt** er Wasser.*

  When Toby is thirsty, he drinks water.

- for actions about to happen in the near future.

  *Ich **suche** zuerst die Taschenlampe.*

  First I am going to look for the flashlight.

- for actions that have already begun and are still going on, particularly after the words **seit** and **seitdem** (*since*).

  *Paul **poliert** seit heute früh die Maschine.*

  Paul has been polishing the machine since early this morning.

- for questions or negatives that use *do* in English.

  *Was **siehst** du, Mimi?*

  What do you see, Mimi?

  *Ich **erinnere mich** nicht.*

  I don't remember.

Plusquamperfekt (*Past Perfect*)

English equivalent also called: Pluperfect
   The past perfect is a compound tense, formed by combining the simple past tense forms of the auxiliary verbs **haben** or **sein** with the past participle of the main verb.

Plusquam- perfekt		Trinken
	Ich	hätte getrunken
	Du	hättest getrunken
	Er/Sie/Es	hätte getrunken
	Wir	hätten getrunken
	Ihr	hättet getrunken
	Sie/sie	hätten getrunken

The majority of German verbs take **haben** as their auxiliary verb, but some (including the following verbs involving motion) take **sein**:

ankommen (to arrive)   **abstürzen** (to crash)
ausgehen (to go out)   **fahren** (to go)
fallen (to fall)   **folgen** (to follow)
gehen (to go, walk)   **kommen** (to come)
reisen (to travel)   **rennen** (to run)
schwimmen (to swim)   **spazieren** (to stroll)
springen (to jump)   **zurückkehren** (to return)

The past perfect tense is used in German in the following situations:

* for describing actions in the past that occurred before other past events, particularly after the word **nachdem** (*after*), before the word **bevor** (*before*, *when*), or before or after the word **als** (*when*).

   Hattest du schon geduscht, als ich anrief?   Had you already showered when I called?

* for describing events in the distant past.

   Die Behörden hatten alles verboten: schwimmen, joggen, ...   The authorities had forbidden everything: swimming, jogging, . . .

xii

Präteritum (*Simple Past*)

Also called: **Imperfekt**. Equivalent English tenses: Imperfect, preterite
The simple past tense is formed by adding the appropriate ending (beginning
-**t**-) to the verb stem.

		Trinken
Präteritum	**Ich**	trank -
	Du	trank st
	Er/Sie/Es	trank -
	Wir	trank en
	Ihr	trank t
	Sie/sie	trank en

The simple past tense is used in German in the following situations:

- to describe actions that happened in the past, particularly in narratives.

Alles, was er schuf, war gut.   **Everything he created was good.**

- to relate events that have already occurred, especially with **haben**, **sein**, and
  the modal verbs.

Ich hoffe, du mochtest das   **I hope you liked the food.**
Essen.

Note: The simple past is more common in written than in spoken German,
though the simple past forms of **haben** (hatte), **sein** (war), and model verbs such
as **können** (könnte), and **mögen** (mochte) are common in speech.

Futur (*Future*)

Also called **Zukunft**. English equivalent also called: Simple future
The future tense is formed by combining the present tense of **werden** with the infinitive.

		Trinken	
Futur	**Ich**	werde	trinken
	Du	wirst	trinken
	Er/Sie/Es	wird	trinken
	Wir	werden	trinken
	Ihr	werdet	trinken
	Sie/sie	werden	trinken

The future is used in German in the following situations:

* for describing actions that will happen in some future time, particularly if no adverb of time is provided.

Ihr werdet genau so malen wie ich!	You are going to paint exactly the way that I do!

* for emphasizing future intentions.

Wir werden rechtzeitig ankommen.	We will (shall) arrive on time.

Note: In German, the present (not future) tense is commonly used to express future meaning, particularly if a time expression is used:

Gleich starten die Läufer.	The runners are about to start.
Morgen schaffe ich die Menschen!	Tomorrow I will create human beings!

Konditional (*Present Conditional*)

Also called **Konjunctiv Futur II**. English equivalent also known as: Future subjunctive II
The conditional tense is formed by combining the subjunctive II form of the auxiliary verb **werden** with the infinitive.

Konditional		Trinken
	Ich	würde trinken
	Du	würdest trinken
	Er/Sie/Es	würde trinken
	Wir	würden trinken
	Ihr	würdet trinken
	Sie/sie	würden trinken

The conditional is used in German in the following situations:

• for softening, or making more polite, a demand or wish.

Ich würde gern selber fahren.   I would like to drive myself.

• for conditional sentences.

Ich würde doch nie im Leben   Of course, I would never lie.
lügen.

• in colloquial speech, for present or future indirect speech (except with auxiliaries, modals).

Sie haben sich gefragt, ob die   They wondered whether the
Polizei kommen würde.   police would come.

Perfekt (*Present Perfect*)

English equivalent also known as: Perfect tense, conversational past

The present perfect is formed by combining the present tense of the auxiliary verb **haben** or **sein** with the past participle of the main verb. The past participle for most verbs is formed by adding the prefix **ge-** and the suffix **-t** or **-en** to the past participle stem. For regular weak verbs, the past participle stem is the same as the infinitive, less **-en**.

		Trinken	
Perfekt	Ich	habe	getrunken
	Du	hast	getrunken
	Er/Sie/Es	hat	getrunken
	Wir	haben	getrunken
	Ihr	habt	getrunken
	Sie/sie	haben	getrunken

The present perfect is used in German in the following situations:

• for actions that happened in the past.

> *Ich habe viele berühmte*
> *Schauspieler dirigiert.*

I have directed a lot of famous actors.

• for completed actions that are referred to in the present.

> *Wir haben schon aufgehört!*

We already quit!

• for questions and negatives about completed actions that use *did* in English.

> *Was hast du mir denn*
> *gebracht?*

What did you bring me?

> *Mimi, gibt es was, was du nicht*
> *gekauft hast?*

Mimi, is there anything you didn't buy?

Note: The present perfect is the standard past tense in spoken German.

Imperativ (*Command*)

English equivalent: Command (imperative mood)

Command forms for du / ihr / Sie are shown in red type below the English verb translation on each conjugation page. The du command form, used to give a command to a single friend, family member, child, or pet, is the same form as the infinitive stem of the verb, to which an -e is sometimes added.

The ihr and Sie command forms are for an order addressed to more than one person, or to a single person in a formal way (such as a teacher, boss, or older person); they are the same as their present tense form.

The du and ihr forms usually don't include the pronoun; the Sie form does, but the subject and verb are inverted.

The imperative mood is used in German for telling someone to do something or not to do something; giving commands, directions, or orders:

Hört bloß auf zu rauchen!	**Just stop smoking!**
Trennen Sie sie, oder sie werden sich umbringen!	**Separate them or they'll kill each other!**

Partizip Präsens (*Present Participle*)

The present participle is shown in olive type below the German infinitive on each conjugation page. It is formed by adding -d to the infinitive. All verbs follow this rule, except **sein** (**seiend**) and **tun** (**tuend**, meaning *doing*). It corresponds to the -*ing* form in English.

The present participle is used in German as an adverb, to describe the manner in which another action is performed:

Tanzend ging ich die Straße entlang.	**I went down the street dancing.**

Note: This form is used much less in German than in English.

Infinitiv (*Infinitive*)

The infinitive is used directly after modal verbs (**dürfen, können, mögen, müssen, sollen, wollen**) without a preposition, and after other verbs followed by prepositions:

Wir müssen unbedingt miteinander sprechen, Mimi!	**We absolutely have to talk to each other, Mimi!**
Hör bitte nicht auf, mich zu küssen.	**Please don't stop kissing me.**

Separable Verbs

Many German verbs contain prefixes, some of which are:

- **inseparable** (including **be-, ent-, er-, ge-, ver-**); these are always written as one word;
- **separable** (including **an-, auf-, ein-, los-, mit-, zurück-, ab-, her-, hin-**);
- and some can be either separable or inseparable (including **durch-, hinter-, über-, um-, unter-, wider-, voll-**).

In many instances (including questions, imperatives, and certain statements), the prefix separates from the verb and is placed at the end of the clause. See example sentences for the following verb conjugations:

#9 **auf-hören** (to quit)   #90 **auf-prallen** (to collide)
#24 **auf-wachen** (to wake up)   #93 **an-zünden** (to light)
#32 **an-kommen** (to arrive)   #97 **auf-nehmen** (to film)
#79 **zurück-kehren** (to return)

Word Order

You will notice throughout this book how German rules on word order impact compound tenses and separable verbs. Here are a few examples:

- Compound tenses consist of more than one part (in this book, the Plusquamperfekt, Futur, Konditional, and Perfekt tenses). In simple sentences, the second part of the verb (the past participle or dependent infinitive) goes at the end of the clause.

Ich habe viele berühmte   I have directed a lot of famous
   Schauspieler dirigiert.   actors.

Ich werde deine Küche   I will always like your cooking!
   immer mögen!

- With subordinate clauses, the entire verb goes at the end of the clause—whether it is a simple verb or compound verb.

Mimi pfiff, während sie den   Mimi whistled as she turned
   Stock drehte.   the stick.

Mimi, gibt es was, was du   Mimi, is there anything you
   nicht gekauft hast?   didn't buy?

- For separable verbs in simple sentences, the separable prefix goes at the end of the main clause. For compound verbs, the prefix is "reattached" to the second part of the verb.

Mimi und Paul ziehen sich für eine Party an.	Mimi and Paul are getting dressed for a party.
Wir haben schon aufgehört.	We already quit!

- For subordinate clauses, the separable prefix also reattaches itself to the verb at the end of the clause.

Als wir heute morgen ausgingen, haben wir an einen solchen Unfall nie erwartet.	When we went out this morning, we never expected an accident like this.

Reflexive Verbs

Some German verbs refer back to the subject of the sentence. English does this, too, for example, as with the English verb *to wash oneself* (*I wash myself, you wash yourself*, etc.). These verbs are called reflexive and use the following reflexive pronouns:

Reflexive Pronouns

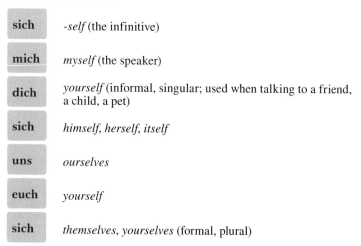

sich	*-self* (the infinitive)
mich	*myself* (the speaker)
dich	*yourself* (informal, singular; used when talking to a friend, a child, a pet)
sich	*himself, herself, itself*
uns	*ourselves*
euch	*yourself*
sich	*themselves, yourselves* (formal, plural)

Check out the example sentences for the following verbs to see how reflexive verbs are conjugated:

#31 **sich anziehen** (to get dressed)
#40 **sich erinnern** (to remember)

Note that some verbs can be both reflexive and non-reflexive, such as:

#30 **sich kämmen** (to comb one's own hair)
kämmen (to comb someone else's hair)

to direct

dirigieren
dirigierend

Sub.	Präsens	Plusquam-perfekt	Präteritum	Futur	Konditional	Perfekt
ich	dirigiere	hatte dirigiert	dirigierte	werde dirigieren	würde dirigieren	habe dirigiert
du	dirigierst	hattest dirigiert	dirigiertest	wirst dirigieren	würdest dirigieren	hast dirigiert
er sie es	dirigiert	hatte dirigiert	dirigierte	wird dirigieren	würde dirigieren	hat dirigiert
wir	dirigieren	hatten dirigiert	dirigierten	werden dirigieren	würden dirigieren	haben dirigiert
ihr	dirigiert	hattet dirigiert	dirigiertet	werdet dirigieren	würdet dirigieren	habt dirigiert
Sie sie	dirigieren	hatten dirigiert	dirigierten	werden dirigieren	würden dirigieren	haben dirigiert

Max dirigiert einen Film über deutsche Verbformen.

Max is directing a movie about German verb forms.

Ich habe viele berühmte Schauspieler dirigiert.

I have directed a lot of famous actors.

1

haben

habend

hab(e)!/habt!/haben Sie!

Sub.	Präsens	Plusquam-perfekt	Präteritum	Futur	Konditional	Perfekt
ich	habe	hatte gehabt	hatte	werde haben	würde haben	habe gehabt
du	hast	hattest gehabt	hattest	wirst haben	würdest haben	hast gehabt
er sie es	hat	hatte gehabt	hatte	wird haben	würde haben	hat gehabt
wir	haben	hatten gehabt	hatten	werden haben	würden haben	haben gehabt
ihr	habt	hattet gehabt	hattet	werdet haben	würdet haben	habt gehabt
Sie sie	haben	hatten gehabt	hatten	werden haben	würden haben	haben gehabt

Andreas **hat** einen grünen Koffer.

Andreas has a green suitcase.

Haben Sie Glück **gehabt**, Andreas?
—Nein!

Did you have any luck, Andreas?
—*No!*

2

to want

woll(e)!/wollt!/wollen Sie!

wollen

wollend

Sub.	Präsens	Plusquam-perfekt	Präteritum	Futur	Konditional	Perfekt
ich	will	hatte gewollt	wollte	werde wollen	würde wollen	habe gewollt
du	willst	hattest gewollt	wolltest	wirst wollen	würdest wollen	hast gewollt
er sie es	will	hatte gewollt	wollte	wird wollen	würde wollen	hat gewollt
wir	wollen	hatten gewollt	wollten	werden wollen	würden wollen	haben gewollt
ihr	wollt	hattet gewollt	wolltet	werdet wollen	würdet wollen	habt gewollt
Sie sie	wollen	hatten gewollt	wollten	werden wollen	würden wollen	haben gewollt

Max **will** nur die teuersten Stühle.

Max only wants the most expensive chairs.

Wir **würden** auch solche Stühle **wollen**.

We would also want chairs like that.

3

können
könnend

to be able to
no commands

Sub.	Präsens	Plusquam-perfekt	Präteritum	Futur	Konditional	Perfekt
ich	kann	hatte gekonnt	konnte	werde können	würde können	habe gekonnt
du	kannst	hattest gekonnt	konntest	wirst können	würdest können	hast gekonnt
er sie es	kann	hatte gekonnt	konnte	wird können	würde können	hat gekonnt
wir	können	hatten gekonnt	konnten	werden können	würden können	haben gekonnt
ihr	könnt	hattet gekonnt	konntet	werdet können	würdet können	habt gekonnt
Sie sie	können	hatten gekonnt	konnten	werden können	würden können	haben gekonnt

Kann ich diesen antiken Stuhl kaufen?

Can I buy this antique chair?

Sie **werden** ihn gleich kaufen **können**.

You'll be able to buy it in a minute.

4

to create
schaffen

Sub.	Präsens	Plusquam-perfekt	Präteritum	Futur	Konditional	Perfekt
ich	schaffe	hatte geschaffen	schuf	werde schaffen	würde schaffen	habe geschaffen
du	schaffst	hattest geschaffen	schufst	wirst schaffen	würdest schaffen	hast geschaffen
er sie es	schafft	hatte geschaffen	schuf	wird schaffen	würde schaffen	hat geschaffen
wir	schaffen	hatten geschaffen	schufen	werden schaffen	würden schaffen	haben geschaffen
ihr	schafft	hattet geschaffen	schuft	werdet schaffen	würdet schaffen	habt geschaffen
Sie sie	schaffen	hatten geschaffen	schufen	werden schaffen	würden schaffen	haben geschaffen

Morgen schaffe ich die Menschen!

Tomorrow I will create human beings!

Alles, was er schuf, war gut.

Everything he created was good.

5

malen

malend

mal(e)!/malt!/malen Sie!

Sub.	Präsens	Plusquam-perfekt	Präteritum	Futur	Konditional	Perfekt
ich	male	hatte gemalt	malte	werde malen	würde malen	habe gemalt
du	malst	hattest gemalt	maltest	wirst malen	würdest malen	hast gemalt
er sie es	malt	hatte gemalt	malte	wird malen	würde malen	hat gemalt
wir	malen	hatten gemalt	malten	werden malen	würden malen	haben gemalt
ihr	malt	hattet gemalt	maltet	werdet malen	würdet malen	habt gemalt
Sie sie	malen	hatten gemalt	malten	werden malen	würden malen	haben gemalt

Ich **male** die Welt so, wie ich sie sehe.

I paint the world the way I see it.

Ihr **werdet** genau so **malen** wie ich!

You are going to paint exactly the way that I do!

6

to dance

tanz(e)!/tanzt!/tanzen Sie!

tanzen

tanzend

Sub.	Präsens	Plusquam-perfekt	Präteritum	Futur	Konditional	Perfekt
ich	tanze	hatte getanzt	tanzte	werde tanzen	würde tanzen	habe getanzt
du	tanzt	hattest getanzt	tanztest	wirst tanzen	würdest tanzen	hast getanzt
er sie es	tanzt	hatte getanzt	tanzte	wird tanzen	würde tanzen	hat getanzt
wir	tanzen	hatten getanzt	tanzten	werden tanzen	würden tanzen	haben getanzt
ihr	tanzt	hattet getanzt	tanztet	werdet tanzen	würdet tanzen	habt getanzt
Sie sie	tanzen	hatten getanzt	tanzten	werden tanzen	würden tanzen	haben getanzt

Mimi tanzt mit dem ganzen Körper.

Mimi dances with her whole body.

Tanzend ging ich die Straße entlang.

I went down the street dancing.

7

lesen

to read

lesend

Sub.	Präsens	Plusquam-perfekt	Präteritum	Futur	Konditional	Perfekt
ich	lese	hatte gelesen	las	werde lesen	würde lesen	habe gelesen
du	liest	hattest gelesen	lasest	wirst lesen	würdest lesen	hast gelesen
er sie es	liest	hatte gelesen	las	wird lesen	würde lesen	hat gelesen
wir	lesen	hatten gelesen	lasen	werden lesen	würden lesen	haben gelesen
ihr	lest	hattet gelesen	last	werdet lesen	würdet lesen	habt gelesen
Sie sie	lesen	hatten gelesen	lasen	werden lesen	würden lesen	haben gelesen

Paul und Mimi **haben** die Speisekarte gemeinsam **gelesen**.

Paul and Mimi read the menu together.

So ein Buch **würdet** ihr nie **lesen**.

You would never read a book like that.

8

Sub.	Präsens	Plusquam-perfekt	Präteritum	Futur	Konditional	Perfekt
ich	höre auf	hatte aufgehört	hörte auf	werde aufhören	würde aufhören	habe aufgehört
du	hörst auf	hattest aufgehört	hörtest auf	wirst aufhören	würdest aufhören	hast aufgehört
er sie es	hört auf	hatte aufgehört	hörte auf	wird aufhören	würde aufhören	hat aufgehört
wir	hören auf	hatten aufgehört	hörten auf	werden aufhören	würden aufhören	haben aufgehört
ihr	hört auf	hattet aufgehört	hörtet auf	werdet aufhören	würdet aufhören	habt aufgehört
Sie sie	hören auf	hatten aufgehört	hörten auf	werden aufhören	würden aufhören	haben aufgehört

Hört bloß **auf** zu rauchen!   Wir **haben** schon **aufgehört**!

Just stop smoking!   *We already quit!*

finden

findend

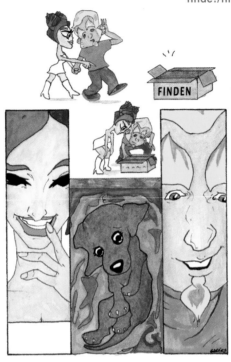

Sub.	Präsens	Plusquam-perfekt	Präteritum	Futur	Konditional	Perfekt
ich	finde	hatte gefunden	fand	werde finden	würde finden	habe gefunden
du	findest	hattest gefunden	fandest	wirst finden	würdest finden	hast gefunden
er sie es	findet	hatte gefunden	fand	wird finden	würde finden	hat gefunden
wir	finden	hatten gefunden	fanden	werden finden	würden finden	haben gefunden
ihr	findet	hattet gefunden	fandet	werdet finden	würdet finden	habt gefunden
Sie sie	finden	hatten gefunden	fanden	werden finden	würden finden	haben gefunden

Was werden Mimi und Paul in dem Karton finden?

What will Mimi and Paul find in the box?

Der kleine, blaue Hund hat sich gefreut, dass sie ihn gefunden hatten!

The little blue dog was happy that they had found him.

10

Sub.	Präsens	Plusquam-perfekt	Präteritum	Futur	Konditional	Perfekt
ich	wachse	war gewachsen	wuchs	werde wachsen	würde wachsen	bin gewachsen
du	wächst	warst gewachsen	wuchsest	wirst wachsen	würdest wachsen	bist gewachsen
er sie es	wächst	war gewachsen	wuchs	wird wachsen	würde wachsen	ist gewachsen
wir	wachsen	waren gewachsen	wuchsen	werden wachsen	würden wachsen	sind gewachsen
ihr	wachst	wart gewachsen	wuchst	werdet wachsen	würdet wachsen	seid gewachsen
Sie sie	wachsen	waren gewachsen	wuchsen	werden wachsen	würden wachsen	sind gewachsen

Toby, der kleine Hund, **wächst** jeden Tag mehr.

Toby, the little dog, grows more every day.

Du **wirst** so lange **wachsen**, bis du so groß bist wie der Baum!

You will keep growing until you are as tall as the tree!

11

bringen

bringend

to bring

bring(e)!/bringt!/bringen Sie!

Sub.	Präsens	Plusquam-perfekt	Präteritum	Futur	Konditional	Perfekt
ich	bringe	hatte gebracht	brachte	werde bringen	würde bringen	habe gebracht
du	bringst	hattest gebracht	brachtest	wirst bringen	würdest bringen	hast gebracht
er sie es	bringt	hatte gebracht	brachte	wird bringen	würde bringen	hat gebracht
wir	bringen	hatten gebracht	brachten	werden bringen	würden bringen	haben gebracht
ihr	bringt	hattet gebracht	brachtet	werdet bringen	würdet bringen	habt gebracht
Sie sie	bringen	hatten gebracht	brachten	werden bringen	würden bringen	haben gebracht

Toby **bringt** mir meine Hausschuhe, und nicht die Zeitung.

Toby brings me my slippers, and not the newspaper.

Was **hast** du mir denn **gebracht**?

What did you bring me?

12

to cook
kochen

koch(e)!/kocht!/kochen Sie!

kochend

Sub.	Präsens	Plusquam-perfekt	Präteritum	Futur	Konditional	Perfekt
ich	koche	hatte gekocht	kochte	werde kochen	würde kochen	habe gekocht
du	kochst	hattest gekocht	kochtest	wirst kochen	würdest kochen	hast gekocht
er sie es	kocht	hatte gekocht	kochte	wird kochen	würde kochen	hat gekocht
wir	kochen	hatten gekocht	kochten	werden kochen	würden kochen	haben gekocht
ihr	kocht	hattet gekocht	kochtet	werdet kochen	würdet kochen	habt gekocht
Sie sie	kochen	hatten gekocht	kochten	werden kochen	würden kochen	haben gekocht

Oh, Mimi, wir haben gestern Abend solche leckeren Sachen gekocht.

Oh, Mimi, we cooked such delicious things last night.

Du kochst ja immer was überraschendes, Paul.

You always cook something surprising, Paul.

13

mögen
mögend

Sub.	Präsens	Plusquam-perfekt	Präteritum	Futur	Konditional	Perfekt
ich	mag	hatte gemocht	mochte	werde mögen	würde mögen	habe gemocht
du	magst	hattest gemocht	mochtest	wirst mögen	würdest mögen	hast gemocht
er sie es	mag	hatte gemocht	mochte	wird mögen	würde mögen	hat gemocht
wir	mögen	hatten gemocht	mochten	werden mögen	würden mögen	haben gemocht
ihr	mögt	hattet gemocht	mochtet	werdet mögen	würdet mögen	habt gemocht
Sie sie	mögen	hatten gemocht	mochten	werden mögen	würden mögen	haben gemocht

Ich hoffe, du **mochtest** das Essen.

I hope you liked the food.

Ich **werde** deine Küche immer **mögen**!

I will always like your cooking!

14

to open
öffne!/öffnet!/öffnen Sie!

öffnen
öffnend

Sub.	Präsens	Plusquam-perfekt	Präteritum	Futur	Konditional	Perfekt
ich	öffne	hatte geöffnet	öffnete	werde öffnen	würde öffnen	habe geöffnet
du	öffnest	hattest geöffnet	öffnetest	wirst öffnen	würdest öffnen	hast geöffnet
er sie es	öffnet	hatte geöffnet	öffnete	wird öffnen	würde öffnen	hat geöffnet
wir	öffnen	hatten geöffnet	öffneten	werden öffnen	würden öffnen	haben geöffnet
ihr	öffnet	hattet geöffnet	öffnetet	werdet öffnen	würdet öffnen	habt geöffnet
Sie sie	öffnen	hatten geöffnet	öffneten	werden öffnen	würden öffnen	haben geöffnet

Paul, warum öffnest du diese Flasche mit den Zähnen?

Paul, why are you opening this bottle with your teeth?

So haben meine Urgroßeltern doch ihre Flaschen geöffnet.

This is how my great-grandparents opened their bottles.

15

trinken

to drink

trinkend

trink(e)!/trinkt!/trinken Sie!

Sub.	Präsens	Plusquam-perfekt	Präteritum	Futur	Konditional	Perfekt
ich	trinke	hatte getrunken	trank	werde trinken	würde trinken	habe getrunken
du	trinkst	hattest getrunken	trankst	wirst trinken	würdest trinken	hast getrunken
er sie es	trinkt	hatte getrunken	trank	wird trinken	würde trinken	hat getrunken
wir	trinken	hatten getrunken	tranken	werden trinken	würden trinken	haben getrunken
ihr	trinkt	hattet getrunken	trankt	werdet trinken	würdet trinken	habt getrunken
Sie sie	trinken	hatten getrunken	tranken	werden trinken	würden trinken	haben getrunken

Wenn Toby Durst hat, trinkt er Wasser.

When Toby is thirsty, he drinks water.

Ich trinke jeden Morgen ein Glas Orangensaft.

Every morning I drink a glass of orange juice.

16

Sub.	Präsens	Plusquam-perfekt	Präteritum	Futur	Konditional	Perfekt
ich	singe	hatte gesungen	sang	werde singen	würde singen	habe gesungen
du	singst	hattest gesungen	sangst	wirst singen	würdest singen	hast gesungen
er sie es	singt	hatte gesungen	sang	wird singen	würde singen	hat gesungen
wir	singen	hatten gesungen	sangen	werden singen	würden singen	haben gesungen
ihr	singt	hattet gesungen	sangt	werdet singen	würdet singen	habt gesungen
Sie sie	singen	hatten gesungen	sangen	werden singen	würden singen	haben gesungen

Paul, du singst unheimlich laut!

Paul, you are singing awfully loud!

Gib uns das Mikrofon und wir werden besser singen.

Give us the microphone and we'll sing better.

schlafen
to sleep

schlafend

schlaf(e)!/schlaft!/schlafen Sie!

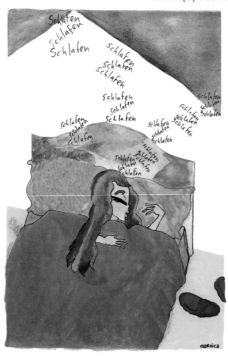

Sub.	Präsens	Plusquam-perfekt	Präteritum	Futur	Konditional	Perfekt
ich	schlafe	hatte geschlafen	schlief	werde schlafen	würde schlafen	habe geschlafen
du	schläfst	hattest geschlafen	schliefst	wirst schlafen	würdest schlafen	hast geschlafen
er sie es	schläft	hatte geschlafen	schlief	wird schlafen	würde schlafen	hat geschlafen
wir	schlafen	hatten geschlafen	schliefen	werden schlafen	würden schlafen	haben geschlafen
ihr	schlaft	hattet geschlafen	schlieft	werdet schlafen	würdet schlafen	habt geschlafen
Sie sie	schlafen	hatten geschlafen	schliefen	werden schlafen	würden schlafen	haben geschlafen

Ich **habe geschlafen**, als du das Bild gemacht hast.

I was sleeping when you took the picture.

Du **wirst** den ganzen Vormittag **schlafen**!
—Ja, ich bin sehr müde.

You're going to sleep all morning!
—Yes, I'm very tired.

18

to go down

geh(e)/geht/gehen Sie hinunter!

hinuntergehen

hinuntergehend

Sub.	Präsens	Plusquam-perfekt	Präteritum	Futur	Konditional	Perfekt
ich	gehe hinunter	war hinunter-gegangen	ging hinunter	werde hinuntergehen	würde hinuntergehen	bin hinunter-gegangen
du	gehst hinunter	warst hinunter-gegangen	gingst hinunter	wirst hinuntergehen	würdest hinuntergehen	bist hinunter-gegangen
er sie es	geht hinunter	war hinunter-gegangen	ging hinunter	wird hinuntergehen	würde hinuntergehen	ist hinunter-gegangen
wir	gehen hinunter	waren hinunter-gegangen	gingen hinunter	werden hinuntergehen	würden hinuntergehen	sind hinunter-gegangen
ihr	geht hinunter	wart hinunter-gegangen	gingt hinunter	werdet hinuntergehen	würdet hinuntergehen	seid hinunter-gegangen
Sie sie	gehen hinunter	waren hinunter-gegangen	gingen hinunter	werden hinuntergehen	würden hinuntergehen	sind hinunter-gegangen

Die Treppe geht in den Keller hinunter.

The stairs go down to the basement.

Max war in den Keller hinuntergegangen.

Max had gone down to the cellar.

sitzen

sitzend

sitz(e)!/sitzt!/sitzen Sie!

Sub.	Präsens	Plusquam-perfekt	Präteritum	Futur	Konditional	Perfekt
ich	sitze	hatte gesessen	saß	werde sitzen	würde sitzen	habe gesessen
du	sitzt	hattest gesessen	saßest	wirst sitzen	würdest sitzen	hast gesessen
er sie es	sitzt	hatte gesessen	saß	wird sitzen	würde sitzen	hat gesessen
wir	sitzen	hatten gesessen	saßen	werden sitzen	würden sitzen	haben gesessen
ihr	sitzt	hattet gesessen	saßt	werdet sitzen	würdet sitzen	habt gesessen
Sie sie	sitzen	hatten gesessen	saßen	werden sitzen	würden sitzen	haben gesessen

Max saß immer sehr gern in seinem
Schaukelstuhl.

*Max always loved to sit in his rocking
chair.*

Wenn Sie lange gesessen haben,
schlafen Sie meistens ein.

*When you have been sitting down for a
long time, you usually fall asleep.*

to play

spielen

spielend

Sub.	Präsens	Plusquam-perfekt	Präteritum	Futur	Konditional	Perfekt
ich	spiele	hatte gespielt	spielte	werde spielen	würde spielen	habe gespielt
du	spielst	hattest gespielt	spieltest	wirst spielen	würdest spielen	hast gespielt
er sie es	spielt	hatte gespielt	spielte	wird spielen	würde spielen	hat gespielt
wir	spielen	hatten gespielt	spielten	werden spielen	würden spielen	haben gespielt
ihr	spielt	hattet gespielt	spieltet	werdet spielen	würdet spielen	habt gespielt
Sie sie	spielen	hatten gespielt	spielten	werden spielen	würden spielen	haben gespielt

Max und seine Kumpels **spielten** die ganze Nacht Karten.

Max and his buddies played cards all night.

Ich **würde** lieber Billard **spielen** als Karten.

I would rather play pool (billiards) than cards.

21

stellen

stellend

stell(e)!/stellt!/stellen Sie!

Sub.	Präsens	Plusquam-perfekt	Präteritum	Futur	Konditional	Perfekt
ich	stelle	hatte gestellt	stellte	werde stellen	würde stellen	habe gestellt
du	stellst	hattest gestellt	stelltest	wirst stellen	würdest stellen	hast gestellt
er sie es	stellt	hatte gestellt	stellte	wird stellen	würde stellen	hat gestellt
wir	stellen	hatten gestellt	stellten	werden stellen	würden stellen	haben gestellt
ihr	stellt	hattet gestellt	stelltet	werdet stellen	würdet stellen	habt gestellt
Sie sie	stellen	hatten gestellt	stellten	werden stellen	würden stellen	haben gestellt

Warum **stellst** du mich vor diese Entscheidung?

Why are you facing me with this decision?

Ich **würde** dir meinen Anwalt gern zur Verfügung **stellen**.

I would be happy to put my lawyer at your disposal.

22

to lose

verlieren

verlierend

Sub.	Präsens	Plusquam-perfekt	Präteritum	Futur	Konditional	Perfekt
ich	verliere	hatte verloren	verlor	werde verlieren	würde verlieren	habe verloren
du	verlierst	hattest verloren	verlorst	wirst verlieren	würdest verlieren	hast verloren
er sie es	verliert	hatte verloren	verlor	wird verlieren	würde verlieren	hat verloren
wir	verlieren	hatten verloren	verloren	werden verlieren	würden verlieren	haben verloren
ihr	verliert	hattet verloren	verlort	werdet verlieren	würdet verlieren	habt verloren
Sie sie	verlieren	hatten verloren	verloren	werden verlieren	würden verlieren	haben verloren

Leider **hat** Max alles **verloren**.

Unfortunately, Max has lost everything.

Hoffentlich **wird** er nie wieder so katastrophal **verlieren**.

Hopefully, he will never lose so disastrously again.

aufwachen

to wake up

aufwachend

wach(e)/wacht/wachen Sie auf!

Sub.	Präsens	Plusquam-perfekt	Präteritum	Futur	Konditional	Perfekt
ich	wache auf	war aufgewacht	wachte auf	werde aufwachen	würde aufwachen	bin aufgewacht
du	wachst auf	warst aufgewacht	wachtest auf	wirst aufwachen	würdest aufwachen	bist aufgewacht
er sie es	wacht auf	war aufgewacht	wachte auf	wird aufwachen	würde aufwachen	ist aufgewacht
wir	wachen auf	waren aufgewacht	wachten auf	werden aufwachen	würden aufwachen	sind aufgewacht
ihr	wacht auf	wart aufgewacht	wachtet auf	werdet aufwachen	würdet aufwachen	seid aufgewacht
Sie sie	wachen auf	waren aufgewacht	wachten auf	werden aufwachen	würden aufwachen	sind aufgewacht

Mimi **wacht** normalerweise früh **auf**.

Mimi usually wakes up early.

Heute Morgen sagt der Wecker:

wach auf!

This morning the alarm clock is saying:

wake up!

24

to run
renn(e)!/rennt!/rennen Sie!

rennen
rennend

Sub.	Präsens	Plusquam-perfekt	Präteritum	Futur	Konditional	Perfekt
ich	renne	war gerannt	rannte	werde rennen	würde rennen	bin gerannt
du	rennst	warst gerannt	ranntest	wirst rennen	würdest rennen	bist gerannt
er sie es	rennt	war gerannt	rannte	wird rennen	würde rennen	ist gerannt
wir	rennen	waren gerannt	rannten	werden rennen	würden rennen	sind gerannt
ihr	rennt	wart gerannt	ranntet	werdet rennen	würdet rennen	seid gerannt
Sie sie	rennen	waren gerannt	rannten	werden rennen	würden rennen	sind gerannt

Mimi, Paul und Toby rannten die Straße entlang.

Mimi, Paul, and Toby were running along the street.

Wer rennt hinter wem her?

Who is running after whom?

25

fallen

to fall

fallend

fall(e)!/fallt!/fallen Sie!

Sub.	Präsens	Plusquam-perfekt	Präteritum	Futur	Konditional	Perfekt
ich	falle	war gefallen	fiel	werde fallen	würde fallen	bin gefallen
du	fällst	warst gefallen	fielst	wirst fallen	würdest fallen	bist gefallen
er sie es	fällt	war gefallen	fiel	wird fallen	würde fallen	ist gefallen
wir	fallen	waren gefallen	fielen	werden fallen	würden fallen	sind gefallen
ihr	fallt	wart gefallen	fielt	werdet fallen	würdet fallen	seid gefallen
Sie sie	fallen	waren gefallen	fielen	werden fallen	würden fallen	sind gefallen

Hilfe! Paul ist in ein Loch gefallen!

Help! Paul has fallen into a hole!

Ich hätte nie gedacht, dass ich in eine Einstiegsschacht fallen würde.

I never thought I would fall into a manhole.

to search, look for

suchen

such(e)!/sucht!/suchen Sie!

suchend

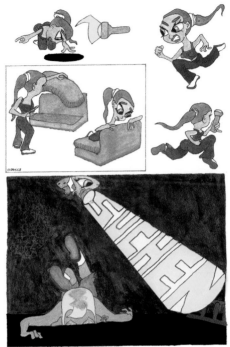

Sub.	Präsens	Plusquam-perfekt	Präteritum	Futur	Konditional	Perfekt
ich	suche	hatte gesucht	suchte	werde suchen	würde suchen	habe gesucht
du	suchst	hattest gesucht	suchtest	wirst suchen	würdest suchen	hast gesucht
er sie es	sucht	hatte gesucht	suchte	wird suchen	würde suchen	hat gesucht
wir	suchen	hatten gesucht	suchten	werden suchen	würden suchen	haben gesucht
ihr	sucht	hattet gesucht	suchtet	werdet suchen	würdet suchen	habt gesucht
Sie sie	suchen	hatten gesucht	suchten	werden suchen	würden suchen	haben gesucht

Ich **suche** zuerste die Taschenlampe.

First I am going to look for the flashlight.

Dann **werde** ich Paul da unten in dem Loch **suchen**.

Then I'll look for Paul down there in the hole.

ausgehen
ausgehend

to go out
geh(e)/geht/gehen Sie aus!

Sub.	Präsens	Plusquam-perfekt	Präteritum	Futur	Konditional	Perfekt
ich	gehe aus	war ausgegangen	ging aus	werde ausgehen	würde ausgehen	bin ausgegangen
du	gehst aus	warst ausgegangen	gingst aus	wirst ausgehen	würdest ausgehen	bist ausgegangen
er sie es	geht aus	war ausgegangen	ging aus	wird ausgehen	würde ausgehen	ist ausgegangen
wir	gehen aus	waren ausgegangen	gingen aus	werden ausgehen	würden ausgehen	sind ausgegangen
ihr	geht aus	wart ausgegangen	gingt aus	werdet ausgehen	würdet ausgehen	seid ausgegangen
Sie sie	gehen aus	waren ausgegangen	gingen aus	werden ausgehen	würden ausgehen	sind ausgegangen

Willst du da unten bleiben oder werden wir heute Abend ausgehen?

Do you want to stay down there, or are we going out tonight?

Als wir heute morgen ausgingen, haben wir an einen solchen Unfall nie erwartet.

When we went out this morning, we never expected an accident like this.

to shower
duschen

dusch(e)!/duscht!/duschen Sie!

duschend

Sub.	Präsens	Plusquam-perfekt	Präteritum	Futur	Konditional	Perfekt
ich	dusche	hatte geduscht	duschte	werde duschen	würde duschen	habe geduscht
du	duschst	hattest geduscht	duschtest	wirst duschen	würdest duschen	hast geduscht
er sie es	duscht	hatte geduscht	duschte	wird duschen	würde duschen	hat geduscht
wir	duschen	hatten geduscht	duschten	werden duschen	würden duschen	haben geduscht
ihr	duscht	hattet geduscht	duschtet	werdet duschen	würdet duschen	habt geduscht
Sie sie	duschen	hatten geduscht	duschten	werden duschen	würden duschen	haben geduscht

Mimi **duscht** jeden Morgen zwanzig Minuten lang.

Mimi showers every morning for twenty minutes.

Hattest du schon **geduscht**, als ich anrief?

Had you already showered when I called?

29

sich kämmen

sich kämmend kämm(e) dich!/kämmt euch!/kämmen Sie sich!

Sub.	Präsens	Plusquam-perfekt	Präteritum	Futur	Konditional	Perfekt
ich	kämme mich	hatte mich gekämmt	kämmte mich	werde mich kämmen	würde mich kämmen	habe mich gekämmt
du	kämmst dich	hattest dich gekämmt	kämmtest dich	wirst dich kämmen	würdest dich kämmen	hast dich gekämmt
er sie es	kämmt sich	hatte sich gekämmt	kämmte sich	wird sich kämmen	würde sich kämmen	hat sich gekämmt
wir	kämmen uns	hatten uns gekämmt	kämmten uns	werden uns kämmen	würden uns kämmen	haben uns gekämmt
ihr	kämmt euch	hattet euch gekämmt	kämmtet euch	werdet euch kämmen	würdet euch kämmen	habt euch gekämmt
Sie sie	kämmen sich	hatten sich gekämmt	kämmten sich	werden sich kämmen	würden sich kämmen	haben sich gekämmt

Mimi **kämmte sich** die langen roten Haare.

Mimi was combing her long red hair.

Ich **kämme** den Hund jeden Abend wenn ich nach Hause komme.

I comb the dog every night when I come home.

to get dressed
sich anziehen

zieh(e) dich/zieht euch/ziehen Sie sich an!

sich anziehend

Sub.	Präsens	Plusquam-perfekt	Präteritum	Futur	Konditional	Perfekt
ich	ziehe mich an	hatte mich angezogen	zog mich an	werde mich anziehen	würde mich anziehen	habe mich angezogen
du	ziehst dich an	hattest dich angezogen	zogst dich an	wirst dich anziehen	würdest dich anziehen	hast dich angezogen
er sie es	zieht sich an	hatte sich angezogen	zog sich an	wird sich anziehen	würde sich anziehen	hat sich angezogen
wir	ziehen uns an	hatten uns angezogen	zogen uns an	werden uns anziehen	würden uns anziehen	haben uns angezogen
ihr	zieht euch an	hattet euch angezogen	zogt euch an	werdet euch anziehen	würdet euch anziehen	habt euch angezogen
Sie sie	ziehen sich an	hatten sich angezogen	zogen sich an	werden sich anziehen	würden sich anziehen	haben sich angezogen

Mimi und Paul **ziehen sich** für eine Party **an**.

Mimi and Paul are getting dressed for a party.

Sogar Toby **zieht sich** gerne schick **an**.

Even Toby likes to dress up.

31

ankommen

to arrive

ankommend

komm(e)/kommt/kommen Sie an!

Sub.	Präsens	Plusquam-perfekt	Präteritum	Futur	Konditional	Perfekt
ich	komme an	war angekommen	kam an	werde ankommen	würde ankommen	bin angekommen
du	kommst an	warst angekommen	kamst an	wirst ankommen	würdest ankommen	bist angekommen
er sie es	kommt an	war angekommen	kam an	wird ankommen	würde ankommen	ist angekommen
wir	kommen an	waren angekommen	kamen an	werden ankommen	würden ankommen	sind angekommen
ihr	kommt an	wart angekommen	kamt an	werdet ankommen	würdet ankommen	seid angekommen
Sie sie	kommen an	waren angekommen	kamen an	werden ankommen	würden ankommen	sind angekommen

Wir **werden** rechtzeitig **ankommen**.

We will (shall) arrive on time.

Sie **sind** erst um 9 Uhr abends **angekommen**.

They didn't arrive until 9 o'clock.

to see

sehen

sehend

Sub.	Präsens	Plusquam-perfekt	Präteritum	Futur	Konditional	Perfekt
ich	sehe	hatte gesehen	sah	werde sehen	würde sehen	habe gesehen
du	siehst	hattest gesehen	sahst	wirst sehen	würdest sehen	hast gesehen
er sie es	sieht	hatte gesehen	sah	wird sehen	würde sehen	hat gesehen
wir	sehen	hatten gesehen	sahen	werden sehen	würden sehen	haben gesehen
ihr	seht	hattet gesehen	saht	werdet sehen	würdet sehen	habt gesehen
Sie sie	sehen	hatten gesehen	sahen	werden sehen	würden sehen	haben gesehen

Was siehst du, Mimi?

What do you see, Mimi?

Sie sah, wie Paul von anderen Frauen umgeben wurde.

She saw Paul surrounded by other women.

33

schreien

schreiend

to scream

schrei(e)!/schreit!/schreien Sie!

Sub.	Präsens	Plusquam-perfekt	Präteritum	Futur	Konditional	Perfekt
ich	schreie	hatte geschrien	schrie	werde schreien	würde schreien	habe geschrien
du	schreist	hattest geschrien	schriest	wirst schreien	würdest schreien	hast geschrien
er sie es	schreit	hatte geschrien	schrie	wird schreien	würde schreien	hat geschrien
wir	schreien	hatten geschrien	schrien	werden schreien	würden schreien	haben geschrien
ihr	schreit	hattet geschrien	schriet	werdet schreien	würdet schreien	habt geschrien
Sie sie	schreien	hatten geschrien	schrien	werden schreien	würden schreien	haben geschrien

Mimi **hat geschrien**. Sie war sehr wütend!

Mimi screamed. She was very angry!

Würden Sie an ihrer Stelle **schreien**?

Would you scream if you were her?

34

to hear
hör(e)!/hört!/hören Sie!

hören
hörend

Sub.	Präsens	Plusquam-perfekt	Präteritum	Futur	Konditional	Perfekt
ich	höre	hatte gehört	hörte	werde hören	würde hören	habe gehört
du	hörst	hattest gehört	hörtest	wirst hören	würdest hören	hast gehört
er sie es	hört	hatte gehört	hörte	wird hören	würde hören	hat gehört
wir	hören	hatten gehört	hörten	werden hören	würden hören	haben gehört
ihr	hört	hattet gehört	hörtet	werdet hören	würdet hören	habt gehört
Sie sie	hören	hatten gehört	hörten	werden hören	würden hören	haben gehört

Paul, mein lieber, **hast** du einen Schrei **gehört**?

Paul, dear, did you hear a scream?

Ja, ich **höre**, wie Mimi schreit.

Yes, I hear Mimi screaming.

kämpfen
kämpfend

to fight

Sub.	Präsens	Plusquam-perfekt	Präteritum	Futur	Konditional	Perfekt
ich	kämpfe	hatte gekämpft	kämpfte	werde kämpfen	würde kämpfen	habe gekämpft
du	kämpfst	hattest gekämpft	kämpftest	wirst kämpfen	würdest kämpfen	hast gekämpft
er sie es	kämpft	hatte gekämpft	kämpfte	wird kämpfen	würde kämpfen	hat gekämpft
wir	kämpfen	hatten gekämpft	kämpften	werden kämpfen	würden kämpfen	haben gekämpft
ihr	kämpft	hattet gekämpft	kämpftet	werdet kämpfen	würdet kämpfen	habt gekämpft
Sie sie	kämpfen	hatten gekämpft	kämpften	werden kämpfen	würden kämpfen	haben gekämpft

Unsere Helden kämpften miteinander!

Our heroes were fighting with each other!

Sie haben bis zum geht nicht mehr gekämpft.

They were fighting to the bitter end.

Sub.	Präsens	Plusquam-perfekt	Präteritum	Futur	Konditional	Perfekt
ich	trenne	hatte getrennt	trennte	werde trennen	würde trennen	habe getrennt
du	trennst	hattest getrennt	trenntest	wirst trennen	würdest trennen	hast getrennt
er sie es	trennt	hatte getrennt	trennte	wird trennen	würde trennen	hat getrennt
wir	trennen	hatten getrennt	trennten	werden trennen	würden trennen	haben getrennt
ihr	trennt	hattet getrennt	trenntet	werdet trennen	würdet trennen	habt getrennt
Sie sie	trennen	hatten getrennt	trennten	werden trennen	würden trennen	haben getrennt

Trennen Sie sie, oder sie werden sich umbringen!

Separate them or they'll kill each other!

Schließlich hat man sie trennen können.

It was finally possible to separate them.

schließen

to close, shut

schließend

schließ(e)!/schließt!/schließen Sie!

Sub.	Präsens	Plusquam-perfekt	Präteritum	Futur	Konditional	Perfekt
ich	schließe	hatte geschlossen	schloss	werde schließen	würde schließen	habe geschlossen
du	schließt	hattest geschlossen	schlossest	wirst schließen	würdest schließen	hast geschlossen
er sie es	schließt	hatte geschlossen	schloss	wird schließen	würde schließen	hat geschlossen
wir	schließen	hatten geschlossen	schlossen	werden schließen	würden schließen	haben geschlossen
ihr	schließt	hattet geschlossen	schlosst	werdet schließen	würdet schließen	habt geschlossen
Sie sie	schließen	hatten geschlossen	schlossen	werden schließen	würden schließen	haben geschlossen

Mimi **hat** Paul die Tür vor der Nase
geschlossen.

Mimi shut the door in Paul's face.

Zum Glück **schließen** die Hotels nie.

Fortunately, hotels never close.

Sub.	Präsens	Plusquam-perfekt	Präteritum	Futur	Konditional	Perfekt
ich	vergesse	hatte vergessen	vergaß	werde vergessen	würde vergessen	habe vergessen
du	vergisst	hattest vergessen	vergaßest	wirst vergessen	würdest vergessen	hast vergessen
er sie es	vergisst	hatte vergessen	vergaß	wird vergessen	würde vergessen	hat vergessen
wir	vergessen	hatten vergessen	vergaßen	werden vergessen	würden vergessen	haben vergessen
ihr	vergesst	hattet vergessen	vergaßt	werdet vergessen	würdet vergessen	habt vergessen
Sie sie	vergessen	hatten vergessen	vergaßen	werden vergessen	würden vergessen	haben vergessen

Paul, **hast** du **vergessen**, warum Mimi so wütend ist?

Paul, have you forgotten why Mimi is so furious?

Ich sollte das nicht vergessen.

I shouldn't forget it.

sich erinnern
to remember

sich erinnernd

erinnere dich!/erinnert euch!/erinnern Sie sich!

Sub.	Präsens	Plusquam-perfekt	Präteritum	Futur	Konditional	Perfekt
ich	erinnere mich	hatte mich erinnert	erinnerte mich	werde mich erinnern	würde erinnern	habe mich erinnert
du	erinnerst dich	hattest dich erinnert	erinnertest dich	wirst dich erinnern	würdest erinnern	hast dich erinnert
er sie es	erinnert sich	hatte sich erinnert	erinnerte sich	wird sich erinnern	würde erinnern	hat sich erinnert
wir	erinnern uns	hatten uns erinnert	erinnerten uns	werden uns erinnern	würden erinnern	haben uns erinnert
ihr	erinnert euch	hattet euch erinnert	erinnertet euch	werdet euch erinnern	würdet erinnern	habt euch erinnert
Sie sie	erinnert sich	hatten uns erinnert	erinnerten sich	werden sich erinnern	würden erinnern	haben sich erinnert

Ich **erinnere mich** nicht.

I don't remember.

Plötzlich **hat** Paul **sich** daran **erinnert**, was am Abend davor alles passiert war.

Suddenly Paul remembered everything that had happened the night before.

to rain   regnen

no commands

regnend

Sub.	Präsens	Plusquam-perfekt	Präteritum	Futur	Konditional	Perfekt
es	regnet	hatte geregnet	regnete	wird regnen	würde regnen	hat geregnet

Es **hat geregnet**; Mimi und Toby waren traurig.

It was raining; Mimi and Toby were sad.

Es **wird** auch Freitag und Samstag **regnen**.

It will rain (on) Friday and Saturday, too.

41

sprechen

sprechend

to talk, speak

sprich!/sprecht!/sprechen Sie!

Sub.	Präsens	Plusquam-perfekt	Präteritum	Futur	Konditional	Perfekt
ich	spreche	hatte gesprochen	sprach	werde sprechen	würde sprechen	habe gesprochen
du	sprichst	hattest gesprochen	sprachst	wirst sprechen	würdest sprechen	hast gesprochen
er sie es	spricht	hatte gesprochen	sprach	wird sprechen	würde sprechen	hat gesprochen
wir	sprechen	hatten gesprochen	sprachen	werden sprechen	würden sprechen	haben gesprochen
ihr	sprecht	hattet gesprochen	spracht	werdet sprechen	würdet sprechen	habt gesprochen
Sie sie	sprechen	hatten gesprochen	sprachen	werden sprechen	würden sprechen	haben gesprochen

Wir müssen unbedingt miteinander sprechen, Mimi!

We absolutely have to talk to each other, Mimi!

Natürlich sprechen sie deutsch!

Of course they're speaking German!

42

to trip, stumble

stolpere!/stolpert!/stolpern Sie!

stolpern
stolpernd

Sub.	Präsens	Plusquam-perfekt	Präteritum	Futur	Konditional	Perfekt
ich	stolpere	war gestolpert	stolperte	werde stolpern	würde stolpern	habe gestolpert
du	stolperst	warst gestolpert	stolpertest	wirst stolpern	würdest stolpern	hast gestolpert
er sie es	stolpert	war gestolpert	stolperte	wird stolpern	würde stolpern	hat gestolpert
wir	stolpern	waren gestolpert	stolperten	werden stolpern	würden stolpern	haben gestolpert
ihr	stolpert	wart gestolpert	stolpertet	werdet stolpern	würdet stolpern	habt gestolpert
Sie sie	stolpern	waren gestolpert	stolperten	werden stolpern	würden stolpern	haben gestolpert

Wenn du hübsche Mädchen siehst,
drehst du dich um und **stolperst**.

*When you see pretty girls, you turn
around and you trip.*

Vorsicht! Stolpere nicht!

Watch out! Don't trip!

43

treten

to kick, shoot

tretend   tritt!/tretet!/treten Sie!

Sub.	Präsens	Plusquam-perfekt	Präteritum	Futur	Konditional	Perfekt
ich	trete	hatte getreten	trat	werde treten	würde treten	habe getreten
du	trittst	hattest getreten	tratest	wirst treten	würdest treten	hast getreten
er sie es	tritt	hatte getreten	trat	wird treten	würde treten	hat getreten
wir	treten	hatten getreten	traten	werden treten	würden treten	haben getreten
ihr	tretet	hattet getreten	tratet	werdet treten	würdet treten	habt getreten
Sie sie	treten	hatten getreten	traten	werden treten	würden treten	haben getreten

Paul war so frustriert, dass er einfach irgendwas treten wollte.

Paul was so frustrated, he just wanted to kick something.

Er hat einen schweren Stein getreten; das hat weh getan!

He kicked a heavy stone; that hurt!

44

to think

denken

denk(e)!/denkt!/denken Sie!

denkend

Sub.	Präsens	Plusquam-perfekt	Präteritum	Futur	Konditional	Perfekt
ich	denke	hatte gedacht	dachte	werde denken	würde denken	habe gedacht
du	denkst	hattest gedacht	dachtest	wirst denken	würdest denken	hast gedacht
er sie es	denkt	hatte gedacht	dachte	wird denken	würde denken	hat gedacht
wir	denken	hatten gedacht	dachten	werden denken	würden denken	haben gedacht
ihr	denkt	hattet gedacht	dachtet	werdet denken	würdet denken	habt gedacht
Sie sie	denken	hatten gedacht	dachten	werden denken	würden denken	haben gedacht

Paul **denkt** und **denkt**: was soll er Mimi sagen?

Paul thinks and thinks: what should he say to Mimi?

Er muss die ganze Zeit daran denken, wie dumm er war.

He can't stop thinking about how stupid he was.

sein
to be

seiend

sei!/seid!/seien Sie!

Sub.	Präsens	Plusquam-perfekt	Präteritum	Futur	Konditional	Perfekt
ich	bin	war gewesen	war	werde sein	würde sein	bin gewesen
du	bist	warst gewesen	warst	wirst sein	würdest sein	bist gewesen
er sie es	ist	war gewesen	war	wird sein	würde sein	ist gewesen
wir	sind	waren gewesen	waren	werden sein	würden sein	sind gewesen
ihr	seid	wart gewesen	wart	werdet sein	würdet sein	seid gewesen
Sie sie	sind	waren gewesen	waren	werden sein	würden sein	sind gewesen

Wer **bin** ich; was **bin** ich?

Who am I; what am I?

Sein oder nicht sein: das ist die Frage!

To be or not to be: that is the question!

to decide

entscheiden

entscheidend

Sub.	Präsens	Plusquam-perfekt	Präteritum	Futur	Konditional	Perfekt
ich	entscheide	hatte entschieden	entschied	werde entscheiden	würde entscheiden	habe entschieden
du	entscheidest	hattest entschieden	entschiedest	wirst entscheiden	würdest entscheiden	hast entschieden
er sie es	entscheidet	hatte entschieden	entschied	wird entscheiden	würde entscheiden	hat entschieden
wir	entscheiden	hatten entschieden	entschieden	werden entscheiden	würden entscheiden	haben entschieden
ihr	entscheidet	hattet entschieden	entschiedet	werdet entscheiden	würdet entscheiden	habt entschieden
Sie sie	entscheiden	hatten entschieden	entschieden	werden entscheiden	würden entscheiden	haben entschieden

Paul **entscheidet** heute seine Zukunft.

Paul is deciding his future today.

Wer **wird** hier tatsächlich **entscheiden**?

Who is actually going to make the decision here?

wissen

wissend

wisse!/wisst!/wissen Sie!

Sub.	Präsens	Plusquam-perfekt	Präteritum	Futur	Konditional	Perfekt
ich	weiß	hatte gewusst	wusste	werde wissen	würde wissen	habe gewusst
du	weißt	hattest gewusst	wusstest	wirst wissen	würdest wissen	hast gewusst
er sie es	weiß	hatte gewusst	wusste	wird wissen	würde wissen	hat gewusst
wir	wissen	hatten gewusst	wussten	werden wissen	würden wissen	haben gewusst
ihr	wisst	hattet gewusst	wusstet	werdet wissen	würdet wissen	habt gewusst
Sie sie	wissen	hatten gewusst	wussten	werden wissen	würden wissen	haben gewusst

Jetzt weiß ich, was ich tun muss.

Now I know what I have to do.

Wissen Sie, wo Paul jetzt hingeht?

Do you know where Paul is going to go now?

to change, swap

tauschen

tausch(e)!/tauscht!/tauschen Sie!

tauschend

Sub.	Präsens	Plusquam-perfekt	Präteritum	Futur	Konditional	Perfekt
ich	tausche	hatte getauscht	tauschte	werde tauschen	würde tauschen	habe getauscht
du	tauschst	hattest getauscht	tauschtest	wirst tauschen	würdest tauschen	hast getauscht
er sie es	tauscht	hatte getauscht	tauschte	wird tauschen	würde tauschen	hat getauscht
wir	tauschen	hatten getauscht	tauschten	werden tauschen	würden tauschen	haben getauscht
ihr	tauscht	hattet getauscht	tauschtet	werdet tauschen	würdet tauschen	habt getauscht
Sie sie	tauschen	hatten getauscht	tauschten	werden tauschen	würden tauschen	haben getauscht

Haben Sie Ihr ganzes Geld **getauscht**?

Did you change all your money?

Die Bank **tauscht** Euro in Dollar.

The bank exchanges euros for dollars.

49

lernen

to learn

lernend

lern(e)!/lernt!/lernen Sie!

Sub.	Präsens	Plusquam-perfekt	Präteritum	Futur	Konditional	Perfekt
ich	lerne	hatte gelernt	lernte	werde lernen	würde lernen	habe gelernt
du	lernst	hattest gelernt	lerntest	wirst lernen	würdest lernen	hast gelernt
er sie es	lernt	hatte gelernt	lernte	wird lernen	würde lernen	hat gelernt
wir	lernen	hatten gelernt	lernten	werden lernen	würden lernen	haben gelernt
ihr	lernt	hattet gelernt	lerntet	werdet lernen	würdet lernen	habt gelernt
Sie sie	lernen	hatten gelernt	lernten	werden lernen	würden lernen	haben gelernt

Was **wirst** du in dieser Schule **lernen**?

What will you learn in this school?

Wir **lernen**, wie man Probleme löst.

We learn how to solve problems.

Sub.	Präsens	Plusquam-perfekt	Präteritum	Futur	Konditional	Perfekt
ich	studiere	hatte studiert	studierte	werde studieren	würde studieren	habe studiert
du	studierst	hattest studiert	studiertest	wirst studieren	würdest studieren	hast studiert
er sie es	studiert	hatte studiert	studierte	wird studieren	würde studieren	hat studiert
wir	studieren	hatten studiert	studierten	werden studieren	würden studieren	haben studiert
ihr	studiert	hattet studiert	studiertet	werdet studieren	würdet studieren	habt studiert
Sie sie	studieren	hatten studiert	studierten	werden studieren	würden studieren	haben studiert

Paul **studiert** dieses Semester Mathematik.

Paul has been studying math this semester (term).

Wer von euch **würde** so was schwieriges **studieren**?

Which of you would study something so difficult?

51

träumen

träumend

träum(e)!/träumt!/träumen Sie!

Sub.	Präsens	Plusquam-perfekt	Präteritum	Futur	Konditional	Perfekt
ich	träume	hatte geträumt	träumte	werde träumen	würde träumen	habe geträumt
du	träumst	hattest geträumt	träumtest	wirst träumen	würdest träumen	hast geträumt
er sie es	träumt	hatte geträumt	träumte	wird träumen	würde träumen	hat geträumt
wir	träumen	hatten geträumt	träumten	werden träumen	würden träumen	haben geträumt
ihr	träumt	hattet geträumt	träumtet	werdet träumen	würdet träumen	habt geträumt
Sie sie	träumen	hatten geträumt	träumten	werden träumen	würden träumen	haben geträumt

Er träumt jede Nacht von Mimi.

He dreams about Mimi every night.

Mimi als Balletttänzerin? Du hast das wohl geträumt!

Mimi as a ballerina? You must have been dreaming!

52

to start
starte!/startet!/starten Sie!

starten
startend

Sub.	Präsens	Plusquam-perfekt	Präteritum	Futur	Konditional	Perfekt
ich	starte	war gestartet	startete	werde starten	würde starten	bin gestartet
du	startest	warst gestartet	startetest	wirst starten	würdest starten	bist gestartet
er sie es	startet	war gestartet	startete	wird starten	würde starten	ist gestartet
wir	starten	waren gestartet	starteten	werden starten	würden starten	sind gestartet
ihr	startet	wart gestartet	startetet	werdet starten	würdet starten	seid gestartet
Sie sie	starten	waren gestartet	starteten	werden starten	würden starten	sind gestartet

Gleich **starten** die Läufer.

The runners are about to start.

Paul **ist** zu früh **gestartet**!

Paul started too soon!

beenden

beendend

to finish

beende!/beendet!/beenden Sie!

Sub.	Präsens	Plusquam-perfekt	Präteritum	Futur	Konditional	Perfekt
ich	beende	hatte beendet	beendete	werde beenden	würde beenden	habe beendet
du	beendest	hattest beendet	beendetest	wirst beenden	würdest beenden	hast beendet
er sie es	beendet	hatte beendet	beendete	wird beenden	würde beenden	hat beendet
wir	beenden	hatten beendet	beendeten	werden beenden	würden beenden	haben beendet
ihr	beendet	hattet beendet	beendetet	werdet beenden	würdet beenden	habt beendet
Sie sie	beenden	hatten beendet	beendeten	werden beenden	würden beenden	haben beendet

Paul **hatte** den Wettlauf **beendet**, als die letzten Läufer um die Kurve kamen.

Paul had finished the race when the last runners came around the bend.

Beende doch, was du angefangen hast!

Finish what you started!

Sub.	Präsens	Plusquam-perfekt	Präteritum	Futur	Konditional	Perfekt
ich	gewinne	hatte gewonnen	gewann	werde gewinnen	würde gewinnen	habe gewonnen
du	gewinnst	hattest gewonnen	gewannst	wirst gewinnen	würdest gewinnen	hast gewonnen
er sie es	gewinnt	hatte gewonnen	gewann	wird gewinnen	würde gewinnen	hat gewonnen
wir	gewinnen	hatten gewonnen	gewannen	werden gewinnen	würden gewinnen	haben gewonnen
ihr	gewinnt	hattet gewonnen	gewannt	werdet gewinnen	würdet gewinnen	habt gewonnen
Sie sie	gewinnen	hatten gewonnen	gewannen	werden gewinnen	würden gewinnen	haben gewonnen

Du **hast** den Wettlauf **gewonnen**.
Herzlichen Glückwunsch!

You won the race. Congratulations!

Ich **werde** Mimis Vertrauen auch wieder **gewinnen**.

I will also win back Mimi's trust.

lügen
lügend

to (tell a) lie
lüg(e)!/lügt!/lügen Sie!

Sub.	Präsens	Plusquam-perfekt	Präteritum	Futur	Konditional	Perfekt
ich	lüge	hatte gelogen	log	werde lügen	würde lügen	habe gelogen
du	lügst	hattest gelogen	logst	wirst lügen	würdest lügen	hast gelogen
er sie es	lügt	hatte gelogen	log	wird lügen	würde lügen	hat gelogen
wir	lügen	hatten gelogen	logen	werden lügen	würden lügen	haben gelogen
ihr	lügt	hattet gelogen	logt	werdet lügen	würdet lügen	habt gelogen
Sie sie	lügen	hatten gelogen	logen	werden lügen	würden lügen	haben gelogen

Lügen Sie mich denn an, junger Mann?

Are you lying to me, young man?

Ich würde doch nie im Leben lügen.

Of course, I would never lie.

56

Sub.	Präsens	Plusquam-perfekt	Präteritum	Futur	Konditional	Perfekt
ich	teste	hatte getestet	testete	werde testen	würde testen	habe getestet
du	testest	hattest getestet	testetest	wirst testen	würdest testen	hast getestet
er sie es	testet	hatte getestet	testete	wird testen	würde testen	hat getestet
wir	testen	hatten getestet	testeten	werden testen	würden testen	haben getestet
ihr	testet	hattet getestet	testetet	werdet testen	würdet testen	habt getestet
Sie sie	testen	hatten getestet	testeten	werden testen	würden testen	haben getestet

Ich habe Ihre Arbeit getestet.

I have evaluated your work.

Testen wir doch, was Sie bis heute alles gelernt haben.

Let's test what you have learned so far.

fahren

to drive

fahrend

GERNICA

Sub.	Präsens	Plusquam-perfekt	Präteritum	Futur	Konditional	Perfekt
ich	fahre	war gefahren	fuhr	werde fahren	würde fahren	bin gefahren
du	fährst	warst gefahren	fuhrst	wirst fahren	würdest fahren	bist gefahren
er sie es	fährt	war gefahren	fuhr	wird fahren	würde fahren	ist gefahren
wir	fahren	waren gefahren	fuhren	werden fahren	würden fahren	sind gefahren
ihr	fahrt	wart gefahren	fuhrt	werdet fahren	würdet fahren	seid gefahren
Sie sie	fahren	waren gefahren	fuhren	werden fahren	würden fahren	sind gefahren

Der Professor **fährt** in seinem alten Auto nach Hause.

The teacher is driving home in his old car.

Ich **würde** gern selber **fahren**.

I would like to drive myself.

58

to count — zählen

zähl(e)!/zählt!/zählen Sie!

zählend

Sub.	Präsens	Plusquam-perfekt	Präteritum	Futur	Konditional	Perfekt
ich	zähle	hatte gezählt	zählte	werde zählen	würde zählen	habe gezählt
du	zählst	hattest gezählt	zähltest	wirst zählen	würdest zählen	hast gezählt
er sie es	zählt	hatte gezählt	zählte	wird zählen	würde zählen	hat gezählt
wir	zählen	hatten gezählt	zählten	werden zählen	würden zählen	haben gezählt
ihr	zählt	hattet gezählt	zähltet	werdet zählen	würdet zählen	habt gezählt
Sie sie	zählen	hatten gezählt	zählten	werden zählen	würden zählen	haben gezählt

Du **zählst** von eins bis zehn tausend.

You are counting from one to ten thousand.

Er gab aber schon auf, als er bis fünf hundert **gezählt hatte**.

He gave up, however, when he counted to five hundred.

ordnen

ordnend

to organize

ordne!/ordnet!/ordnen Sie!

Sub.	Präsens	Plusquam-perfekt	Präteritum	Futur	Konditional	Perfekt
ich	ordne	hatte geordnet	ordnete	werde ordnen	würde ordnen	habe geordnet
du	ordnest	hattest geordnet	ordnetest	wirst ordnen	würdest ordnen	hast geordnet
er sie es	ordnet	hatte geordnet	ordnete	wird ordnen	würde ordnen	hat geordnet
wir	ordnen	hatten geordnet	ordneten	werden ordnen	würden ordnen	haben geordnet
ihr	ordnet	hattet geordnet	ordnetet	werdet ordnen	würdet ordnen	habt geordnet
Sie sie	ordnen	hatten geordnet	ordneten	werden ordnen	würden ordnen	haben geordnet

Paul ordnete sorgfältig seine Akten.

Paul carefully organized his files.

Wirst du deine Sachen endlich ordnen?

Will you finally organize your things?

60

to build

bau(e)!/baut!/bauen Sie!

bauen

bauend

Sub.	Präsens	Plusquam-perfekt	Präteritum	Futur	Konditional	Perfekt
ich	baue	hatte gebaut	baute	werde bauen	würde bauen	habe gebaut
du	baust	hattest gebaut	bautest	wirst bauen	würdest bauen	hast gebaut
er sie es	baut	hatte gebaut	baute	wird bauen	würde bauen	hat gebaut
wir	bauen	hatten gebaut	bauten	werden bauen	würden bauen	haben gebaut
ihr	baut	hattet gebaut	bautet	werdet bauen	würdet bauen	habt gebaut
Sie sie	bauen	hatten gebaut	bauten	werden bauen	würden bauen	haben gebaut

Jetzt baut Paul eine Maschine.

Now Paul is building a machine.

Ich habe sie mit meinen eigenen Werkzeugen gebaut!

I built it with my own tools!

61

putzen

to clean

putzend

putz(e)!/putzt!/putzen Sie!

Sub.	Präsens	Plusquam-perfekt	Präteritum	Futur	Konditional	Perfekt
ich	putze	hatte geputzt	putzte	werde putzen	würde putzen	habe geputzt
du	putzt	hattest geputzt	putztest	wirst putzen	würdest putzen	hast geputzt
er sie es	putzt	hatte geputzt	putzte	wird putzen	würde putzen	hat geputzt
wir	putzen	hatten geputzt	putzten	werden putzen	würden putzen	haben geputzt
ihr	putzt	hattet geputzt	putztet	werdet putzen	würdet putzen	habt geputzt
Sie sie	putzen	hatten geputzt	putzten	werden putzen	würden putzen	haben geputzt

Mimi wird staunen, dass ich die Maschine so gründlich **geputzt habe**.

Mimi will be amazed at how thoroughly I have cleaned the machine.

Er **putzt** nicht einmal in der Wohnung.

He doesn't even do any cleaning in the apartment.

62

to polish

polieren

polier(e)!/poliert!/polieren Sie!

polierend

Sub.	Präsens	Plusquam-perfekt	Präteritum	Futur	Konditional	Perfekt
ich	poliere	hatte poliert	polierte	werde polieren	würde polieren	habe poliert
du	polierst	hattest poliert	poliertest	wirst polieren	würdest polieren	hast poliert
er sie es	poliert	hatte poliert	polierte	wird polieren	würde polieren	hat poliert
wir	polieren	hatten poliert	polierten	werden polieren	würden polieren	haben poliert
ihr	poliert	hattet poliert	poliertet	werdet polieren	würdet polieren	habt poliert
Sie sie	polieren	hatten poliert	polierten	werden polieren	würden polieren	haben poliert

Paul poliert seit heute früh die Maschine.

Paul has been polishing the machine since early this morning.

Kann mir jemand helfen, sie zu polieren?

Can someone help me polish it?

schreiben

schreibend

to write

schreib(e)!/schreibt!/schreiben Sie!

Sub.	Präsens	Plusquam-perfekt	Präteritum	Futur	Konditional	Perfekt
ich	schreibe	hatte geschrieben	schrieb	werde schreiben	würde schreiben	habe geschrieben
du	schreibst	hattest geschrieben	schriebst	wirst schreiben	würdest schreiben	hast geschrieben
er sie es	schreibt	hatte geschrieben	schrieb	wird schreiben	würde schreiben	hat geschrieben
wir	schreiben	hatten geschrieben	schrieben	werden schreiben	würden schreiben	haben geschrieben
ihr	schreibt	hattet geschrieben	schriebt	werdet schreiben	würdet schreiben	habt geschrieben
Sie sie	schreiben	hatten geschrieben	schrieben	werden schreiben	würden schreiben	haben geschrieben

In der Zwischenzeit schreibt Mimi einen sehr langen Brief an Paul.

In the meantime, Mimi is writing Paul a very long letter.

Morgen werde ich E-Mail schreiben.

Tomorrow I will write e-mail.

64

to receive
erhalte!/erhaltet!/erhalten Sie!

erhalten
erhaltend

Sub.	Präsens	Plusquam-perfekt	Präteritum	Futur	Konditional	Perfekt
ich	erhalte	hatte erhalten	erhielt	werde erhalten	würde erhalten	habe erhalten
du	erhältst	hattest erhalten	erhieltest	wirst erhalten	würdest erhalten	hast erhalten
er sie es	erhält	hatte erhalten	erhielt	wird erhalten	würde erhalten	hat erhalten
wir	erhalten	hatten erhalten	erhielten	werden erhalten	würden erhalten	haben erhalten
ihr	erhaltet	hattet erhalten	erhieltet	werdet erhalten	würdet erhalten	habt erhalten
Sie sie	erhalten	hatten erhalten	erhielten	werden erhalten	würden erhalten	haben erhalten

Unterschreiben Sie bitte hier, dass Sie diesen riesigen Brief **erhalten haben**.

Please sign here that you have received this enormous letter.

Wird er meine Nachricht **erhalten**?

Will he receive my message?

65

geben
gebend

to give

gib!/gebt!/geben Sie!

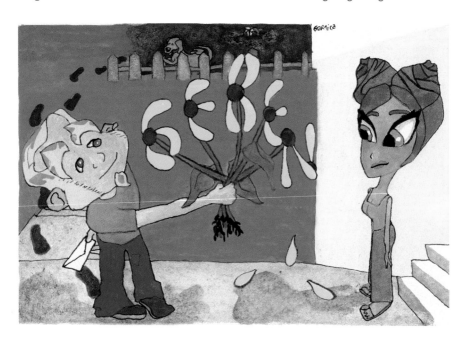

Sub.	Präsens	Plusquam-perfekt	Präteritum	Futur	Konditional	Perfekt
ich	gebe	hatte gegeben	gab	werde geben	würde geben	habe gegeben
du	gibst	hattest gegeben	gabst	wirst geben	würdest geben	hast gegeben
er sie es	gibt	hatte gegeben	gab	wird geben	würde geben	hat gegeben
wir	geben	hatten gegeben	gaben	werden geben	würden geben	haben gegeben
ihr	gebt	hattet gegeben	gabt	werdet geben	würdet geben	habt gegeben
Sie sie	geben	hatten gegeben	gaben	werden geben	würden geben	haben gegeben

Paul **gibt** Mimi fünf gelbe Blumen.

Paul gives Mimi five yellow flowers.

Es ist so süß, dass du mir diese Blumen **gibst**.

It's so sweet of you to give me these flowers.

66

to show
zeig(e)!/zeigt!/zeigen Sie!

zeigen
zeigend

Sub.	Präsens	Plusquam-perfekt	Präteritum	Futur	Konditional	Perfekt
ich	zeige	hatte gezeigt	zeigte	werde zeigen	würde zeigen	habe gezeigt
du	zeigst	hattest gezeigt	zeigtest	wirst zeigen	würdest zeigen	hast gezeigt
er sie es	zeigt	hatte gezeigt	zeigte	wird zeigen	würde zeigen	hat gezeigt
wir	zeigen	hatten gezeigt	zeigten	werden zeigen	würden zeigen	haben gezeigt
ihr	zeigt	hattet gezeigt	zeigtet	werdet zeigen	würdet zeigen	habt gezeigt
Sie sie	zeigen	hatten gezeigt	zeigten	werden zeigen	würden zeigen	haben gezeigt

Jetzt **zeige** ich dir meine Erfindung!

And now I will show you my invention!

Du **hast** mir eine Zeitmaschine **gezeigt**!

You have shown me a time machine!

küssen

küssend

to kiss

küss(e)!/küsst!/küssen Sie!

Sub.	Präsens	Plusquam-perfekt	Präteritum	Futur	Konditional	Perfekt
ich	küsse	hatte geküsst	küsste	werde küssen	würde küssen	habe geküsst
du	küsst	hattest geküsst	küsstest	wirst küssen	würdest küssen	hast geküsst
er sie es	küsst	hatte geküsst	küsste	wird küssen	würde küssen	hat geküsst
wir	küssen	hatten geküsst	küssten	werden küssen	würden küssen	haben geküsst
ihr	küsst	hattet geküsst	küsstet	werdet küssen	würdet küssen	habt geküsst
Sie sie	küssen	hatten geküsst	küssten	werden küssen	würden küssen	haben geküsst

Mimi hat Paul im ganzen Gesicht geküsst.

Mimi kissed Paul all over his face.

Hör bitte nicht auf, mich zu küssen.

Please don't stop kissing me.

to buy   kaufen

kauf(e)!/kauft!/kaufen Sie!   kaufend

Sub.	Präsens	Plusquam-perfekt	Präteritum	Futur	Konditional	Perfekt
ich	kaufe	hatte gekauft	kaufte	werde kaufen	würde kaufen	habe gekauft
du	kaufst	hattest gekauft	kauftest	wirst kaufen	würdest kaufen	hast gekauft
er sie es	kauft	hatte gekauft	kaufte	wird kaufen	würde kaufen	hat gekauft
wir	kaufen	hatten gekauft	kauften	werden kaufen	würden kaufen	haben gekauft
ihr	kauft	hattet gekauft	kauftet	werdet kaufen	würdet kaufen	habt gekauft
Sie sie	kaufen	hatten gekauft	kauften	werden kaufen	würden kaufen	haben gekauft

Wir **kaufen** Anziehsachen für eine Reise.

We're buying clothes for a trip.

Mimi, gibt es was, was du nicht **gekauft hast**?

Mimi, is there anything you didn't buy?

69

zahlen

zahlend

zahl(e)!/zahlt!/zahlen Sie!

Sub.	Präsens	Plusquam-perfekt	Präteritum	Futur	Konditional	Perfekt
ich	zahle	hatte gezahlt	zahlte	werde zahlen	würde zahlen	habe gezahlt
du	zahlst	hattest gezahlt	zahltest	wirst zahlen	würdest zahlen	hast gezahlt
er sie es	zahlt	hatte gezahlt	zahlte	wird zahlen	würde zahlen	hat gezahlt
wir	zahlen	hatten gezahlt	zahlten	werden zahlen	würden zahlen	haben gezahlt
ihr	zahlt	hattet gezahlt	zahltet	werdet zahlen	würdet zahlen	habt gezahlt
Sie sie	zahlen	hatten gezahlt	zahlten	werden zahlen	würden haben	haben gezahlt

Mimi **hat** im Supermarkt bar **gezahlt**.

At the supermarket, Mimi paid cash.

Wer **würde** denn so viel **zahlen**?

Who would pay that much?

to take off, start
losgehen

geh(e)!/geht!/gehen Sie los!

Sub.	Präsens	Plusquam-perfekt	Präteritum	Futur	Konditional	Perfekt
ich	gehe los	war losgegangen	ging los	werde losgehen	würde losgehen	bin losgegangen
du	gehst los	warst losgegangen	gingst los	wirst losgehen	würdest losgehen	bist losgegangen
er sie es	geht los	war losgegangen	ging los	wird losgehen	würde losgehen	ist losgegangen
wir	gehen los	waren losgegangen	gingen los	werden losgehen	würden losgehen	sind losgegangen
ihr	geht los	wart losgegangen	gingt los	werdet losgehen	würdet losgehen	seid losgegangen
Sie sie	gehen los	waren losgegangen	gingen los	werden losgehen	würden losgehen	sind losgegangen

Gleich **geht**'s **los**!

We're about to take off!

Jetzt **wird** unsere Reise in die Zukunft **losgehen**.

Our trip to the future will begin now.

71

heiraten
heiratend

to get married
heirate!/heiratet!/heiraten Sie!

Sub.	Präsens	Plusquam-perfekt	Präteritum	Futur	Konditional	Perfekt
ich	heirate	hatte geheiratet	heiratete	werde heiraten	würde heiraten	habe geheiratet
du	heiratest	hattest geheiratet	heiratetest	wirst heiraten	würdest heiraten	hast geheiratet
er sie es	heiratet	hatte geheiratet	heiratete	wird heiraten	würde heiraten	hat geheiratet
wir	heiraten	hatten geheiratet	heirateten	werden heiraten	würden heiraten	haben geheiratet
ihr	heiratet	hattet geheiratet	heiratetet	werdet heiraten	würdet heiraten	habt geheiratet
Sie sie	heiraten	hatten geheiratet	heirateten	werden heiraten	würden heiraten	haben geheiratet

Toby will dabei sein, wenn Paul und Mimi heiraten.

Toby wants to be there when Paul and Mimi get married.

Würdet ihr denn auf diese Weise heiraten?

Would you get married like that?

to forbid, prohibit

verbieten

verbiete!/verbietet!/verbieten Sie!

verbietend

Sub.	Präsens	Plusquam-perfekt	Präteritum	Futur	Konditional	Perfekt
ich	verbiete	hatte verboten	verbot	werde verbieten	würde verbieten	habe verboten
du	verbietest	hattest verboten	verbotest	wirst verbieten	würdest verbieten	hast verboten
er sie es	verbietet	hatte verboten	verbot	wird verbieten	würde verbieten	hat verboten
wir	verbieten	hatten verboten	verboten	werden verbieten	würden verbieten	haben verboten
ihr	verbietet	hattet verboten	verbotet	werdet verbieten	würdet verbieten	habt verboten
Sie sie	verbieten	hatten verboten	verboten	werden verbieten	würden verbieten	haben verboten

Die Behörden **hatten** alles **verboten**:
schwimmen, joggen, ...

The authorities had forbidden everything:
swimming, jogging, . . .

Gnädige Frau, ich **verbiete** Ihnen, dieses
Schild runter zu nehmen.

Madam, I forbid you to take down
that sign.

73

schwimmen

schwimmend schwimm(e)!/schwimmt!/ schwimmen Sie!

Sub.	Präsens	Plusquam-perfekt	Präteritum	Futur	Konditional	Perfekt
ich	schwimme	war geschwommen	schwamm	werde schwimmen	würde schwimmen	bin geschwommen
du	schwimmst	warst geschwommen	schwammst	wirst schwimmen	würdest schwimmen	bist geschwommen
er sie es	schwimmt	war geschwommen	schwamm	wird schwimmen	würde schwimmen	ist geschwommen
wir	schwimmen	waren geschwommen	schwammen	werden schwimmen	würden schwimmen	sind geschwommen
ihr	schwimmt	wart geschwommen	schwammt	werdet schwimmen	würdet schwimmen	seid geschwommen
Sie sie	schwimmen	waren geschwommen	schwammen	werden schwimmen	würden schwimmen	sind geschwommen

Paul **schwimmt** mit den Delfinen.

Paul is swimming with the dolphins.

Schwimmen Sie lieber im Ozean oder im Schwimmbad?

Do you prefer to swim in the sea or in the pool?

74

to love

lieben

lieb(e)!/liebt!/lieben Sie!

liebend

Sub.	Präsens	Plusquam-perfekt	Präteritum	Futur	Konditional	Perfekt
ich	liebe	hatte geliebt	liebte	werde lieben	würde lieben	habe geliebt
du	liebst	hattest geliebt	liebtest	wirst lieben	würdest lieben	hast geliebt
er sie es	liebt	hatte geliebt	liebte	wird lieben	würde lieben	hat geliebt
wir	lieben	hatten geliebt	liebten	werden lieben	würden lieben	haben geliebt
ihr	liebt	hattet geliebt	liebtet	werdet lieben	würdet lieben	habt geliebt
Sie sie	lieben	hatten geliebt	liebten	werden lieben	würden lieben	haben geliebt

Paul **liebt** Mimi und er **liebt** den Strand.

Sie **lieben** sich zutiefst.

Paul loves Mimi and he loves the seaside.

They love each other deeply.

springen to jump

springend

Sub.	Präsens	Plusquam-perfekt	Präteritum	Futur	Konditional	Perfekt
ich	springe	war gesprungen	sprang	werde springen	würde springen	bin gesprungen
du	springst	warst gesprungen	sprangst	wirst springen	würdest springen	bist gesprungen
er sie es	springt	war gesprungen	sprang	wird springen	würde springen	ist gesprungen
wir	springen	waren gesprungen	sprangen	werden springen	würden springen	sind gesprungen
ihr	springt	wart gesprungen	sprangt	werdet springen	würdet springen	seid gesprungen
Sie sie	springen	waren gesprungen	sprangen	werden springen	würden springen	sind gesprungen

Paul, du **springst** ja so hoch!

Paul, you're jumping so high!

Ich dachte, er **war** vor Freude **gesprungen**.

I thought he was jumping for joy.

76

to turn

drehen

dreh(e)!/dreht!/drehen Sie!

drehend

Sub.	Präsens	Plusquam-perfekt	Präteritum	Futur	Konditional	Perfekt
ich	drehe	hatte gedreht	drehte	werde drehen	würde drehen	habe gedreht
du	drehst	hattest gedreht	drehtest	wirst drehen	würdest drehen	hast gedreht
er sie es	dreht	hatte gedreht	drehte	wird drehen	würde drehen	hat gedreht
wir	drehen	hatten gedreht	drehten	werden drehen	würden drehen	haben gedreht
ihr	dreht	hattet gedreht	drehtet	werdet drehen	würdet drehen	habt gedreht
Sie sie	drehen	hatten gedreht	drehten	werden drehen	würden drehen	haben gedreht

Mimi pfiff, während sie den Stock drehte.

Mimi whistled as she turned the stick.

Hör auf zu drehen! Ich werde krank!

Stop turning! I'm getting sick!

77

bewachen

to observe, supervise

bewachend

bewach(e)!/bewacht!/bewachen Sie!

Sub.	Präsens	Plusquam-perfekt	Präteritum	Futur	Konditional	Perfekt
ich	bewache	hatte bewacht	bewachte	werde bewachen	würde bewachen	habe bewacht
du	bewachst	hattest bewacht	bewachtest	wirst bewachen	würdest bewachen	hast bewacht
er sie es	bewacht	hatte bewacht	bewachte	wird bewachen	würde bewachen	hat bewacht
wir	bewachen	hatten bewacht	bewachten	werden bewachen	würden bewachen	haben bewacht
ihr	bewacht	hattet bewacht	bewachtet	werdet bewachen	würdet bewachen	habt bewacht
Sie sie	bewachen	hatten bewacht	bewachten	werden bewachen	würden bewachen	haben bewacht

Diese verdammten Kameras **bewachen** uns bei Schritt und Tritt.

These blasted cameras are supervising every step we take.

Wer **bewacht** Mimi und Paul, und warum?

Who is observing Mimi and Paul, and why?

Sub.	Präsens	Plusquam-perfekt	Präteritum	Futur	Konditional	Perfekt
ich	kehre zurück	war zurückgekehrt	kehrte zurück	werde zurückkehren	würde zurückkehren	bin zurückgekehrt
du	kehrst zurück	warst zurückgekehrt	kehrtest zurück	wirst zurückkehren	würdest zurückkehren	bist zurückgekehrt
er sie es	kehrt zurück	war zurückgekehrt	kehrte zurück	wird zurückkehren	würde zurückkehren	ist zurückgekehrt
wir	kehren zurück	waren zurückgekehrt	kehrten zurück	werden zurückkehren	würden zurückkehren	sind zurückgekehrt
ihr	kehrt zurück	wart zurückgekehrt	kehrtet zurück	werdet zurückkehren	würdet zurückkehren	seid zurückgekehrt
Sie sie	kehren zurück	waren zurückgekehrt	kehrten zurück	werden zurückkehren	würden zurückkehren	sind zurückgekehrt

Unsere Freunde **kehren** in die Gegenwart **zurück**.

Our friends are returning to the present.

Wir **sind** tatsächlich **zurückgekehrt**!

We have actually returned!

gehen

gehend

to walk

geh(e)!/geht!/gehen Sie!

Sub.	Präsens	Plusquam-perfekt	Präteritum	Futur	Konditional	Perfekt
ich	gehe	war gegangen	ging	werde gehen	würde gehen	bin gegangen
du	gehst	warst gegangen	gingst	wirst gehen	würdest gehen	bist gegangen
er sie es	geht	war gegangen	ging	wird gehen	würde gehen	ist gegangen
wir	gehen	waren gegangen	gingen	werden gehen	würden gehen	sind gegangen
ihr	geht	wart gegangen	gingt	werdet gehen	würdet gehen	seid gegangen
Sie sie	gehen	waren gegangen	gingen	werden gehen	würden gehen	sind gegangen

Mimi **geht** in der Stadt herum.

Mimi is walking around town.

Ich kann in diesen hohen Hacken nur langsam **gehen**.

I can only walk slowly in these high heels.

to ask (for)
bitte!/bittet!/bitten Sie!

bitten
bittend

Sub.	Präsens	Plusquam-perfekt	Präteritum	Futur	Konditional	Perfekt
ich	bitte	hatte gebeten	bat	werde bitten	würde bitten	habe gebeten
du	bittest	hattest gebeten	batest	wirst bitten	würdest bitten	hast gebeten
er sie es	bittet	hatte gebeten	bat	wird bitten	würde bitten	hat gebeten
wir	bitten	hatten gebeten	baten	werden bitten	würden bitten	haben gebeten
ihr	bittet	hattet gebeten	batet	werdet bitten	würdet bitten	habt gebeten
Sie sie	bitten	hatten gebeten	baten	werden bitten	würden bitten	haben gebeten

Der Bettler Max **hat** Paul um Geld für eine Wurst **gebeten**.

The beggar Max asked Paul for money for a sausage.

Jetzt **bittet** er den Kellner um ein teures Abendessen.

Now he is asking the waiter for an expensive dinner.

eintreten
eintretend

to enter, go in

tritt/tretet/treten Sie ein!

Sub.	Präsens	Plusquam-perfekt	Präteritum	Futur	Konditional	Perfekt
ich	trete ein	war eingetreten	trat ein	werde eintreten	würde eintreten	bin eingetreten
du	trittst ein	warst eingetreten	trat(e)st ein	wirst eintreten	würdest eintreten	bist eingetreten
er sie es	tritt ein	war eingetreten	trat ein	wird eintreten	würde eintreten	ist eingetreten
wir	treten ein	waren eingetreten	traten ein	werden eintreten	würden eintreten	sind eingetreten
ihr	tretet ein	wart eingetreten	tratet ein	werdet eintreten	würdet eintreten	seid eingetreten
Sie sie	treten ein	waren eingetreten	traten ein	werden eintreten	würden eintreten	sind eingetreten

Nico, der Einbrecher, **tritt** durch das Fenster ins Haus **ein**.

Nico, the burglar, enters the house through the window.

Wie **ist** er denn so leicht **eingetreten**?

How did he enter so easily?

82

ruf(e)!/ruft!/rufen Sie!

rufend

Sub.	Präsens	Plusquam-perfekt	Präteritum	Futur	Konditional	Perfekt
ich	rufe	hatte gerufen	rief	werde rufen	würde rufen	habe gerufen
du	rufst	hattest gerufen	riefst	wirst rufen	würdest rufen	hast gerufen
er sie es	ruft	hatte gerufen	rief	wird rufen	würde rufen	hat gerufen
wir	rufen	hatten gerufen	riefen	werden rufen	würden rufen	haben gerufen
ihr	ruft	hattet gerufen	rieft	werdet rufen	würdet rufen	habt gerufen
Sie sie	rufen	hatten gerufen	riefen	werden rufen	würden rufen	haben gerufen

Mimi **hat** die Polizei **gerufen**.

Mimi called the police.

Paul **ruft** den Hund.

Paul calls the dog.

kommen
kommend

to come
komm(e)!/kommt!/kommen Sie!

Sub.	Präsens	Plusquam-perfekt	Präteritum	Futur	Konditional	Perfekt
ich	komme	war gekommen	kam	werde kommen	würde kommen	bin gekommen
du	kommst	warst gekommen	kamst	wirst kommen	würdest kommen	bist gekommen
er sie es	kommt	war gekommen	kam	wird kommen	würde kommen	ist gekommen
wir	kommen	waren gekommen	kamen	werden kommen	würden kommen	sind gekommen
ihr	kommt	wart gekommen	kamt	werdet kommen	würdet kommen	seid gekommen
Sie sie	kommen	waren gekommen	kamen	werden kommen	würden kommen	sind gekommen

Komm, Toby! Such nach Indizien!

Come here, Toby! Look for clues (evidence)!

Sie haben sich gefragt, ob die Polizei kommen würde.

They wondered whether the police would come.

to follow

folg(e)!/folgt!/folgen Sie!

folgen

folgend

Sub.	Präsens	Plusquam-perfekt	Präteritum	Futur	Konditional	Perfekt
ich	folge	war gefolgt	folgte	werde folgen	würde folgen	bin gefolgt
du	folgst	warst gefolgt	folgtest	wirst folgen	würdest folgen	bist gefolgt
er sie es	folgt	war gefolgt	folgte	wird folgen	würde folgen	ist gefolgt
wir	folgen	waren gefolgt	folgten	werden folgen	würden folgen	sind gefolgt
ihr	folgt	wart gefolgt	folgtet	werdet folgen	würdet folgen	seid gefolgt
Sie sie	folgen	waren gefolgt	folgten	werden folgen	würden folgen	sind gefolgt

Die Polizisten **sind** den Fußabdrücken **gefolgt**.

The policemen followed the footprints.

Diese Seite **folgt** der vorigen Seite (Verb #84, kommen).

This page follows the previous one (verb #84, to come).

verhaften
to arrest

verhaftend

verhafte!/verhaftet!/verhaften Sie!

Sub.	Präsens	Plusquam-perfekt	Präteritum	Futur	Konditional	Perfekt
ich	verhafte	hatte verhaftet	verhaftete	werde verhaften	würde verhaften	habe verhaftet
du	verhaftest	hattest verhaftet	verhaftetest	wirst verhaften	würdest verhaften	hast verhaftet
er sie es	verhaftet	hatte verhaftet	verhaftete	wird verhaften	würde verhaften	hat verhaftet
wir	verhaften	hatten verhaftet	verhafteten	werden verhaften	würden verhaften	haben verhaftet
ihr	verhaftet	hattet verhaftet	verhaftetet	werdet verhaften	würdet verhaften	habt verhaftet
Sie sie	verhaften	hatten verhaftet	verhafteten	werden verhaften	würden verhaften	haben verhaftet

Sie **haben** Nico schließlich für den Einbruch **verhaftet**.

They finally arrested Nico for the burglary.

Verhaften Sie mich doch bitte nicht!

Please don't arrest me!

to wait

warten

Sub.	Präsens	Plusquam-perfekt	Präteritum	Futur	Konditional	Perfekt
ich	warte	hatte gewartet	wartete	werde warten	würde warten	habe gewartet
du	wartest	hattest gewartet	wartetest	wirst warten	würdest warten	hast gewartet
er sie es	wartet	hatte gewartet	wartete	wird warten	würde warten	hat gewartet
wir	warten	hatten gewartet	warteten	werden warten	würden warten	haben gewartet
ihr	wartet	hattet gewartet	wartetet	werdet warten	würdet warten	habt gewartet
Sie sie	warten	hatten gewartet	warteten	werden warten	würden warten	haben gewartet

Nico **wird** lange auf seine Befreiung **warten**.

Nico will have to wait a long time for his release.

Wie lange **warte** ich schon?

How long have I been waiting already?

winken

winkend

Sub.	Präsens	Plusquam- perfekt	Präteritum	Futur	Konditional	Perfekt
ich	winke	hatte gewinkt	winkte	werde winken	würde winken	habe gewinkt
du	winkst	hattest gewinkt	winktest	wirst winken	würdest winken	hast gewinkt
er sie es	winkt	hatte gewinkt	winkte	wird winken	würde winken	hat gewinkt
wir	winken	hatten gewinkt	winkten	werden winken	würden winken	haben gewinkt
ihr	winkt	hattet gewinkt	winktet	werdet winken	würdet winken	habt gewinkt
Sie sie	winken	hatten gewinkt	winkten	werden winken	würden winken	haben gewinkt

Paul und Mimi haben zuerst gewinkt.

Paul and Mimi waved first.

Ihre Freunde winken jetzt alle zurück.

Now their friends are all waving back.

to travel   reisen

reis(e)!/reist!/reisen Sie!   **reisend**

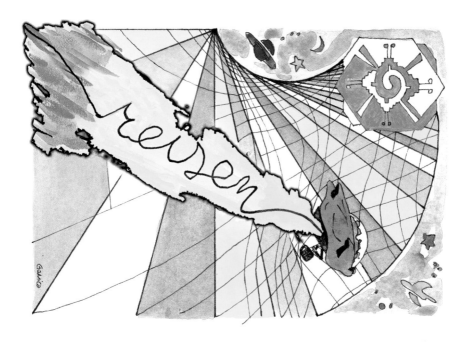

Sub.	Präsens	Plusquam-perfekt	Präteritum	Futur	Konditional	Perfekt
ich	reise	war gereist	reiste	werde reisen	würde reisen	bin gereist
du	reist	warst gereist	reistest	wirst reisen	würdest reisen	bist gereist
er sie es	reist	war gereist	reiste	wird reisen	würde reisen	ist gereist
wir	reisen	waren gereist	reisten	werden reisen	würden reisen	sind gereist
ihr	reist	wart gereist	reistet	werdet reisen	würdet reisen	seid gereist
Sie sie	reisen	waren gereist	reisten	werden reisen	würden reisen	sind gereist

Reisen sie denn in die Zukunft?

Are they travel(l)ing to the future?

Nein, diesmal **werden** sie in die Vergangenheit **reisen**.

No, this time they are going to travel to the past.

aufprallen

to collide, crash into

aufprallend

prall(e) auf!/prallt auf!/prallen Sie auf!

Sub.	Präsens	Plusquam-perfekt	Präteritum	Futur	Konditional	Perfekt
ich	pralle auf	war aufgeprallt	prallte auf	werde aufprallen	würde aufprallen	bin aufgeprallt
du	prallst auf	warst aufgeprallt	pralltest auf	wirst aufprallen	würdest aufprallen	bist aufgeprallt
er sie es	prallt auf	war aufgeprallt	prallte auf	wird aufprallen	würde aufprallen	ist aufgeprallt
wir	prallen auf	waren aufgeprallt	prallten auf	werden aufprallen	würden aufprallen	sind aufgeprallt
ihr	prallt auf	wart aufgeprallt	pralltet auf	werdet aufprallen	würdet aufprallen	seid aufgeprallt
Sie sie	prallen auf	waren aufgeprallt	prallten auf	werden aufprallen	würden aufprallen	sind aufgeprallt

Die Zeitmaschine **ist** mit einem Asteroid **aufgeprallt**, dann ist abgestürzt.

The time machine collided with an asteroid and then crashed.

Ich kann es nicht fassen, dass wir **aufgeprallt** mit etwas **sind**.

I can't believe we crashed into something.

to repair

reparier(e)!/repariert!/reparieren Sie!

reparieren

reparierend

Sub.	Präsens	Plusquam-perfekt	Präteritum	Futur	Konditional	Perfekt
ich	repariere	hatte repariert	reparierte	werde reparieren	würde reparieren	habe repariert
du	reparierst	hattest repariert	repariertest	wirst reparieren	würdest reparieren	hast repariert
er sie es	repariert	hatte repariert	reparierte	wird reparieren	würde reparieren	hat repariert
wir	reparieren	hatten repariert	reparierten	werden reparieren	würden reparieren	haben repariert
ihr	repariert	hattet repariert	repariertet	werdet reparieren	würdet reparieren	habt repariert
Sie sie	reparieren	hatten repariert	reparierten	werden reparieren	würden reparieren	haben repariert

Paul, kannst du die Maschine wirklich reparieren?

Paul, can you really repair the machine?

Natürlich! Ich werde sie sofort reparieren!

Of course! I'll repair it right away!

91

schweigen

to be quiet

schweig(e)!/schweigt!/schweigen Sie!

Sub.	Präsens	Plusquam-perfekt	Präteritum	Futur	Konditional	Perfekt
ich	schweige	hatte geschwiegen	schwieg	werde schweigen	würde schweigen	habe geschwiegen
du	schweigst	hattest geschwiegen	schwiegst	wirst schweigen	würdest schweigen	hast geschwiegen
er sie es	schweigt	hatte geschwiegen	schwieg	wird schweigen	würde schweigen	hat geschwiegen
wir	schweigen	hatten geschwiegen	schwiegen	werden schweigen	würden schweigen	haben geschwiegen
ihr	schweigt	hattet geschwiegen	schwiegt	werdet schweigen	würdet schweigen	habt geschwiegen
Sie sie	schweigen	hatten geschwiegen	schwiegen	werden schweigen	würden schweigen	haben geschwiegen

Toby, du musst schweigen. Und bewege dich nicht!

Toby, you have to be quiet. And don't move!

Wenn wir schweigen , wird das Tier uns in Ruhe lassen.

If we are quiet, the animal will leave us alone.

Sub.	Präsens	Plusquam-perfekt	Präteritum	Futur	Konditional	Perfekt
ich	zünde an	hatte angezündet	zündete an	werde anzünden	würde anzünden	habe angezündet
du	zündest an	hattest angezündet	zündetest an	wirst anzünden	würdest anzünden	hast angezündet
er sie es	zündet an	hatte angezündet	zündete an	wird anzünden	würde anzünden	hat angezündet
wir	zünden an	hatten angezündet	zündeten an	werden anzünden	würden anzünden	haben angezündet
ihr	zündet an	hattet angezündet	zündetet an	werdet anzünden	würdet anzünden	habt angezündet
Sie sie	zünden an	hatten angezündet	zündeten an	werden anzünden	würden anzünden	haben angezündet

Paul, kannst du das Holz denn anzünden?

Paul, can you get the wood to burn?

Wenn ich ein Streichholz hätte, würde ich es sofort anzünden.

If I had a match, I would light it right away.

93

tragen
to carry

tragend

trag(e)!/tragt!/tragen Sie!

Sub.	Präsens	Plusquam-perfekt	Präteritum	Futur	Konditional	Perfekt
ich	trage	hatte getragen	trug	werde tragen	würde tragen	habe getragen
du	trägst	hattest getragen	trugst	wirst tragen	würdest tragen	hast getragen
er sie es	trägt	hatte getragen	trug	wird tragen	würde tragen	hat getragen
wir	tragen	hatten getragen	trugen	werden tragen	würden tragen	haben getragen
ihr	tragt	hattet getragen	trugt	werdet tragen	würdet tragen	habt getragen
Sie sie	tragen	hatten getragen	trugen	werden tragen	würden tragen	haben getragen

Tut es nicht weh, wenn du diese schweren Feuersteine **trägst**?

Doesn't it hurt if you carry these heavy flintstones?

Diese Steine **haben** wir von weitem **getragen**, aber es lohnt sich.

We carried these stones from far away, but it's worth it.

to cut

schneiden

schneide!/schneidet!/schneiden Sie!

schneidend

Sub.	Präsens	Plusquam-perfekt	Präteritum	Futur	Konditional	Perfekt
ich	schneide	hatte geschnitten	schnitt	werde schneiden	würde schneiden	habe geschnitten
du	schneidest	hattest geschnitten	schnittest	wirst schneiden	würdest schneiden	hast geschnitten
er sie es	schneidet	hatte geschnitten	schnitt	wird schneiden	würde schneiden	hat geschnitten
wir	schneiden	hatten geschnitten	schnitten	werden schneiden	würden schneiden	haben geschnitten
ihr	schneidet	hattet geschnitten	schnittet	werdet schneiden	würdet schneiden	habt geschnitten
Sie sie	schneiden	hatten geschnitten	schnitten	werden schneiden	würden schneiden	haben geschnitten

Mimi hat das Papier mit einer Schere geschnitten.

Mimi cut the paper with scissors.

Mimi, du schneidest ein sehr schönes Muster.

Mimi, you're cutting a very pretty pattern.

machen

machend

to make

mach(e)!/macht!/machen Sie!

Sub.	Präsens	Plusquam-perfekt	Präteritum	Futur	Konditional	Perfekt
ich	mache	hatte gemacht	machte	werde machen	würde machen	habe gemacht
du	machst	hattest gemacht	machtest	wirst machen	würdest machen	hast gemacht
er sie es	macht	hatte gemacht	machte	wird machen	würde machen	hat gemacht
wir	machen	hatten gemacht	machten	werden machen	würden machen	haben gemacht
ihr	macht	hattet gemacht	machtet	werdet machen	würdet machen	habt gemacht
Sie sie	machen	hatten gemacht	machten	werden machen	würden machen	haben gemacht

Paul würde eine elegante Skulptur machen, wenn er nur Zeit hätte.

Paul would make an elegant sculpture if only he had time.

Paul hat einen schrecklichen Lärm gemacht!

Paul made a dreadful noise!

Sub.	Präsens	Plusquam-perfekt	Präteritum	Futur	Konditional	Perfekt
ich	nehme auf	hatte aufgenommen	nahm auf	werde aufnehmen	würde aufnehmen	habe aufgenommen
du	nimmst auf	hattest aufgenommen	nahmst auf	wirst aufnehmen	würdest aufnehmen	hast aufgenommen
er sie es	nimmt auf	hatte aufgenommen	nahm auf	wird aufnehmen	würde aufnehmen	hat aufgenommen
wir	nehmen auf	hatten aufgenommen	nahmen auf	werden aufnehmen	würden aufnehmen	haben aufgenommen
ihr	nehmt auf	hattet aufgenommen	nahmt auf	werdet aufnehmen	würdet aufnehmen	habt aufgenommen
Sie sie	nehmen auf	hatten aufgenommen	nahmen auf	werden aufnehmen	würden aufnehmen	haben aufgenommen

Wir **nehmen** einen Film über Cleopatra **auf**.

We're filming a movie about Cleopatra.

Die nächste Reise **werde** ich unbedingt **aufnehmen**.

I will definitely film our next trip.

essen

to eat

essend

Sub.	Präsens	Plusquam-perfekt	Präteritum	Futur	Konditional	Perfekt
ich	esse	hatte gegessen	aß	werde essen	würde essen	habe gegessen
du	ißt	hattest gegessen	aßest	wirst essen	würdest essen	hast gegessen
er sie es	ißt	hatte gegessen	aß	wird essen	würde essen	hat gegessen
wir	essen	hatten gegessen	aßen	werden essen	würden essen	haben gegessen
ihr	eßt	hattet gegessen	aßt	werdet essen	würdet essen	habt gegessen
Sie sie	essen	hatten gegessen	aßen	werden essen	würden essen	haben gegessen

Mimi und Paul **aßen** eine Kleinigkeit.

Mimi and Paul were having a snack.

Der Löwe fragte sich: wieso **essen** diese Menschen so langsam?

The lion asked itself: why do these human beings eat so slowly?

to stroll, go for a walk

spazieren

spazier(e)!/spaziert!/spazieren Sie!

spazierend

Sub.	Präsens	Plusquam-perfekt	Präteritum	Futur	Konditional	Perfekt
ich	spaziere	war spaziert	spazierte	werde spazieren	würde spazieren	bin spaziert
du	spazierst	warst spaziert	spaziertest	wirst spazieren	würdest spazieren	bist spaziert
er sie es	spaziert	war spaziert	spazierte	wird spazieren	würde spazieren	ist spaziert
wir	spazieren	waren spaziert	spazierten	werden spazieren	würden spazieren	sind spaziert
ihr	spaziert	wart spaziert	spaziertet	werdet spazieren	würdet spazieren	seid spaziert
Sie sie	spazieren	waren spaziert	spazierten	werden spazieren	würden spazieren	sind spaziert

Paul **spaziert** mit Mimi durch den Park.

Paul is strolling through the park with Mimi.

Was sind das für Menschen, die neben uns **spazieren**?

What kind of people are those walking next to us?

99

wohnen

wohnend

wohn(e)!/wohnt!/wohnen Sie!

Sub.	Präsens	Plusquam-perfekt	Präteritum	Futur	Konditional	Perfekt
ich	wohne	hatte gewohnt	wohnte	werde wohnen	würde wohnen	habe gewohnt
du	wohnst	hattest gewohnt	wohntest	wirst wohnen	würdest wohnen	hast gewohnt
er sie es	wohnt	hatte gewohnt	wohnte	wird wohnen	würde wohnen	hat gewohnt
wir	wohnen	hatten gewohnt	wohnten	werden wohnen	würden wohnen	haben gewohnt
ihr	wohnt	hattet gewohnt	wohntet	werdet wohnen	würdet wohnen	habt gewohnt
Sie sie	wohnen	hatten gewohnt	wohnten	werden wohnen	würden wohnen	haben gewohnt

Wo werden wir wohnen?

Where shall we live?

Wir könnten in England, Kanada, den USA, ... wohnen.

We could live in England, Canada, the United States, . . .

to stop

stoppen

stopp(e)!/stoppt!/stoppen Sie!

stoppend

Sub.	Präsens	Plusquam-perfekt	Präteritum	Futur	Konditional	Perfekt
ich	stoppe	hatte gestoppt	stoppte	werde stoppen	würde stoppen	habe gestoppt
du	stoppst	hattest gestoppt	stopptest	wirst stoppen	würdest stoppen	hast gestoppt
er sie es	stoppt	hatte gestoppt	stoppte	wird stoppen	würde stoppen	hat gestoppt
wir	stoppen	hatten gestoppt	stoppten	werden stoppen	würden stoppen	haben gestoppt
ihr	stoppt	hattet gestoppt	stopptet	werdet stoppen	würdet stoppen	habt gestoppt
Sie sie	stoppen	hatten gestoppt	stoppten	werden stoppen	würden stoppen	haben gestoppt

Paul, warum **stoppst** du die Zeitmaschine?

Paul, why are you stopping the time machine?

Dieses Verb **hat** unsere Geschichte **gestoppt**.

This verb has stopped our story.

101

German Verb Index

The 101 verbs in blue throughout this Index are verbs you've seen conjugated within the text. A further 150 common German verbs are also included, cross-referenced to a verb in the book that follows the same pattern. Note that separable-prefix verbs are marked by • after their separable prefix.

English Verb Index

This index allows you to look up German verbs by their English meaning. Each English verb is matched to a German equivalent; a German verb in blue is one of the 101 sample conjugations found within the text, while verbs in black follow the pattern of the verb on the cross-referenced page. Note that separable-prefix verbs are marked by • after their separable prefix.

to accompany begleiten 54
to advise informieren 54
to allow erlauben 54
to annoy ärgern 75
to answer antworten 75
to arrest verhaften 86
to arrive an•kommen 32
to ask fragen 75; ask (for) bitten 81
to ask for fordern 75

to bathe baden 75
to be sein 46
to be able to können 4
to be missing fehlen 75
to be of use dienen 75
to be quiet schweigen 92
to beat klopfen 75
to believe glauben 75
to belong gehören 54
to bring bringen 12
to build bauen 61
to buy kaufen 69

to call rufen 83
to carry tragen 94
to celebrate feiern 75
to change ändern 75; schalten 75; tauschen 49; verändern 54
to check prüfen 75
to choose wählen 75
to clean putzen 62
to climb klettern 75
to close schließen 38
to collect sammeln 75
to collide auf•prallen 90
to comb sich kämmen 30
to come kommen 84
to complain klagen 75
to concentrate konzentrieren 54
to consider über•legen 93

to construct bauen 61
to cook kochen 13
to cost kosten 75
to count zählen 59
to crash auf•prallen 90
to create schaffen 5
to cry weinen 75
to cut schneiden 95

to damage schaden 75
to dance tanzen 7
to deal with behandeln 54
to decide entscheiden 47
to deliver liefern 75
to develop entwickeln 54
to direct dirigieren 1
to disappoint enttäuschen 54
to discover entdecken 54
to discuss diskutieren 54
to display aus•stellen 93
to disturb stören 75
to divide teilen 75
to doubt zweifeln 75
to draw zeichnen 75
to dream träumen 52
to drink trinken 16
to drive fahren 58

to earn verdienen 54
to eat essen 98
to eat breakfast frühstücken 75
to enter ein•treten 82
to establish fest•sellen 93; gründen 75
to estimate rechnen 75
to exchange wechseln 75
to excuse entschuldigen 54
to exist existieren 54
to expect erwarten 54
to explain erklären 54

105

to fall **fallen** 26; stürzen 75
to fear fürchten 75
to feel fühlen 75
to fetch holen 75; ab•holen 93
to fight **kämpfen** 36
to fill füllen 75
to find **finden** 10
to finish **beenden** 54
to follow **folgen** 85
to forbid **verbieten** 73
to forget **vergessen** 39
to function funktionieren 54

to get holen 75
to get dressed **sich an•ziehen** 31
to get married **heiraten** 72
to give **geben** 66; schenken 75
to go down **hinunter•gehen** 19
to go in **ein•treten** 82
to go out **aus•gehen** 28
to go shopping **ein•kaufen** 93
to grasp fassen 75
to greet **winken** 88; begrüßen 54;
    grüßen 75
to grow **wachsen** 11

to handle an•fassen 93
to happen passieren 54; to happen
    (to someone) sich ereignen 30
to have **haben** 2
to hear **hören** 35
to heat heizen 75
to hope hoffen 75
to hurry sich beeilen 30

to improve verbessern 54
to increase erhölen 54
to inform mit•teilen 93
to inspect besichtigen 54
to install ein•setzen 93
to interest interessieren 54
to introduce vor•stellen 93

to jump **springen** 76

to kick **treten** 44
to kill töten 75
to kiss **küssen** 68
to know **wissen** 48

to last (time) dauern 75
to laugh lachen 75

to lay legen 75
to lead führen 75
to learn **lernen** 50
to lie (tell a) **lügen** 56
to light an•zünden 93
to like **mögen** 14
to listen to zü•horen 93
to live **wohnen** 100; leben 75
to look schauen 75
to look after besorgen 54
to look at an•schauen 93
to look for **suchen** 27
to lose **verlieren** 23
to love **lieben** 75

to maintain behaupten 54
to make **machen** 96
to mean bedeuten 54; meinen 75
to meet begegnen 54
to mention erwähnen 54

to need brauchen 75
to notice bemerken 54; merken
    75

to obey beachten 54
to observe **bewachen** 78;
    beobachten 54
to obstruct behindern 54
to occur sich ereignen 30
to open **öffnen** 15
to order bestellen 54
to organize **ordnen** 60;
    ein•richten 93

to pack packen 75
to paint **malen** 6
to pass über•holen 93
to pay bezahlen 54; **zahlen** 70
to persuade überzeugen 54
to phone **rufen** 83
to plan planen 75
to play **spielen** 21
to polish **polieren** 63
to prepare bereiten 54;
    vor•bereiten 93
to press drücken 75
to protect schützen 75
to put **stellen** 22; setzen 75

to quit **auf•hören** 9

Comments from Teachers
About the *101 Verbs* Series

"The colo(u)r-coding in this book makes for quick identification of tenses, and the running stories provided by the pictures are an ideal mnemonic device in that they help students visualize each word. I would heartily recommend this fun verb book for use with pupils in the early stages of language learning and for revision later on in their school careers. . . . This is a praiseworthy attempt to make Spanish verbs more easily accessible to every schoolboy and girl in the country."

—DR. JOSEP-LLUÍS GONZÁLEZ MEDINA,
HEAD OF SPANISH, ETON COLLEGE, ENGLAND

"This book is easy to refer to and very good for learning the raw forms of the verbs and the pictures are a great help for triggering the memory. The way the story comes together is quite amazing and students found the colo(u)r-coded verb tables extremely useful, allowing the eye to go straight to the tense they are working on . . ."

—SUE TRICIO, THURROCK & BASILDON COLLEGE,
ENGLAND

"Verbs are brought to life in this book through skillful use of humorous storytelling. This innovative approach to language learning transforms an often dull and uninspiring process into one which is refreshing and empowering."

—KAREN BROOKS, SPANISH TEACHER,
PENRICE COMMUNITY COLLEGE, ENGLAND

"The understanding and learning of verbs is probably the key to improving communication at every level. With this book verbs can be learnt quickly and accurately."

—R. PLACE, TYNE METROPOLITAN COLLEGE, ENGLAND

"No more boring grammar lessons!!! This book is a great tool for learning verbs through excellent illustrations. A must-have for all language learners."

—LYNDA MCTIER, LIPSON COMMUNITY COLLEGE,
ENGLAND

Way~

all the best.

A masterful blend of stark realism and thrilling adventure, you won't find yourself crying foul on how the events play out. An excellent grasp of the concepts of society and survival are on full display. This wasn't just a book for me, it was an experience!

– Colin Webster,
author of *Blood and Tequila* –

Skip Coryell has done it again. Not only is *The Shadow Militia* a fast-paced, thrill-a-minute, strap-in-or-you'll-be-thrown-off action novel, it is a sometimes raw and often endearing commentary on love, patriotism and all-out survival. Coryell's rich characterization and compelling, real-life speak makes this second installment in The Thousand Year Night trilogy a more than worthy sequel to *The God Virus*. One can only imagine what Coryell has up his sleeve for the finale.

.– Josh Clark, author of
The McGurney Chronicles
and the *Dakota Lester* books

The wait is over! If you've been hollering for Book Two ever since you finished *The God Virus*, your time has come. Skip Coryell has outdone himself with *The Shadow Militia*. Once again, this is not a book for the faint-hearted, but if you love a fast-moving, believable action-adventure story - this one's for you. Now, the bad news: just when you think Good has triumphed over Evil and our heroes (and heroines) can take a breath - the book ends with the warning that the next peril is on the way.

– Mary Mueller author of
The Redemption of Matthew Ryersen–

The
Shadow
Militia

The Golden Horde Advances…

Skip

Coryell

Published by White Feather Press. (www.whitefeatherpress.com)

ISBN 978-1-61808-030-1

Printed in the United States of America

Cover design created by Ron Bell of AdVision Design Group (www.advisiondesigngroup.com)

White Feather Press

Reaffirming Faith in God, Family, and Country!

Books by Skip Coryell

We Hold These Truths
Bond of Unseen Blood
Church and State
Blood in the Streets
Laughter and Tears
RKBA: Defending the Right to Keep and Bear Arms
Stalking Natalie
The God Virus
The Shadow Militia

For Sara Sunbreak.

The light of my life.

What has gone before…

In book one of this series, *The God Virus*, a cyber terrorist attack takes out the American power grid, leaving the entire country in darkness, death and widespread chaos. Dan Branch and his son, Jeremy, have to drive through Northern Wisconsin to the Michigan Lower Peninsula to the safety of his Uncle Rodney's home. Uncle Rodney, an eccentric, hardcore prepper and Vietnam vet tries to rescue Dan but fails.

It takes Dan and his son six months to reach the safety of the northern Lower Peninsula. On the way Dan is forced to kill many men. He also rescues Jackie, a damsel in distress, and marries her. When they finally reach Iroquois City, Uncle Rodney announces he is the commanding general of *The Shadow Militia* and a mob of over a thousand cut throats and thieves will be attacking within the week.

Welcome home. And thus, the story begins where it left off. I am proud to give you … *The Shadow Militia*!

CHAPTER 1

The Golden Horde Advances

DAN **B**RANCH SAT NERVOUSLY around the big conference table at the old, red brick courthouse that he'd passed thousands of times before in his youth. The old world, the one with electricity, now seemed like a million miles ago. So much had happened since those innocent days of his youth, but, if he was honest about it, even then, there'd been nothing innocent or carefree about growing up with his Uncle Rodney.

And now he knew why.

Way back then he'd always known there was something different about his uncle, something strange, something vague, maybe even something special, but … General Branch? His own uncle, the leader of the Shadow Militia? He mulled it over in his mind as Uncle Rodney pulled out a pack of Camel nonfiltereds from his front breast pocket. Rodney reached in his jeans to pull out his trusty Zippo, but Colonel MacPherson already had a Bic lighter out in front of him, suspended over the table, its flame reaching up toward the dead, fluorescent lighting in the ceiling above.

The big window curtains on both walls of the corner room were wide open, letting in the rare March sunshine. Dan gazed out at the courthouse lawn. A small crowd had gathered around the two Apache attack helicopters resting there, flanked on all four sides by Shadow Militia soldiers in full battle gear bearing M4 carbines. The Huey had already been dispatched to take Jeremy and Jackie to the Sheriff's house to be with his wife, Marge, until this meeting was over. Then, they'd be picked up again for the final move to Uncle Rodney's house in the woods a few miles outside of town.

Dan had no idea what would happen then. Things had changed. No, everything had changed. His anticipation of a tedious, difficult life of survival had been dashed when they'd flown over the small city of Greenville, Michigan, a few hours ago. The carnage he'd seen there still made him shiver inside.

"Why do you smoke in here, Rodney? You know I don't like it."

General Branch looked over at his friend and smiled. "God came to me in a dream, Sheriff, and he told me it was my purpose in life to teach you patience."

Sheriff Leif cocked his head and raised his left eyebrow.

"Yeah, right. To teach me patience." He mumbled under his breath. "Those things are going to kill you."

Rodney ignored the comment and looked over at Dan and his face grew serious.

"Dan, I feel I need to apologize to you. I kept a lot of things from you while you were growing up. I led a bit of a double life, but there were things I just couldn't tell you. I wanted to spare you the complication, and we just couldn't risk the security compromise."

The General then glanced over at Joe Leif. "You too, Sheriff. I just couldn't tell you everything back then. It would've put you in an awkward position as the head law enforcement officer of the county, because I was doing things in violation of federal and state laws."

Sheriff Leif watched the thick, blue smoke drift up from the cigarette until it stopped at the ceiling and billowed out toward the walls.

"I think I understand. You didn't want to be arrested for illegal arms trafficking." He nodded out the window at the lawn and the growing crowd. "You know, little things like a fleet of attack helicopters, battle tanks, and only God knows what else." The Sheriff gritted his teeth and ground them slightly. "For all I know you could have a bunch of ICBMs buried in your back yard!"

The Sheriff noticed his voice was rising, so he clamped his mouth shut and looked away. Rodney smiled sympathetically. "Don't be silly, Joe." And then he grinned. "I would never stockpile nuclear weapons on my own property. I'd put them in the state forest where they couldn't be traced back to me."

The two men locked eyes like bulls in an arena. Then, the Sheriff's eyes softened, and he looked down at the table top. When he finally spoke again, it was with a great sense of reluctance in his voice.

"So, are you going to help me save my people or not?"

General Branch glanced over at the Colonel where their eyes met briefly. From across the table, Dan sensed the two men had communicated in that single, short glance in ways he'd never known possible. He thought to himself, *They have a long history.*

Rodney leaned back in his chair and snuffed out his half-smoked cigarette by rolling the burning ash between his fingers. He put the butt into his breast pocket.

Colonel MacPherson was speaking now. "Sheriff Leif. The Shadow Militia has the highest respect for the office of Sheriff. The office of Sheriff is the one remaining constitutionally mandated and elected office in this county, perhaps even in the whole state for all we know." He paused.

"You are in charge of Iroquois County. We are here simply to advise and assist."

Sheriff Leif looked up from the table. He met eyes with the Colonel and then with Rodney Branch.

"Are you serious, Colonel?"

Colonel MacPherson nodded. "We are at your service, sir."

The hint of a smile moved across Sheriff Joe's lips. "Okay then. I'd like you to take ten of those attack helicopters and annihilate the mob heading toward us."

The Colonel didn't answer. His lips pursed tightly together.

General Branch leaned forward again, placing his elbows on the table with both fists on either side of his chin.

"We can't do that, Joe."

Sheriff Leif's chair slid backward into the wall as he stood. "What! You can't? What does that mean? You said you commanded them. What's going on here, Rodney?"

Suddenly, Rodney felt the need for the other half of his cigarette, but he denied himself the urge. He let his hands fall down onto the table. Dan Branch watched as his uncle's eyes grew frozen-stone cold before speaking. Dan shivered at the change.

"There are certain things we know, but cannot divulge. The things we know demand we not tip our hand. We cannot deploy our forces in mass. It would jeopardize not just Iroquois County, but the entire Midwest."

Moving both arms up to his chest, Sheriff Leif folded them together and looked down at the two military men.

"What kind of a cock and bull story is that?"

Rodney looked down at the table top, and when he spoke, his voice carried an apologetic tone. "I can't tell you, Joe, and you're just going to have to trust me."

"What!" The Sheriff slammed his right fist down on the table top as he screamed. Then he made an effort to regain his composure before he spoke again. Sheriff Leif bit down on his lip, and Dan thought for sure it was going to bleed. Against his better judgment, he decided to get involved.

"Uncle Rodney, please. We have a thousand murderers heading this way to rape our women and kill our children. Don't keep us guessing. Exactly what *are* you allowed to do? How *can* you help us?"

General Branch glanced over at the Colonel as if they

were mind melding again. Dan thought he saw his uncle give a slight nod, but he couldn't be sure. Finally, Colonel MacPherson turned back to the Sheriff and spoke.

"We can help arm you. We can train you."

Sheriff Leif looked over at him in disbelief. "How are you going to do that when they'll be here in just over a week?"

The Colonel's eyes locked onto the Sheriff like a laser. "We can also slow them down."

Joe Leif leaned his shoulders against the wall behind him as he thought. Finally, he sat back down in his chair and scooted it back up to the table.

"Okay. You can slow them down. How much? How much time can you give us?"

Slowly, a smile spread across the Colonel's face. When his grin reached full bloom, he exclaimed, "A month. We can give you thirty days."

☆ ☆ ☆ ☆

They were all back at Uncle Rodney's house now, seated on the front porch and no one was talking. The Colonel had flown away with his three helicopters, purportedly to make some arrangements and prepare for the county's defense. Jackie felt more vulnerable now that he and his soldiers were gone. She wondered, *Perhaps we should have stayed in Escanaba where it's safe?*

She held baby Donna on her lap now. The pain in her broken leg had subsided, but her skin underneath the cast was starting to itch like crazy. Dan's Uncle Rodney had relinquished his old rocking chair to her with a gentlemanly smile. Jeremy sat a few feet away with his right elbow propped up on the wooden railing. The big German Shepherd named Moses was lying beside him as the boy stroked his massive head.

"So shouldn't we be doing something right now? Like training, practicing, shooting our guns or something? I mean, hey, we've got a thousand screaming bad guys coming straight at us, and they want to kill us all."

Uncle Rodney laughed out loud. "I like your son, Dan. He's a straight shooter. He doesn't mince words, and I respect that in a man." Rodney glanced over and nodded at Jackie a few feet away before adding, "And from a woman as well."

Jackie smiled back nervously. She just didn't quite know what to think of Uncle Rodney. He seemed like the kind of man who could open the door for a lady with one hand while shooting a man in the back with the other. But at the same time, she had a feeling that he would die for Dan, and even for her and Jeremy and baby Donna, simply because Dan loved them, and that trait alone made him one of the good guys.

"I'm interested to hear everything that happened to you after leaving Menomonie, but you must be tired from all the travel …"

Rodney let the sentence trail off into the breeze around them. Dan smiled, knowing it was his invitation, that the General wanted to hear a full debriefing of his exploits. Dan thought to himself, *I have a few questions of my own, old man.* Dan stood up abruptly, and ran his left hand through his lengthening, blonde hair from forehead to neck. He glanced over at Jackie, all the while, smiling with his eyes.

"Honey, do you mind if I walk with my uncle for a while? We have a lot to talk about."

The concerned look was still on her face, but Jackie forced a smile and a nod.

"Can I come too, Dad?"

"Better not, Son. We need a man here to watch after the place. We won't be far though. Just fire a shot if you need help."

The two men walked off the porch and down the drive. When they reached the dirt road in front of the house, they turned left and walked away. Jackie watched them until they disappeared, all the while wondering what kind of fate was about to fall on her and her baby.

* * * *

"So what happened to your other wife, Debbie?"

Uncle Rodney's voice was emotionless as they both walked down the dirt side trail through the woods. Dan answered him curtly.

"She killed herself with a drug overdose."

Rodney thought for a moment and nodded.

"No offense on the dead, but that doesn't surprise me a bit. I never liked that woman."

Dan didn't say anything at first. Then he answered shortly. "You were right about her."

His uncle took a pack of cigarettes out of his pocket and started to shake one out, but he hesitated and then replaced them in his pocket. Dan gave him a quizzical look.

"You're not smoking?"

The old man shook his head. "Nope. I'm cutting back. I have to stay alive for now."

Then he continued his questioning. "The boy seems like good stock. Has he proven himself yet?"

Dan nodded. "Unfortunately, yes." And then he recounted the story of how Jeremy had shot and killed the man on the snowmobile and after that the man on the river.

Rodney grunted and reached up to his lips to remove the cigarette that wasn't there. "And you? How many did you have to kill to make it here?"

"Nine."

Rodney stopped walking. He stared directly into his nephew's eyes. Then he nodded and started walking again. "I recognized the look. I knew you were different. I trust they all needed killing." It wasn't a question, but more a statement of fact.

"And the woman. If she's going to live with us I need to know it all."

This time it was Dan who stopped walking. He looked deeply into his uncle's eyes before talking.

7

"She's the best. I place my life in her hands. I would die for her."

Uncle Rodney contemplated his answer and finally nodded. "She looks Muslim to me. I don't trust Muslims. You know that."

Dan nodded. "Yes, I know. Her father was a Christian. Her mother was a Muslim who converted to Christianity when they both fell in love. The Muslims murdered Jackie's father, and she grew up with her paternal grandparents here in America after that. She went to a Christian college, married a missionary. They were together when I ran across them."

Rodney looked down at the sand and then back up again. "So where is her husband now?"

"He's dead. I shot him."

Uncle Rodney reached back up to his shirt pocket for a cigarette but caught himself halfway.

"You killed Jackie's husband and then married her?"

Dan nodded briefly.

"How exactly does that work, young Daniel?"

A big sigh escaped Dan's lips. He didn't want to go into this, but he knew he had to satisfy his uncle.

"They were both strapped to chairs in their cabin. She was pregnant and due. The man was torturing them. He needed killing and I obliged him. The bullet passed through and hit her husband. I tried to save him, but he was gut shot."

The old man looked over to his left and off through the bare trees. It would be another month before leaves started to take limb.

"So you delivered her baby and holed up in the cabin until March?"

Dan nodded.

"And she forgave you?"

Dan nodded again.

"That's not the Muslim way."

Then he looked back at his nephew with frankness in his

eyes. "Listen, Daniel, I've never been married. Don't know the way of men and women, so I won't presume to pass judgment on the two of you. So just tell me straight out. Does she love You?"

The right side of Dan's lips turned up as he nodded.

"Would she die for you?"

"I believe she would."

Dan watched as the wheels and gears twisted and turned inside his uncle's head. He'd expected this, all the while knowing his uncle wasn't equipped to live with a woman in the house much less children. Dan added the clincher.

"If she goes - I go."

The face of the old man tightened into a grimace, his wrinkles coming together like the confluence of a million dry creek beds. Finally he nodded his head and slumped his shoulders.

"All right then. It's settled. But you're responsible for her. The little baby too. I don't want her crying at night. No getting into my stuff. And everybody pulls their weight. I'm not running a homeless shelter here."

Dan hesitated. Then his next words surprised even him.

"Uncle Rodney, listen to me. We'll agree to stay and help you out here. But you have to understand that we're a family, and we want you to be part of that family too. Jeremy is my son, Donna is my daughter, and Jackie is my wife. That's a sacred thing of God."

Rodney raised his left hand up to scratch his chin in thought. Dan went on.

"And you're going to have to be a good grampa to the kids. No cussing in front of them, church once a week and no smoking in the house."

Rodney's left eyebrow raised up involuntarily in a reflex action at the last statement, as if to say, *Oh really? You're going to tell me what to do in my own house?* But the old man didn't say that. He thought silently to himself for a full minute, scratching the stubble on his chin, his eyes wandering off into the woods. The longer he waited, the more nervous Dan became.

Finally, a smile spread across his uncle's face. His left hand moved over to his breast pocket and pulled out the pack of Camel unfiltereds. He started to shake one out, but then he abruptly stopped. The cigarettes suddenly crushed and crumpled as Rodney's hand squeezed shut. Then he tossed the crumpled-up pack to the side of the trail.

The old man placed his hand on Dan's shoulders and turned him around to face the way they'd come.

"Welcome home, Daniel."

They walked away down the trail, not saying another word until they reached the house.

CHAPTER 2

The Sniper

"THAT'S HIM? THAT'S THE GUY
who's going to give us an extra month to prepare?"

Sheriff Leif looked over at Rodney in disbelief. "One guy? That's all you can spare for us?"

Rodney, wearing a heavy, green wool shirt and flannel-lined jeans, just smiled.

"He's not *just* one guy. He's a highly trained Marine Corps sniper. That man is a force of one, capable of head shots almost a mile out."

The Sheriff nodded. "Okay, that's fine. But we've got a thousand bad guys headed our way. How many of them can he kill?"

Rodney smirked. "As many as we let him. But who he kills is more important than how many. That simple, unassuming man is here to cut the head off the snake."

Donny Brewster was wearing a tattered pair of faded, black jeans and a green T-shirt that read *Jesus Saves*. He walked straight up to Rodney, snapped to attention and saluted crisply. Rodney reached out his right hand.

"No more saluting, son. We're in a war zone now."

Donny Brewster accepted his general's handshake.

"It's an honor, sir."

Rodney pointed at Joe Leif. "Thanks for coming, Sergeant.

This is Joe Leif, Sheriff of Iroquois County. We are here at his discretion."

Donny turned and offered his hand. Joe accepted it, feeling firsthand the strength in the man's grip. That was when he noticed the power in the man's upper body. Even though the T-shirt was large and loose, it was obvious Donny Brewster worked out.

"Thank you for coming, Mr. Brewster."

Donny smiled broadly. "It's my pleasure, sir, and I mean that in every sense of the word."

Joe thought to himself, *What does he mean by that?* But he said nothing. Just then Dan Branch walked up behind them. Joe was surprised when the two men embraced.

"Good to see you again, Donny! Jeremy knows you're coming and he's excited about it."

Donny smiled. "Roger that, Marine. Maybe we can get together before I head out." The sniper glanced quickly over at his general, who nodded slightly.

"Dinner at my place tonight at 1800 hours, Sergeant. You can have some down time, then we'll brief you tomorrow and get you on your way."

Just then the crew chief from the Blackhawk helicopter walked up carrying a duffle bag. He threw it down at Donny's feet. "You still have those two footlockers in there, Donny, but I know better than to touch a sniper's gear."

Donny laughed out loud. "Good call. I'll get them myself."

"I'll help." Dan stepped forward and walked with Donny over to the Blackhawk where they began unloading the two, large, plastic footlockers.

"This one's pretty light. What's in it?"

Donny smiled. "Just my Ghillie, and some clothes."

Dan nodded at the one Donny was now unloading. "And what ya got in there?"

The sergeant's face became more serious. "These are my babies. No one touches my babies."

Dan laughed out loud. "You snipers are such stoics."

As the two men walked back to the General, towing the footlockers behind them, Joe Leif looked on thoughtfully, all the while wondering. *How could things change so fast? Six months ago I'd probably be arresting this man, but now he's our greatest hope?* He looked down at the ground and sighed. These days he was just holding on for the ride, never knowing what the new day would bring.

"Ma'am, I gotta tell ya. This is for sure the best damn food I've had in ages." Donny Brewster shoveled another spoonful of food into his mouth. A piece of venison fell off his lips and onto the table, but Donny seemed not to notice.

Across from the table, Dan smiled quietly as his wife winced at the sniper's lack of table manners. Jackie thought to herself, *If he's around for very long, I'll have to do something about that.*

Jeremy sat beside his new idol, smiling broadly, secretly wanting to go into battle with his new friend. Uncle Rodney looked on from the head of the table and thought to himself, *I have to order Sergeant Brewster not to cuss in front of women and children.* General Branch was a man of few words, thinking multitudes, but saying very little. For him, Stoicism was a serious religion. He'd learned long ago that the only words regretted were the ones spoken.

"Thank you, Sergeant Brewster. It's just goulash." She couldn't stop herself from glancing over at Dan's uncle as she spoke. "We seem to have an amazing supply of food here."

Dan laughed out loud. "Didn't I tell you, honey? My Uncle Rodney is a prepper par excellence! He's been preparing for this since Noah stepped off the boat."

Jackie nodded. "I can see that. And we have electricity, hot and cold running water, even toilets that flush." She glanced over at Uncle Rodney suspiciously. "I haven't seen that in over six months."

Uncle Rodney locked eyes with her, his whole face taking on the countenance of granite. Jackie couldn't help but think, *He's sizing me up. Give him something to think about.* Jackie and Rodney's eyes remained locked for a full ten seconds. No one spoke. Dan looked up and felt his chest tighten, all the while thinking to himself, *Don't challenge him, honey. Back down.* But he couldn't say it out loud, so he had to helplessly watch the silent battle. Slowly, he reached his hand over and placed it on her knee. He squeezed softly, and was surprised when she pulled her leg away.

Finally, Jackie ended the confrontation with an almost imperceptible wink of her left eye before turning away. Uncle Rodney picked up his fork again and smiled deep inside, all the while thinking, *She's an alpha. How interesting.*

Jeremy, oblivious to the tension, shattered it with his next question. "Donny, can I go with you on your mission? I want to help."

Dan looked up abruptly, his eyes immediately turning to steel. "No!" Then he faltered, realizing how loud and abrupt his objection had been. Donny stopped eating and glanced up at Dan. Finally, he smiled.

"Not this time, champ. This one is a solo run." He looked over at his general as if to glean direction, but received none. "But as soon as I get back, I'll teach you some sniper secrets." Donny paused. "We got a deal?"

Jeremy's face broke into a grin as he reached his hand over. Donny gave him a firm handshake to seal the new covenant. Dan relaxed and slouched his shoulders down a bit. The relief was etched all over his face.

Jackie bent down to pick up baby Donna who'd been crawling under her chair. She scooped her up and drew her close to her face. All this testosterone was getting on her nerves. *Why can't men just relax?*

General Branch placed his fork beside his plate and pushed

it away as if signaling the meal was over. Sergeant Brewster saw this out of the corner of his eye, and took two big gulps of food before doing the same. Jackie looked on, amazed at how clearly the pecking order was established. She wondered to herself how Donny, a strong, capable man in his prime, could so completely give himself over to Rodney's will.

General Branch reached into the front breast pocket of his flannel shirt and pulled out three sheets of paper. He handed one to Dan and another to Jeremy. He kept the last for himself.

"This is the standard duty roster. It outlines all the daily tasks that must be done here at the base, how they are to be done and at what time they are to be accomplished." Rodney's voice had suddenly taken on a commanding tone. He was in commanding officer mode now.

Dan looked over at Jackie and saw her face flushed red with anger. The look scared him, and he was surprised he'd never seen her like this before. Then he thought for a moment. *Yes, Uncle Rodney has a polarizing effect on everyone he meets. Why would Jackie be any different?*

"You forgot to give me a copy."

Rodney ignored her statement.

"Jeremy, you'll take the first watch from twenty-two-hundred hours to zero-one-hundred hours. I'll take the second watch, and Dan, you get the third. Reveille is always at zero-seven-hundred hours, no excuses, no exceptions."

Jackie cleared her throat, but Uncle Rodney continued to ignore her. She spoke anyway. "General, doesn't it make sense for me to take a shift too? That way everyone pulls a two-hour shift instead of three."

They locked eyes again. Rodney tried to stare her down, but she wouldn't budge.

"Don't you need a good night's sleep so you can take care of the baby all day, cook the meals and clean the house? I would think you'd welcome a full night's sleep."

Jeremy looked across the table and watched his new mother smile. It frightened him. Jackie shook her head defiantly. "I can do the job of any man here, and I'm not a slacker. If I'm going to stay here, then I want equal work and responsibility."

Uncle Rodney smiled back, but his smile contained something secret, no malice, no fear, just the simple statement, *I'm in charge and I know things you don't.* He pushed back his chair and got up. Slowly, he walked toward the front door. When he reached it, he opened the door and motioned with his left hand. "After you, me lady ."

Jeremy looked nervously at his father. Dan looked nervously at Donny. Donny looked up at Jackie and smiled.

She pushed her chair back and it tipped over behind her onto the floor. Jackie thrust the baby into her husband's arms. "Take care of the baby! I'll be right back!"

She picked up her crutches leaning against the wall and headed for the door. When the door closed behind Rodney and Jackie, the air pressure in the room seemed to lesson. Jeremy was the first to speak. "Dad? Is he going to kill her?"

Dan looked over at Donny imploringly, who just laughed out loud.

"What are you looking at me for? He's *your* uncle!"

Dan nodded, "Yes, but he's *your* general." He looked longingly at the door. "Besides, I don't really know who's out there right now. Is it the General, or my Uncle Rodney?"

Donny shrugged. "Doesn't matter. There's a couple storms a brewin' and one's a typhoon and the other's a tornado."

Then he turned back and started shoveling more goulash onto his plate. "Besides, nothing we can do about it. Gives me a chance to eat more carbs."

Dan looked over at his son and then back at Sergeant Brewster. "My wife is out there with a tornado, and all you care about is food?"

Donny laughed again. "I never been married, but why is it that most men underestimate their women?" He waited, but Dan said nothing. Jeremy looked over at his father, then started to scoop out more food onto his own plate.

"Yeah, Dad. Why do you do that?"

Then Jeremy and Donny laughed, giving each other a high five. Dan's face turned red and he slammed his palm down hard on the table.

"Donny! My wife's out there with a mad man and he's angry!"

Donny calmly took a bite and chewed fully before swallowing. "Hey, listen, man. You don't understand. When I said one of them's a tornado and the other's a typhoon, I was talking about your wife too." He paused, giving Dan time to cool down. "General Branch would never hit a lady. And, besides, she'd probably kick his butt anyway."

He went back to eating.

"That woman's tough! I can tell. She's got that look."

☆ ☆ ☆ ☆

Once outside, Jackie followed Rodney as best she could on crutches down a trail to the left of the house. They passed a small swamp and then walked up a hill. Jackie found herself out of breath and struggling, but her pride drove her on. Every few minutes Rodney would get way ahead of her and have to stop and wait. A half mile later, Rodney stopped and turned to face her. He could see that the time and distance hadn't ebbed her resolve in the least.

Rodney sat down on the ground and leaned his back up against the trunk of a Jack Pine. He let out a deep breath.

"Man I'm gettin' old." He looked up at Jackie and she just stood there, towering above him, leaning forward on her crutches. "Please, Jackie, please sit down with me."

Jackie became suspicious of his change in demeanor, but felt stupid standing over him. She plopped herself down six feet away with her back to a scrub oak. They both looked out towards the woods in front of them. There was silence for several minutes. All of a sudden, Jackie could hear the wind in the trees as night began to set in around them. The snow was still a foot deep inside the trees, with patches of bare ground where the sun shone in and reached the ground. She felt the cold and wet soaking through her jeans and wondered why it didn't seem to bother the old man.

A bright, red Cardinal landed on a branch a few feet from Rodney's head. Jackie watched and was surprised to see him smile at the little bird. He reached out his right arm with his forefinger extended, but the bird flitted away. The old man's smile faded and disappeared. His face turned stone cold as he turned his head toward Jackie.

"So, young lady. What's it going to take to move you from the liability column to the asset column?"

She answered his question with a question.

"Have you always been this arrogant?"

Rodney turned his head away, thought for a moment and then turned back again. "Okay, I could have worded that better. Let's try it again." He paused. "Jackie, why do you want to sit up watching the darkness for two hours in the dead of night when you could be sleeping in a nice, warm bed?"

She looked at him blankly, afraid to show any emotion in front of him, but she answered him nonetheless.

"Because it's my duty to my family to pull my weight. As a mother and wife, it's my job to help protect my family. I am honor bound to protect the weak and to defend the helpless. My daughter is helpless. She needs me strong, not lying in a safe, warm bed while others sacrifice on our behalf."

The old man cocked his head to one side and smiled softly. He thought for a moment. "And what taught you this deep sense of honor?"

Jackie pursed her lips tightly together, and then she moved her long, black hair off her neck so it flowed down around her. "Six months in the wilderness watching two men risk their lives and shed their blood and sweat for the safety of my daughter, myself and my husband. We were strangers, but they took us in. They would have died for us. And now … I'll die for them."

Uncle Rodney nodded in confirmation and smiled broadly. "Now you're talking my language." He groaned as he got up stiffly and stood before her. "But let's hope it doesn't come to that." Then he changed the subject abruptly, as if it was the most natural transition in the world. "Can you shoot a pistol?"

Three-quarters of a mile away Dan and Jeremy heard the gun shots. Dan flinched, then stood up and headed for the door at a run, but Donny's commanding voice halted him in his tracks.

"Dan! Stop! Think!"

Dan turned around at the door and looked back at him. "Didn't you just hear those shots?"

Donny nodded. He walked up to Dan and put his hand on his shoulder and squeezed tightly. "If you and I are going into battle together, we have to trust each other. I trust General Branch and I trust your wife. C'mon, Marine. You have to do the same. Step up. Control your emotions."

Dan hesitated, then walked slowly back to the table and sat down. Donny joined him there in his chair beside Jeremy. Then, out of the blue, he asked an unrelated question.

"So, what do you guys miss most about the good old days before the end of the world?"

Jeremy laughed and spoke right away. "I miss Tonya, the girl from next door."

His father shot him a deadly stare, and Jeremy quickly backtracked. "It's her smile. I miss her smile and her white teeth. They were very straight. It was amazing really."

Donny laughed again. "Okay, must be a story there, but I won't ask. What about you, Dan?"

Dan sighed and slumped down in his chair with his arms on the table.

"Ice, cold, Mocha Frappuccino. And man could I ever use

one about now."

"I think if you tighten up your grip with your weak hand, it'll give you a more stable shooting platform and you'll be able to hold a tighter group."

Jackie smiled and nodded. "Yeah, that's a good point. I'll try that. Thanks."

Rodney slowed his pace as they reached the driveway, and Jackie followed his lead. "So can you shoot an AR like that, too? You're a pretty good shot with a pistol."

Jackie shook her head. "No, I wish I could, but Jeremy and Dan seem to be the snipers in the family."

The old man stopped in the sandy driveway. He reached out and touched Jackie's shoulder with the finger tips of his left hand. His command voice returned, but this time without the sharp edges. "Don't worry about it. I have some videos you can watch, and we'll take you out for some private instruction. You'll be a long-distance marksman in no time."

Jackie bowed her head down as she remembered the old man reaching his fingertips out to the little bird. She thought to herself, *That's how I'll choose to see him from now on.*

"Listen, General Branch, I'm sorry for acting the way I did. It's not my normal way."

The old man nodded. "I know. These are tough times. But do me a favor, please."

She nodded apprehensively. "Okay, what is it?"

"When Sergeant Brewster or any other soldier is present, please treat me with respect and don't question my orders. But when we're alone or just family, please call me Uncle Rodney. Then you can speak your mind in any tone you like."

Jackie nodded and smiled. "Of course, Uncle Rodney. I understand. There's a war on. Command presence prevails."

Rodney smiled. "So is there anything else we need to discuss privately before we go back inside with the others?"

She took a step closer before answering. "Just one other

thing. I need to thank you for raising my husband and for taking us all in. I appreciate your kindness." And with that, she reached out and hugged the grizzled, old soldier. Rodney's back straightened as he came to attention, not quite knowing how to respond. He couldn't remember the last time he'd been hugged. So much had changed. And more change was coming. Nervously, he moved his right hand up to pat her back. After a few seconds, they separated and walked up the drive, onto the steps and back into the house as darkness fell all around them.

CHAPTER 3

Taking Action

THE ALARM WENT OFF BESIDE Rodney's bed, but he could barely hear it. He slept on a cot with a thin mattress on top and a sleeping bag. There was a small, pot-bellied stove that he fired up each night before turning in that kept the small room warm. His bedroom was only ten-feet square with a low ceiling. Even before the power grid crash, he'd kept the room dark and simple. There was a metal, olive drab, military locker against one wall with an old, wooden foot locker beside it. A clean change of olive drab utilities along with his boots rested neatly on top, waiting impatiently for the start of a new day. On this particular morning, a full battle pack and M16 rifle sat off to one side next to the locker.

The night before, he'd shaved and asked Jackie to cut his hair close to his scalp with a razor. He looked more military now, and he felt tighter and more in control of himself.

The alarm kept ringing, and Rodney reached over clumsily to tap the button on top. It was an old, wind-up alarm clock he'd had since just after boot camp. That made the clock over fifty years old. It was an antique, but, like him, it was still simple and very dependable.

Rodney threw open his sleeping bag and swung his feet out and onto the bare, cement floor. Somewhere around fifty years old he'd noticed his feet still hurt even after a full night's sleep.

The older he got, the tougher it was to find enough reason to get out of bed in the morning. Then around sixty he'd begun to understand the lure of death's appeal. The old man had long considered it cruel that finally, after all these decades, when he knew enough to merit his existence, his body was falling apart around him. Here he was, getting ready to lead and fight the greatest battles of his time, but only after he'd grown old and nearly useless.

He turned the small lamp on beside his bed, and it lit up the room with little more than a dimness. It was connected to a car battery beneath the cot and would last for days, since he spent very little time inside the room. Over the years he'd collected dozens of car batteries which he constantly trickle charged off a solar panel array on the sunny side of the hill. Two walls of the house were surrounded by dirt banks all the way up and onto the roof. It looked a little like one of Tolkien's Hobbit houses from *The Lord of the Rings*. The main part of the house, with the dining room, kitchen, living room and bathroom were on the main circuit powered by much larger batteries. There were three other bedrooms branching off the main house that relied on car batteries for light just like his own. By last year's standards, his energy set-up was archaic, but now, after the power crash, he was one of a select few with electricity, and he was very careful not to advertise that fact.

But the real purpose of Rodney's bedroom was not to sleep, but to guard the below-ground level of the house. The solid, steel door to the left of his cot was protected by three heavy padlocks. The door frame was reinforced and solidly anchored into the cement wall behind his cot. It was clearly a custom addition that Rodney had built himself. No one knew of it save himself and Daniel.

He grabbed the clothes off the footlocker and hurriedly dressed in the same way, in the same sequence that he had for the last fifty years. The last thing to strap on was his nylon duty belt with his 45 caliber 1911 pistol and two extra magazines. He was truly neat, meticulous, and a creature of habit. Normally he would have lit up a cigarette by now, but, not today, not anymore. Never again.

With his boots laced up, he stood and donned the pack, grabbed the M16 and the handheld field radio and took the padlock off the door leading to the rest of the house. Others would no doubt think it strange that he padlocked himself into his bedroom each night, but that's the way he'd done it for years, and he wasn't about to change now. It was a security issue, and he never compromised on security. To say he'd never really been one to care what others thought of him was a gross understatement. Besides, everyone who'd been calling him a kook for decades now relied on him for protection.

Quietly, he stepped out of his bedroom and into the living room where he quickly padlocked the door from the outside. Everyone else was sleeping except Daniel who should be on the roof with a radio, his rifle, binoculars and night vision.

The phlegm in his chest was nagging at him now, but he held the coughing at bay until he opened the door and walked outside into the pre-dawn blackness. Daniel would have heard the door open, so he called him now on the radio.

"Hawks Nest this is HQ Actual, over."

The response was almost immediate, and Rodney smiled with satisfaction at his nephew.

"HQ Actual, this is Hawks Nest, go ahead, over."

"Hawks Nest, be advised I'm exiting through the front and you should hold fire, over."

"Roger that, HQ Actual. Will comply."

Rodney wanted to chat with him, just because he hadn't gotten much of a chance since his return. Everything had been moving at light speed, and would continue to do so. But, even though the radios were encrypted, he couldn't break procedure and condone personal chatter on the airwaves. No exceptions. But, for some reason, he just wanted to hear his boy's voice.

"Thanks, Hawks Nest. Sit Rep, please."

"All is quiet, HQ Actual. No incidents to report. It was a good night. Over."

The old man smiled and keyed his mic one last time.

"Roger that, Hawks Nest. Will return by noon chow. Over."

"Roger that, HQ Actual. This is Hawks Nest, out."

Rodney fastened the radio inside a pocket on his packstrap and headed for the road. His upper body was still in pretty good shape, for a man of his advancing years, but his lungs were going to need some work. He'd been smoking for decades, and hadn't really done a lot of hiking. Today would be the first of many pre-dawn, solitary force marches.

A mile into the woods, when he was sure Hawks Nest could no longer hear him, he knelt down and coughed out all the phlegm from his lungs onto the dried oak leaves. He should have stopped smoking years ago, but he hadn't. And now, when the world needed him most, he was less than his best.

Slowly, he stood up and wiped the slobber from his mouth and chin. With his rifle in his left hand, he looked up at the hill in front of him like it was Mount Everest and began the long climb.

☆ ☆ ☆ ☆

"Dan, I want you set up on that hilltop over there with your AR15 and your binoculars. Make sure your radio is on the right frequency, and don't transmit unless you see a security risk. Understood?"

Dan Branch nodded and smiled. "Am I supposed to salute you now, Uncle Rodney?"

The old man laughed out loud. He was wearing a quilted, green, flannel shirt and blue jeans to ward off the mid march northern Michigan chill. It was almost dark now, and they were expecting the Huey at any moment."

"Just get up there and do your job, Marine."

Dan turned to Sergeant Donny Brewster and held out his

right hand. The two men shook firmly and locked eyes for a moment.

"You stay cool out there, Donny." Donny nodded but didn't say anything. "I want you to know that I appreciate what you're doing for my family and for my home. I really do."

Donny smiled. "Semper Fi, Marine. You take care of the wife and kids, cuz I want a hot, home-cooked meal when I get back from the boonies."

"You got it, Donny." Dan looked at him one last time, wondering if he'd ever see him again. Then he turned and strode up the hill to set up the lookout post.

"Don't take any unnecessary chances, Sergeant. Give us as much information and time as you can, but don't get killed in the process." He hesitated. "And that's an order."

Donny was wearing RealTree camo with a wool sweater underneath. He reached up and pulled his boonie hat down over his eyes just a tad. His pack lay on the ground beside him, and his rifle was still encased. A 9mm Glock was strapped to his right thigh, and his suppressed M4 leaned against Rodney's truck. Rodney had insisted on driving twenty miles away from town to the most secluded area in the county. He didn't want anyone to associate military helos with his home town.

"General, that's one order I plan to follow to the letter."

Off in the distance, they heard the heavy blades of the Huey in the dense air getting closer. General Branch reached out his hand and the two men shook in silence. As the helicopter touched down, Rodney backed away. Donny grabbed his gear and walked over to the Huey with his head down. The blades lowered the wind chill, but Donny was acclimated from the long, hard winters of the Upper Peninsula. In a few seconds, the helicopter took off again and headed east ten miles and then turned to the south.

A few minutes later Dan climbed into the truck beside his

uncle.

"Did you see anything, son?"

Dan shook his head.

"Good. At least we got off to a positive start."

Uncle Rodney fired up the diesel engine and drove out of the small field and onto the two-track logging road back into the safety of the trees.

With all the nonchalance of a Sunday drive, Uncle Rodney asked, "So what is that wife of yours serving us for chow tonight?"

A smile spread across Dan's face as he answered.

"It's a surprise. You're going to love it."

General Branch frowned. "I don't like surprises. It's not healthy in my line of work."

The two men grew silent, both contemplating the future and the tasks at hand. So much was riding on Donny Brewster's shoulders.

CHAPTER 4

A State of Flux - State Forest Refugee Camp

"YOU FOLKS GATHER ROUND ME,
now, ya hear?"

Sheriff Leif dropped the mic down a bit with his left hand as he waited for people to pull in closer around his police cruiser. Rodney Branch stood behind the open door on the passenger side. Joe looked out across the sea of tents spread out before him. The refugees kept coming up from the south, trying to stay ahead of the horde of looters and murderers. Last week there had been only one hundred people here at the campgrounds, but now, he guessed the number had tripled. "Keep coming in, folks. I need you all to hear what I have to say."

Once they were all in, the Sheriff felt a little intimidated. He glanced over at Rodney for support. For some reason, he just felt safer when the old man was around. He cleared his throat, clicked the mic on and began his rehearsed speech.

"We had another break-in back near town last night. That's the third one this week. I'm here to ask if any of you have any information about it."

The crowd murmured among themselves, but no one spoke to him. "I'm not accusing anyone, I just need to know if any of you can help me out with information."

A man near the front snickered. "Sure sounds like an accusation to me, Sheriff."

Sheriff Leif made eye contact with him, trying to stare the man down, but it didn't work. The crowd took a step closer. They looked at him like he was the bad guy, and he just couldn't believe what he was seeing. A year ago these were probably all good folks, but now … anything was possible.

"We didn't do anything wrong, and we have a right to be here. This is state land, and you don't have any jurisdiction in the game area."

This time it was a different man than the one who'd first spoken out. There were four rough-looking men flanking him. All of them were armed with rifles and shotguns.

Joe held up his hand in a calming gesture. "Yes, I know you have a right to be here. But you have to understand my first loyalty is to the citizens of Iroquois County. They elected me, and I answer to them and them alone."

He stared into the man's eyes for a few seconds, then moved from man to man. He thought to himself, *Don't let them smell your fear. Command presence. Sell it or you're dead meat.*

"Martial law was declared long ago, so I *do* have jurisdiction here. But let's not argue that. I'm just here to tell you that my men have orders to shoot any looters on sight with no questions asked. So please be careful when you wander off state land here and onto private property. The people are getting pretty nervous and they might do something less than prudent."

Five men stepped forward and another six filled in the gap behind them. They came to within fifteen feet of the cruiser before stopping.

"We don't like your tone, Sheriff. And we don't answer to you or anyone else." The man was a head taller than six feet with massive shoulders and chest muscles. Apparently the food shortage hadn't effected his diet. The men behind him wore confident smiles.

"Listen folks, we don't want any trouble. I'm just trying to do my job here."

The big man folded his muscled arms across his chest.

"Neither do we, Sheriff. But unless you're here to bring us food or medicine or extra blankets, then … well, we just got no use for you here."

The Sheriff glanced over at Rodney for moral support, but the General was already easing himself back into the cruiser.

Joe looked back over at the crowd and pasted his best relax-and-have-a-nice-day smile on his face. But the men pressed in closer, moving to within ten feet of the car.

Just as Joe was about to speak, something came flying out the passenger side window of his cruiser. It landed on the ground in front of the advancing men. He glanced over at Rodney just in time to hear a deafening explosion. The shock wave pressed up against him, and he felt sand and gravel hit him full in the face.

Someone yelled "Grenade!" and the men stopped advancing and started to retreat back as fast as they could. Several more grenades came out Rodney's window as Joe quickly jumped into the cruiser and closed the door behind him.

As more explosions went off in front of the car, Joe fired up the engine and backed out as fast as he could. Uncle Rodney was still pitching grenades out the window as they turned around and pulled away. Joe looked in the rear-view mirror but all he saw was thick, white smoke billowing out and up totally obscuring the campgrounds. They heard gunshots, but nothing hit the car as they sped away.

Once they were on the main road again, Joe looked over at Rodney. "What did you just do? You just killed dozens of innocent people back there!"

Uncle Rodney just smiled. "No, I don't think so. Those were just flash-bangs. Just enough bang and noise to disorient them long enough for us to get the hell out of there before you got us both killed with all your flowery speech. The last two were smoke grenades. I got 'em on eBay."

Rodney slammed on the brakes and the car skidded to a halt on the pavement. Uncle Rodney took his hands off the dash and stopped smiling.

"Why do you always get so emotional about things, Joe. I thought you did pretty good, considering those folks are starving, homeless and afraid for their wives and children. You walked into a no-win situation. What did you expect?"

Joe pursed his lips together but didn't answer.

"Did you actually expect them to hand over the bad guys to you on a silver platter? Right now the line between good and bad is a little blurry."

Joe thought about it for a second, but he couldn't fight off the anger he still felt about what Rodney had just done.

"I can't believe you just did that. They could've been hurt back there."

Rodney folded his arms across his chest. "Did it occur to you at all that we were outmanned and outgunned, not to mention outflanked, and those men weren't coming in closer to shake your hand, Sheriff. You and I were about to die, and I saved your sorry ass!"

Joe pressed down on the accelerator again. "Maybe. We'd better get out of here in case they're following us." Joe shook his head back and forth. "I just … nobody ever did that to me before. It's like nobody respects the law anymore."

Rodney looked at the road ahead, and, after he'd calmed down a bit, he began to feel sorry for his friend.

"Joe, it's not that people have lost respect for the law, it's that the law has changed. People aren't sure what it is anymore. The law is in a state of flux. Right now anything that doesn't help people survive is meaningless to them."

The Sheriff looked over at him with a confused look on his face. "What do you mean? It's always been against the law to attack a law enforcement officer. That hasn't changed."

Rodney shrugged his shoulders. "Yeah, well, maybe. But you have to start looking at it from their perspective if you want to understand it. Most of those men have a wife and kids who got ran out of their homes. They lost their jobs, lost their way of life, and now they can't even put a roof over their heads and feed them a decent meal. That takes away a man's self respect and replaces it with something more dangerous, something more violent."

Rodney looked out the window at the passing trees. "You just handled it wrong, that's all. You set them off like flames in a powder magazine."

For the next mile Joe didn't say anything. Finally, he gripped the wheel tighter, making his knuckles turn white.

"Okay, so my way didn't work out. I can see that. I'm not too proud to admit when I'm wrong."

Rodney nodded and snickered to himself. "Did you see the look on that big guy's face when he saw that grenade land between his legs?"

The Sheriff thought for a moment and then smiled slightly. "I think his life was flashing before his eyes, and it wasn't pretty."

The old man laughed before reaching into his breast pocket for a cigarette. He quickly realized they weren't there, and dropped his hand back down again.

"So, how many deputies do we have now to defend the county?"

The Sheriff's smile faded away. "I deputized three hundred men, but last week when I mustered them, only seventy-nine showed up."

"That's a problem."

"No kidding."

Uncle Rodney thought for a few seconds. Then he looked over at Joe and smiled. "I think I know how we can get us some more fighters."

A concerned look came over Joe's face.

"Okay, I'm listening."

The next day they returned to the state campgrounds with three truckloads of food, blankets and basic medicine. They were quickly surrounded by armed men, but very calmly got out of their cabs and started throwing cases of MREs out onto the ground in front of them.

The people pounced on the boxes of food like a swarm of locust.

Once all the trucks were unloaded, the big man from the day before walked up. Rodney met him with an extended right hand. The man hesitated, then met Rodney eye for eye before gripping his hand firmly.

"We have extra, at least for now, and it just didn't seem right to keep it all to ourselves while good people went hungry."

The man's stone face finally relaxed. "Okay, that's nice, and we appreciate it. But what's the catch?"

Rodney smiled knowingly. This guy was more than big and strong. He was also very smart.

"Is there a place where you and I can talk?"

The man nodded and turned to leave. Rodney fell in behind him. They came to a large tent with the flaps tied open. A campfire burned about ten feet away from the entrance. The whole scene reminded Rodney of old black and white tintype photos he'd seen of Civil War campsites.

"C'mon inside and sit down."

Rodney followed him in and soon both men were sitting across from each other at a small, folding card table.

"My name is Rodney Branch. I got a place a few miles west of Iroquois City."

The big man nodded. "Jason Little. Grand Rapids."

And then the two men talked.

Thirty minutes later Rodney walked away with the promise of one hundred fighting men to help defend the county. In return, he'd promised sanctuary and permanent homes for a select number of families from the campsite.

Over the next few days people formally applied for permanent residency to Iroquois County. There were already fifty homes in the area where the owners had either died or were unaccounted for since the collapse. These houses would be turned over to refugees who could demonstrate a key skill or resource critical to the defense and well being of the county. In many cases simply a willing fighter with a good firearm and extra ammo was enough to foot the bill.

Once the new residents had been chosen, Rodney and the Sheriff held a formal swearing in ceremony at the camp. Each man, woman and child raised their right hand and swore the following oath:

> *"I hereby declare, on oath, that I absolutely and entirely will support and defend the Constitution of the United States of America and the laws of Iroquois County against all enemies, foreign and domestic; that I will bear true faith and allegiance to the same; that I will bear arms on behalf of Iroquois County and that I take this obligation freely without any mental reservation or purpose of evasion; so help me God."*

In that way, the camp was nearly emptied out in three days time. The rash of burglaries stopped.

CHAPTER 5

Bad Moon on the Rise

SERGEANT **D**ONNY **B**REWSTER peered down the hill just north of Greenville. He couldn't believe what he was seeing. He estimated the camp at twelve hundred, most of them able-bodied men. And their numbers seemed to be growing as he watched. At this rate, by the time they reached Iroquois, General Branch would be fighting against an army of three thousand men.

The large parking lot surrounding the warehouse was filled with a hodge-podge of vehicles with everything from military HumVees to snow plows and semi trucks and trailers. Off to one side there appeared to be a group of twenty quads. The pavement of the parking lot was bare of snow, and fires now burned in dozens of places interspersed across the landscape. Wooden pallets from inside the warehouse had been dragged outside and set on fire to keep the rank and file soldiers warm.

Donny had thrown a white, vinyl tarp over himself and his gear, allowing only his face to show. He also wore white gloves and a white ski mask. Beyond thirty yards, he was nearly invisible, even from the air. After being dropped off by the helo, he'd hiked in the last ten miles and dug into the top of this hill. Now, he was ready to lay perfectly still at a distance of seven hundred yards for the next ten hours, watching, taking notes, analyzing, probing for weakness. Donny

Brewster was on the hunt.

That night, just after sundown, Donny quietly broke camp. After moving back into the trees and stretching his tired muscles, he packed up a few choice supplies and walked around the encampment to the far side of the warehouse. He'd already mapped out the camp's security, complete with the location of each guard. From a military standpoint it was pretty relaxed, so he easily slipped into the front parking lot and from there into the back lot where all the troops were staged. Once inside their perimeter, it was easy to move from campfire to campfire, listening intently to anything he wanted so long as he didn't bring attention to himself.

As Donny sat just outside the light of the fire and listened, he heard a mixture of sounds: diesel generators, men talking, laughter, anger, the screams of a woman, and the unmistakable sound of his favorite band, Credence Clearwater Revival. He just sat there for a few minutes enjoying the words.

> *Don't go around tonight,*
> *Well, it's bound to take your life,*
> *There's a bad moon on the rise.*

"So when we pullin' outta this place, Mikey?"

Donny's ears perked up as he listened to the two men talk just a few yards away from him.

"Boss says tomorrow. He wants to keep headin' north fer some reason."

"Why we keep headin' north for? It's cold up there and most the people are south. I don't get it."

Donny heard the man hack up some phlegm and spit before answering. "Yeah, you don't get it cuz yer so stupid! The reason we left Grand Rapids is cuz we had no choice!"

There was a pause. "What? Ya mean cuz of that other gang? We could of taken 'em."

Donny leaned in closer.

"Maybe. Maybe not. Boss said it weren't worth the risk. GR was bout tapped out anyway. Sides, the others got most of the military hardware. Boss says we need more of our own and the smaller cities north got plenty of stuff. If ya wanna live high on the hog like this, ya gotta keep movin' on."

The other man nodded in the darkness. Donny moved away from the fire and walked slowly toward the warehouse. He was wearing a green poncho that hung down to his knees. It helped hide his tactical vest laden with his suppressed M4 on a 3-point sling in front of him, his 9mm suppressed Glock, and a variety of other ordinance including smoke grenades, thermite, C4 and fragmentation grenades.

Donny didn't like coming in close like this, but he knew that after tonight security would tighten up and things would have to be done from longer distances. This was his one best shot at inflicting massive damage and chaos.

He worked his way up slowly, but then stopped and waited outside the fire closest to the warehouse. Security seemed to tighten up around the entrances to the building. He knew from his daytime surveillance that each door leading in was guarded by two men. And up on the roof, there was a man with a rifle stationed at each wall. He would assume they had night vision.

Donny sat down with his back leaning up against the big tires of a semi trailer to wait for everyone in camp to fall asleep. Just then the back door of the trailer opened wide and something was thrown out onto the ground. It landed just a few feet away from Donny. He looked down at the young woman, naked and unmoving. Her face was battered, bruised and bleeding.

"How many more guys we got? Raise your hand if you haven't gone yet."

Thirteen men clustered by the fire raised their hands. "Okay, Jim. Bring us another one. Should be the last of it for tonight. I need some sleep."

Donny looked down at the woman lying beside him on the ground. She wasn't moving. As discreetly as possible, he reached his hand over and placed his fingers on her carotid artery. There was no pulse.

"Next in line."

Harold Steffens stepped up slowly to the table on the courthouse lawn. He was a tall, thin man, nothing but skin and bones, frail and old, wearing an ancient United States Army uniform. Over his right shoulder, on a sling, draped a large rifle that was older than most of the men who'd already volunteered for the Iroquois County Home Guard. Harold stood proudly at attention in front of the Sheriff who looked at him and shook his head.

"Harold, what are you doing?"

The old man looked him straight in the eye with a fierceness that belied his age. "I'm here to serve my county."

Joe Leif placed his elbows up on the white, plastic table and rested his chin on his folded hands. "How old are you, Harold?"

Harold slumped his shoulders slightly but didn't give in. "I wasn't aware there was an age requirement, Sheriff. But I have ID and can prove I'm at least eighteen."

The Sheriff stood up and walked around in front of the table. He gently placed his hand on the man's shoulder and leaned in closer.

"Harold, does Myra know you're doing this?"

The man's lips pursed together, and the deep wrinkles around his eyes tightened with anger. "Myra's been dead for two months, Joe. She caught pneumonia just after Christmas."

Joe nodded and lowered his head in sadness. "I'm sorry, Harold. I didn't know."

"That doesn't matter. I'm here to serve. I'll fight and die if I have to. I'm healthy and I still got my eyes. I can shoot as good as any man you got standing here."

General Rodney Branch had been watching from twenty feet away, waiting to see how the Sheriff would handle this. Finally, he walked up and stood in front of Harold Steffens. The old man saw Rodney's uniform and suddenly stiffened to attention and immediately saluted. General Branch returned the salute smartly and crisply.

"At ease, soldier."

Rodney looked the old man up and down. "That's a nice M1 Garand you have there, Sergeant. Where'd you get it?"

The old man's wrinkled lips smiled slightly.

"At a small beach in France, sir."

Rodney nodded. "I see you were with the 3rd Armored Division. That means you saw a lot of action."

The old man nodded resolutely. "Yes, sir. We called ourselves The Third Herd. We lost a lot of good men on that continent."

The General's mouth frowned, but his eyes continued to sparkle. He looked over to Sheriff Leif. "Sheriff, can you spare this man? I need to assign him to a special unit. We're short noncoms, and this man has the training and experience I need for an important mission."

Joe Leif looked off to the left. A stiff, cool breeze picked up from the north, causing a chill to run through his bones. Finally, he stuck his arm out and shook hands with Harold Steffens. "Welcome to the Home Guard, Sergeant Steffens."

The old man smiled, and a thousand wrinkles smiled with him.

"May I speak with you privately, General Branch?"

Rodney motioned for Harold to sit down and wait for him in the chair beside the table. As soon as the two men were out of earshot, Joe cut loose on Rodney.

"What the hell do you think you're doing? That man is eighty-some years old! He won't last a day on the battlefield!"

General Branch nodded. "I expect you're right, Sheriff."

"Well, then …"

Rodney interrupted him.

"You're right when you say he won't last a day on the battlefield, but this battle will be over in less than a day. So, maybe, just maybe, he might have a fighting chance. Besides, if we lose this battle, he'll be dead anyway. At least this way we give him a reason to live."

Sheriff Leif stood there unmoving, trying desperately to figure out what Rodney had planned for the old man.

"Let me put it to you another way, Sheriff Leif. This man fought his way from Normandy all the way through France, into Belgium and Nazi Germany." Rodney paused to let it sink in. "Did you see those medals on his chest? The Purple Heart? The Silver Star? That man shed his blood for both of us. They don't give those medals away. You have to earn them."

Joe Leif looked down at the ground. "Yes, Rodney, I know. It's just … that man was my grandfather's best friend. I just don't want to see him get hurt."

Rodney's eyes softened a bit, but he didn't let up. "From now on, anyone you deem too old for combat, just send them to me. Sergeant Steffens will lead them into battle. And he'll make us proud. And the very worst that can happen is he dies with honor instead of wheezing helplessly sick in a bed all alone."

General Branch turned and walked back over to the old man. The man stood up and snapped back to attention.

"Do you have a few minutes, Sergeant Steffens? I have a few ideas I'd like to discuss. We have a battle to plan."

☆ ☆ ☆ ☆

It was 4:00 a,m, and Donny Brewster was flat against the east wall of the warehouse, standing at the base of a ladder leading up to the roof. After taking one final look around, he moved up the ladder and climbed thirty feet to the rooftop. Just before peering over the top, he flipped down his night vision and turned it on.

When he peeked over the rooftop, he saw the first sentry leaning up against the three-foot ledge with his back turned. Donny had already removed his poncho, so he quietly swung up onto the rooftop, rotated his M4 up to his chest and took aim. A few seconds later he heard the sound of the rifle action opening and closing, then a thud as the guard hit the tar and gravel-covered rooftop.

He quickly moved to the south wall and dispatched the second sentry who was carelessly smoking a cigarette. The west sentry was just as simple. But when he closed in on the north wall, something wasn't right. He couldn't find the guard. He waited five minutes, but still - no movement. He picked up a small stone and threw it forty feet out towards the wall. Still - no sign of the sentry.

After another five minutes of scanning and waiting, Donny flipped back his night vision and pulled a small infrared monocular from a pocket in his tactical vest. He looked through it, scanning first the far end of the wall, working his way back. Only then did he see the small, red blotch sticking out from behind the upraised ceiling vent. Now that he knew where to look, Donny put away the IR and flipped his generation 4 NVIS back down over his eyes. It was obvious now. There was a boot-covered foot about twenty feet away from him. He rotated his M4 around behind him and unholstered his 9mm Glock. As he walked slowly and carefully over the gravel, his footsteps sounded to him much louder than they really were, so he moved slowly. Upon reaching the foot, he peeked around the vent and saw the man asleep on the job. He calculated the angle and quickly put one round through the man's left eye socket. Donny thought to himself, *You'll sleep much better now.*

With all four sentries dispatched, Donny descended quickly down the hatch and into the heart of the building. From there, he moved from the warehouse portion into the front offices. He holstered his nine millimeter and drew his suppressed 22 caliber pistol from the front of his tactical vest. With stealth derived from practice, he moved from office to office, almost noiselessly dispatching every man he found. Most of them were lying on mattresses or cots, and a few of them had naked women beside them. The sound of the smaller action on his 22 caliber pistol was much quieter, allowing him to leave the women alive. He presumed most of them were unwilling participants.

After eliminating fourteen men, he moved past a conference room with papers rolled out onto a big table. He looked down at the map and saw a large, red, felt pen circle around Traverse City. Donny smiled, pulled out his cell phone and snapped a picture. After finishing his sweep of the building, he climbed back up onto the roof and exited the camp the way he'd come.

Before first light, he was back on the hill, totally concealed in his hidey hole, ready to watch all hell break loose with the coming dawn.

CHAPTER 6

The Blind Man and Hannibal Lecter

THE BLIND MAN SAT AT THE HEAD of the large, rectangular mahogany table. His high-backed chair was plush leather that seemed to rise up and envelop him. Also at the table were six other men. They were seated rigidly and uncomfortably in small, metal folding chairs. Behind each regional leader was his second in command, and behind him was his personal bodyguard. So the room was a bit crowded.

At that moment, several women came in and cleared away the remnants of the gourmet meal they'd just consumed. Within thirty seconds the table was empty and wiped clean except for a small paper cup of wine in front of each leader.

Behind the blind man was his assistant, Sammy Thurmond, but no one knew his real name save the blind man, and the blind man's real name was Jared Thompson. But no one knew that either, except for a few hand-picked dead people.

Jared was wearing dark sun glasses and a black suit with white shirt and tie as was his assistant. Sammy touched his boss on the shoulder signifying all was ready then looked straight ahead.

"I trust all of you had a good meal?"

No one answered, though a few glanced around the table nervously. By now all of them knew it was the blind man who'd created the thousand-year night. They also knew the demise of the rich, Arab Sheik who'd hired him to bring down the power grid. Most of them were prepared to swear allegiance in order to share in Jared's power and to avoid the Sheik's fate. But there was one holdout.

"And now, I propose a toast."

Jared picked up his own long-stemmed crystal goblet and raised it up. The other six men hesitated, but then, one by one, as if falling to an unseen pressure, each man slowly raised the paper cup of wine in front of him. Jared smiled and thought to himself, *As if they have a choice.*"

"By drinking this wine you signify your allegiance to me and only me. You will serve me like slaves, unwavering and unfailing. You will obey me and only me. If you succeed I will reward you. If you fail, I will kill you."

The blind man raised his glass.

"To loyalty and unity."

At first, no one moved. Then Jared drank and put his glass back on the table. Finally, the man to his left drank as well. Then, one by one, all capitulated to Jared's will … save one man.

Walter Herwath was from Los Angeles, and he now ruled all of southern California with an iron fist. The once beautiful and depraved paradise was in a shambles. After the fall, it had become disease-ridden, looted, and burning. But Walter had risen to the top of the herd, destroyed his competitors and re-stored cosmos from all the chaos. Walter Herwath was proud, and he never shared power.

"Wonderful! I'm happy that we're all on the same page. And now …"

But Jared stopped in mid sentence as Sammy reached down and tapped him gently on the shoulder then leaned down and whispered in his ear. Jared frowned.

"I see."

And then he laughed out loud.

"I made a joke. Don't you get it? I said 'I see'. I'm blind!"

He kept laughing as he spoke. "I see said the blind man."

But no one else laughed. They just looked around nervously. Finally, when the room was quiet again Walter spoke out.

"You're just a weak blind man who can't read the writing on the wall. Southern California is mine because I earned it. And no one is coming in just because they think they can." He looked around the room at each man and then straight over at Sammy. "You can have southern California, over my dead body!"

Jared smiled.

"Please count down for me."

Sammy raised up his wrist and lifted his sleeve revealing his watch. Then, in his Hannibal Lecter voice, he began to count down. "Seven. Six. Five."

The men around the table began to squirm in their cheap, metal folding chairs. But Walter jumped up from his chair in anger.

"Four. Three. Two."

Walter yelled as loud as he could while drawing his pistol from his shoulder rig. "This is bull!"

"One."

Walter's gun slipped from his hand and fell onto the expensive mahogany table top. He clutched at his chest and began to cough. Blood and foam bubbled out his mouth and spilled on the table in a crimson pool. Walter's eyes rolled up into his head as he came down hard on the table. They didn't re-open.

Jared heard the thud and smiled. "Oh, I'm sorry. I'm not being a good host. It would be rude of me not to explain."

He folded his hands on the table in front of him. "You see, I took the liberty of lacing the chicken and the prime rib with a deadly toxin. I needed to know who would be loyal to me, so I put the antidote in the glass of wine Walter just refused to drink. The rest of you will live though since you toasted to our loyalty and unity."

Jared then looked in the direction of Walter's second in

command. "And what about you, Carlos? It would seem with the death of Walter you've just inherited a regional empire. Would you like to relinquish your independence and pledge your obedience to a mere blind man?"

Carlos looked down at Walter's dead body and shook his head in disbelief. "You are a crazy man."

Jared made a clicking sound with his tongue against the roof of his mouth. "Oh my. Now that's not very polite."

Carlos was large for a Mexican, standing six feet five inches in height. He had dark hair and eyes with a neatly trimmed beard and moustache.

"Southern California will stand against you, and my brothers from the south will rise up and join me."

Jared glanced over his shoulder and nodded. Just then a TV screen began to drop slowly down through the white-painted ceiling. "I want you to see something, Mr. Ramirez."

The television turned on, showing a panoramic view of the Los Angeles skyline. Jared laughed. "So Carlos, how can you stand *against* me when there's nothing left for you to stand *for*?"

The camera view panned out to a distance of about twenty miles. There was an explosion, a very large explosion. The mushroom cloud rose up and then billowed out as all of Los Angeles melted and burned in the uranium-induced heat wave.

Carlos' mouth dropped open in shock. Sammy Thurmond pulled out his pistol in one smooth motion and put one shot into Carlos' brain. The second in command's lifeless body dropped down onto that of his boss.

Jared smiled again.

"Well … okay. That was an interesting development." He hesitated before going on. "It would appear there is no one to lead southern California. But …" The blind man threw up his hands. "That doesn't really matter since Los Angeles no longer exists."

He waited a few seconds, allowing everyone to look at the

malignant cloud filling the big screen. Jared knew, that they knew, Los Angeles could just as easily be the fate of Chicago, or New York or Miami … Jared let that realization sink in.

"And, now that we're all on the same page, my staff will pass out some information and fill you in on the details of what you will be doing over the next few months."

Jared stood and Sammy pulled away his chair. "So, if there are no further disagreements, I'll be on my way."

The blind man walked slowly out of the conference room with one hand on Sammy's elbow to lead him. As he left, the blood of Walter and Carlos joined together, mingled and became one before pouring off onto the floor. In the background, the sound of uranium thunder filled the room as what was left of Los Angeles melted and burned.

CHAPTER 7

The Warehouse of Death

"HOW DID THIS HAPPEN?" MANNY
looked down at his fallen leader. There was a tiny
bullet hole in his left temple and no exit wound. He
covered his nose with his sleeve. It was already starting to
stink inside.

"We don't know. I guess somebody broke in and shot him."

Manny looked up and over at his next in command. He
was a moron, but he was a loyal moron. "So you're telling me
that one man broke in here and killed forty-three men without
being seen or heard?"

Buster Bancroft squirmed under the scrutiny of his new
boss. "Ah, well, I guess it's really forty-eight if ya count the
four guys on the roof." The two men behind him snickered under their breath. Buster was loyal and big, huge actually and
very strong, but not the sharpest tool in the shed. His father
had told him repeatedly as a child, "Son, you couldn't think
your way out of a wet, paper bag!"

But he'd killed his father with his bare hands, so that no
longer mattered and Buster had forgiven him since then. He
looked down sheepishly when he heard everyone snicker.
"It's forty-seven, ain't it, Manny."

Manny smiled. "Doesn't matter, Buster. Those men are
just jealous of your physical attributes."

Buster smiled. "Yeah, it's always been big like that."

Manny looked down at the swollen body of his dead boss and thought for a moment. This was unfortunate and a bit disconcerting, but ... it also saved him the trouble of doing it himself. Ever since they'd left Grand Rapids he'd been forming a plan to kill his boss and take over, but now ... someone else had done it for him.

But the million-dollar question was ... who? And was he coming back?

Manny spent the next two hours going from room to room, studying the carnage, trying to glean clues and figure out exactly how this had happened. At one point, he'd even pulled out his knife and dug into a man's brain to retrieve the bullet. He'd read somewhere that the best assassins used 22 caliber to maintain silence.

Perhaps the rival gang in Grand Rapids had sent someone after them? Manny shook his head. No, he didn't think so. This was something else.

He cleaned the blood off his hands and sat down to think. *What should he do? More importantly, what was in his best interest?* Manny wasn't like most of the others in this encampment. The majority of them were just hoodlums, punks, gangbangers, druggies, sex fiends, while a few were certifiably crazy or just plain evil. But Manny was different. Sure, he could kill with the best of them. He could rape, sodomize, kill, steal and destroy ... but those were just tools of the trade. These other guys did it for enjoyment, or worse yet because they had to obey the voices inside their heads. With Manny, it was just business, a means to an end. So he killed often, and with purpose and discretion. But, more importantly, he always made a plan and stuck to it so long as it advanced the cause of Manny. Selfish ambition was Manny's sole, defining characteristic.

He sat down at a small desk out at the loading dock and quickly drew up a list of everyone he knew and trusted. His entire chain of command would have to be set up all over again. Of course, most of it was already in his head anyway, since he'd been planning for this day, but he'd never suspected that everyone would be killed. In fact, the only reason Manny had survived was just dumb luck. The boss had sent him on a raiding party to get more women and supplies. Anyone could have done it, and he hadn't really been necessary for the menial task. But ... the dead and bloating gang leader had trusted only Manny. And that trust had been Manny's salvation.

Manny gave the list to Buster. "Go get these people and bring them to me right now."

Buster nodded and started to walk away. "Buster!" The big man turned around and stared at his boss. "And get somebody to haul all these bodies out of here. Put them in the back of a semi and dump them two miles from here in that gravel pit we passed on the way in. No need to bury them. I just don't want the guys to see."

Buster nodded again and walked out to follow his orders. Buster Bancroft may not have been very smart, but he was loyal, and smart enough to know when to ask questions and when to do as he was told.

Iroquois City - A Town in Training

"No! In this situation you hold the knife like this and let the man come to you. He'll be out of control, hyped up on adrenalin, but you have to keep your cool."

General Rodney Branch was wearing newly pressed and starched olive-drab fatigues. They were the same fatigues he'd worn in Vietnam, and he looked like General Patton on steroids. Rodney rotated the small bayonet in his right hand like a drum major twirling a baton. The knife's balance was off, but Rodney held on to it like a pro. He put up his fists in a classic fighting stance with the knife pointing down at the ground.

"And when the man comes forward, you punch at his face. He'll try to block you with his arms. And that's when you slice through the arteries in his wrist. Once he starts bleeding out, you follow up with a punch to his throat, taking out the carotid and his windpipe." Rodney went through the motions fluidly, defined into muscle memory through a lifetime of mindful practice. "And then you quickly move on to the next enemy soldier." He handed the knife back to Jason Little. Jason smiled.

"You've done this before. Are you really a general?" Jason Little stood towering over Rodney, but somehow, despite the man's obvious hugeness, Rodney was not diminished, and Jason knew it. Jason smiled. "Are you always the toughest man in the room?"

Rodney's face looked grim and determined, as if the pending battle were happening in fifteen minutes instead of several weeks. He didn't answer either of Jason's questions.

"Jason, what did you do for a living back before The Day?"

The big man tried rolling the knife around in his palm the way Rodney had done, but it fumbled to the ground and stuck in the dirt. He bent down sheepishly to pick it up. "I was an accountant for a bakery. We made mostly cereal, Pop-Tarts, Toaster Strudels, all kinds of breakfast foods." He hesitated. "Why does it matter?"

Rodney met his gaze. He'd been working out hard now for almost two weeks and much of his former toughness and bearing had returned. "Because we don't need any accountants in Iroquois County. We need warriors. We need leaders. We need you to learn how to kill like it's second nature, like you've been doing it your whole life. And you have to make it look effortless."

There were eighty-five men and a few of the tougher women surrounding him in a circle as he spoke with their leader, teaching them all how to kill. He looked around at the motley crew seated on the grass. They'd already been through hell just getting this far north, and their old lives and ways were shattered, replaced by something brutal and riddled with chaos. General Branch thought to himself at breakneck speed.

What could he offer them? What did they need most at this particular moment in time?

"Are there really a thousand people coming to kill us?"

Rodney looked over toward a woman seated on the ground with her legs crossed Indian style. She was slight of frame, with long, blonde hair that reached down to the middle of her back. He recognized her eyes. He'd seen the likes of them before many times in the dark of night, just before a battle. She had the look of a woman who knew she was going to die.

"Stand up!"

She obeyed his command; because he was at the top of the pecking order; because it was law of the jungle, and because he could kill her with a simple twist of his hands.

"Step forward!"

She once again complied. Rodney could see her shaking almost uncontrollably. He reached his right hand out to Jason Little and motioned with a twitch of his fingertips.

"Give me the knife."

Jason looked at him with a single unspoken question in his eyes. *What are you going to do to her?*

General Branch swiveled his head on his shoulders quicker than a hawk looking for prey. "The knife!"

Jason reluctantly handed Rodney the small bayonet. He held it in his hand like an old friend come home to visit. Rodney turned to the woman.

"What is your name?"

She looked down, avoiding the intensity of his gaze, but Rodney quickly admonished her. "Stand like a man! Look me in the eye!"

The woman looked around at her peers, but no one moved. She felt all alone in the vise-like talons of a mad man. Then she looked into Rodney's eyes, and what she saw there made her blood turn to ice. It was the coldness. It was the enigmatic maelstrom in his eyes that caused her to shudder in fear and revulsion.

"What did you do before The Day?"

Rodney caused his eyes to soften, knowing she needed his prompting to speak. He asked her again. "What did you do before The Day?"

Finally, she found her voice. "I was a mom to my daughter and a wife to my husband."

Rodney smiled and nodded. "That's a noble profession and worthy of all your attention." He hesitated. "But today, you are a warrior. You are here to kill or be killed."

She said nothing, and Rodney looked deep into her eyes, sizing her up, testing her mettle, wondering what she was capable of. "Where is your daughter now?"

She looked up quickly and immediately met his gaze as if being challenged. "She's safe with a friend." She went quiet again, but Rodney sensed she had more to say.

"Speak your mind, soldier."

Her words were short and crisp.

"I don't know if I can kill anyone."

Out of the corner of his eye, Rodney saw several others nodding their heads slightly. He looked up and they quickly stopped. Then he met the woman's gaze once more.

"What is your name?"

"My name is Lisa."

"And your daughter?"

"She's five years old. Her name is Sam."

The General nodded. "Yes, good. Now here's what I want you to do. I want you to close your eyes. I'm going to paint a picture for you. Let the picture play out in your mind. Can you do that, Lisa?"

Lisa looked at him with questions in her mind, but finally nodded and closed her blue eyes.

"You're at your house here in Iroquois. In the middle of the night you hear a scream. You run to your daughter's bedroom and see a man. He has Sam on the bed. She is screaming and struggling, but the man is too strong for her. She is pinned down and he begins to rip off her pajamas. Sam is screaming as loud as she can, 'Mommy! Mommy! Help me!' But you are too scared to help, and you don't have the training necessary to kill him. You are too decent and pure to take another human life, so you let the man rape your daughter. And while your daughter dies in pain, terror and torment, you look on, because you don't have the will or the courage to stop him."

Lisa looked up. There were tears in her eyes, but the sheep-like countenance was gone, replaced with a mixture of both fear and anger. Rodney thought to himself, *It's a start*. And then he handed Lisa the knife. She hesitated, then reached out and accepted it from his open palm. Lisa looked at it and rolled it in her hand, then hefted it from first one hand and then back to the other.

"Lisa, the man in your daughter's bedroom is coming to town. He's coming for Sam. What are you going to do? Are you going to learn to fight him? Or, are you going to cower and die while her helpless screams echo in your ears for eternity?"

The door to a secret room in Lisa's mind swung open with a creak. It was a part of her she'd never felt before. She looked up and the fear was gone. She replied coldly with two words.

"Teach me."

Then Lisa fell down to her knees in front of him, not in worship, but in voluntary submission. She held the knife out to him with both palms facing up.

The General nodded and took the knife. He stepped quietly behind her and grasped her long, beautiful,blonde hair in his left hand. He squeezed and pulled it out behind her.

"Lisa, I do this now as a symbol of your loyalty and commitment. You are now a mother … and a warrior."

The razor-sharp knife came down and severed her hair with one, quick slice. Lisa stood to her feet and turned to face the old man. Rodney let the hair fall to the ground, before handing her the knife.

She turned and walked over to the other seven women in the crowd. They all stood, as if on some unspoken command, and turned, dropping to their knees. One by one, Lisa cut their hair, letting it fall to the ground before being carried away on the breeze.

"You are a warrior."

The hair separated and fell.

"You are a warrior."

Step to the next woman.

"You are a warrior."

Again.

"You are a warrior."

Seven times the knife came down.

Seven times a warrior rose up.

Seven women.

Seven warriors.

Lisa turned and walked back to the General with all seven trailing in her wake. They stood at attention before him, and only then did Rodney sigh in relief.

Jason Little looked on in awe.

"How did you do that? I can't even get my wife to cook me dinner."

General Branch ignored his question.

"Jason, for the next two hours I want you to review and practice the proper use of rifle and bayonet with the men. Pay particular attention to the horizontal butt stroke, the diagonal slash, and the basic jab."

The big man nodded. "Ah, okay."

General Branch turned and walked away. Eight warriors followed him to begin their special training.

CHAPTER 8

Domestic Drudgery

"BUT I DON'T UNDERSTAND WHY HE won't let me fight! He's letting other women work right alongside the men, and those eight he chose out last week are being trained like some kind of Special Forces team or something."

Dan Branch looked at his wife helplessly. She was strong willed, and this was one of those arguments he knew would never go well for either of them. As far as Dan was concerned, it was a lose-lose.

"I don't know, honey. You'll have to ask Uncle Rodney. I just don't know why he does all the things he does." He shrugged his shoulders. "Does anybody?"

But that wasn't good enough for Jackie Branch. "But you know more about him than anyone does. He raised you! He's your blood! He shares more with you than with anyone else."

But in his heart, Dan knew her last statement wasn't accurate. His Uncle Rodney was in commanding general mode now, and there were many aspects of him Dan was learning for the first time, despite the thirty-some years they'd known each other.

"Honey, I love you, but you know I've gotta get going. Uncle Rodney wants me to find all those supplies by the end of the week."

Jackie folded her arms across her chest and stuck out her

lower lip in defiance. Dan smiled. "Did I ever tell you how sexy Lebanese women look when they're angry?"

They were outside the house, and the weather had turned mild, so the baby was playing on a blanket beside the porch with some pine cones and sticks. She was at the stage now where everything went into her mouth. The dog, Moses, was lying on the wooden decking of the porch on an old rug. Jackie turned her back on Dan before speaking.

"Don't sweet talk me Dan Branch. You haven't heard the last of me on this one."

Of that Dan was sure. He placed his hands on her shoulders and kissed the back of her head. His only reward was a mouthful of coarse, black hair. He lingered behind her long enough to smell the scented olive oil she combed into it each morning. She was quite the woman, and he was madly in love with her, despite, or maybe because of, her fiery ways. His wife was not a woman to be trifled with. He shuddered to think what might happen if she ever found out the real reason she didn't train with the others.

In the end, Jackie watched as he walked off down the path toward town. Most everyone walked to town these days as gas had become scarce. Most people had a small supply, but were hoarding it in case of emergency, whatever that might entail. Of course, Uncle Rodney had more than most, as was the case with just about everything else. But, for some reason, he insisted they lead the same lifestyle as everyone else.

Jackie looked down at baby Donna and frowned. She loved her daughter, but ... for some reason, she still wanted to contribute, to pull her own weight, not just by cooking and cleaning and doing laundry and watching babies, but by preparing to fight like everyone else.

Dan had moved the old ringer washing machine out onto the front deck for her as he did every week. She sighed and dropped down onto the blanket to play with the baby.

"Hi honey. Do you love me even if I can't fight like everybody else?"

Baby Donna laughed and bit down on a pine cone. She was teething again. Jackie played with her a few more minutes before walking up the deck steps to the old ringer washing machine. They were lucky to have it as most people were without electricity and had to wash their clothes on a rock down by a river or stream. Because of Rodney's foresight and hard work, they were one of the few families to have any considerable amount of electricity to work with.

Jackie was lucky, no, more than that; she was blessed. By all rights her and her daughter should have been tortured and killed in that isolated Wisconsin cabin last fall. Instead, Dan Branch and his son, Jeremy, had rescued them. Then Dan had fallen in love with her, and her with him.

For some reason, no one in town asked her why her baby was black. Maybe they thought she was adopted, or maybe that her first husband had been black. But, as far as she knew, none of the townspeople knew the truth: that she'd cheated on her first husband on a mission trip to Haiti. But Dan knew, and Jeremy knew. And probably by now Uncle Rodney as well. He suspected the men were protecting her reputation as best they could. And she loved all three of them for it.

She turned on the garden hose and heard the water pump kick on as the small electric motor worked to suck up water from thirty feet below the surface. Jackie measured out a cup of lye soap flakes that she'd cut up from a bar last night and dumped it into the water. Once the tub was full, she pushed in the clothes and turned on the agitator. It moved slower than her Maytag back home, so it took longer for the clothes to get clean, but time was something she had more of now. Life was slower, and that was one part of her new world that she liked.

While the machine worked, she watched her baby play. Then she glanced over at the sentry post at three o'clock about thirty yards into the woods. She could see him high up in the tree, but only because she already knew he was there. Uncle

Rodney seemed to have a knack for camouflage. She guessed he could make just about anything, big or small, seem near invisible.

The sentry post was manned twenty-four seven. At night by Dan, Jeremy, herself and Uncle Rodney, but by a Shadow Militia member during the day when the men went off to train for war. She had more questions than answers about the Shadow Militia. To her they seemed like the Masons on steroids. So secretive, so strong, always so disciplined and ready to follow any order Rodney gave them. She had no doubt any of its members would run into a hail of gunfire upon their general's command. She wondered now, *How had he gained that much loyalty?*

For the rest of the morning she did laundry, but her mind was free to analyze and plot, *How do I get past Uncle Rodney? How do I persuade him to let me train with the others?*

All the while, it never occurred to her that most people wouldn't want to fight, that they'd be thankful for the domestic drudgery she was now living through. But, for some reason, to Jackie, it felt like a life sentence with no chance of parole.

Donny Brewster - Master Sniper

Donny lay there in the prone position with the butt of his Crusader Broadsword rifle tucked firmly into his shoulder. The trigger came back ever so slowly and gently. Finally, Donny felt the recoil, and took one quick peek through the ACOG 4x scope. The man was lying on the ground, motionless, with the top half of his head no longer intact. Donny thought to himself, *It's true, snipers do get more head!*

He quickly packed up, and started moving to his fallback position. Out on the road he heard the quads fire up and begin the chase. This was Donny's third week in the bush, and he'd grown quite a beard and become a bit gamey smelling.

It had taken the mob almost a week to re-organize enough to get moving again, and they were now traveling at a snail's pace about twenty miles north of Big Rapids. Their present course and rate of speed would put them just south of Iroquois within two weeks. That said, Donny had accomplished his mission. He only hoped it was enough.

The first week Donny had been able to kill dozens of men each day, but they'd begun to adapt to his guerilla tactics, taking good advantage of the speed and all-terrain mobility of the quads. The longer he kept this up, the more dangerous it would become. Eventually, if they got lucky, Donny would be captured or killed. But Donny had no intention of letting that happen.

As the sound of the quads came near, Donny scrambled into the river and grabbed onto the rope he'd pre-positioned for his getaway. Most of his gear was on the other bank, and the nearest bridge was miles away. Even if they knew where to look, he'd be far away setting up the next ambush by the time they got across the deep river. By strapping his rifle onto his back, he was able to pull himself hand over hand within a few minutes.

Thirty minutes later he was four miles away down inside a trench with branches on top of him. He had claymores set up all around him just in case they stumbled onto him. In the confusion of the mine going off, shooting out its load of deadly buckshot, Donny would be able to melt slowly again back into the ever-thickening north woods of Michigan. He'd stay there until dark, sleeping in dry clothes and a down-filled mummy bag, recharging his batteries, staying warm, gathering up as much sanity as he could muster, and, more importantly, planning his next ambush.

Yes, Donny Brewster was a Master Sniper. And he was the best.

Manny Makes a Plan

"You say he does it this way every time? Just shoots one guy and then falls back?"

Manny looked over at the little man before him and nodded

his head. "Yes, just like this every day, usually in the morning when the sun is at his back. We can't see him because the sun blinds us, and by time we get the quads up there he's long gone. He's really starting to piss me off!"

The little man laughed. "If I was you, Mr. Manny, I'd be more than pissed. I'd be afraid."

Manny grit his teeth and ground them slowly back and forth to keep from swearing. He needed this man and his talents. Finally, after gaining his composure, he was able to talk again. "Just tell me straight out. Can you kill him?"

Robbie looked up at the hillside where the sun was now well over the treeline. He could easily pick out the best spot for the sniper to strike. Robbie pointed to a little indentation in the hillside about six hundred yards away.

"Leave me here with a week's supplies, and I'll do the rest."

Manny looked over at the little man like he was crazy. "Leave you here? In the middle of nowhere? Don't you want a quad or some more men?"

Robbie laughed again, and the laugh infuriated Manny. But the gang leader kept his cool this time. "I work alone. Just get me some MREs and I'll be fine." He started to walk up the hill, then hesitated and turned back around. "Just leave the food here in the ditch. I'll pick them up after I'm done scouting around up there." Then he added, almost as an afterthought. "This man's good, but he's on foot. Instead of stopping at every little town to rape and pillage, you should go as fast as you can today without stopping. He'll have to march all night long to catch up. By morning he'll be exhausted and in a hurry, more likely to make mistakes. I can exploit that."

And then Robbie turned and walked up the hill without looking back.

That day, Manny tried to do as Robbie suggested, but his men were undisciplined and it was tough to sell. The men were used to stopping at every house they saw along the highway and killing the men and raping the women. He didn't begrudge them their fun as it didn't really hurt anything, and it kept them happy and compliant. So long as Manny led them where they wanted to go, he knew they would follow. That was an immutable gang law he knew he couldn't break. So instead of fifty miles, they made only twenty miles by nightfall. He hoped to himself, *Maybe it will be enough.* But he knew, even as he thought it, that it was a hope in vain.

That morning, just as they were pulling out, the lead truck blew a front tire. When the driver got out to examine it, Manny was watching safely from one-hundred yards to the rear. He shook his head from side to side in disgust. *Don't they know by now?* The second shot came down off the hillside and the driver was knocked to the ground. The .308 match-grade bullet went through the heart and then the spine. Everyone else scrambled for cover, and soon the annoying whine of the quads drowned out all else as they raced up the hill.

Robbie had positioned himself perfectly higher up the hill and further down by only two hundred yards. Usually he didn't like getting this close; it was just too risky. But after examining and studying the sniper's ambush site yesterday morning, he knew the best shot he'd get was probably a sniper on the run. And moving targets required less recoil and a higher rate of fire. Not to mention the fact he was working under less than ideal circumstances with sub-par equipment. When Manny had come to him with the job, he'd been hesitant to accept it. Unfortunately, it had been made clear there were only two choices: kill the sniper and be richly rewarded, or turn the job down and receive a bullet for his impudence. Robbie had lost all three of his sniper rifles in the chaos following The Day, so the best he could scrounge up for this job was a stock AR-15 with a nice Leupold scope. It was better than nothing, and, along with the element of surprise, he would be able to kill his opponent.

Without the second shot into the driver, Robbie never would have seen Donny Brewster's location. It was that well hidden. As soon as he saw the tiny flash of movement, he brought up his rifle scope and cursed to himself for not being faster. The man was already on the move. Robbie tucked in his 5.56 mm semi-automatic rifle and unloaded the thirty-round magazine into the fleeing sniper.

Donny Brewster was surprised when he felt the bullet thud against his left arm,and even more surprised when another bullet came through his left ear, leaving a ragged hole. He stumbled, then ran again. Another bullet hit him in the butt, but he kept moving as bullets kicked up in the dirt all around him. After fifty yards of running into the thick woods, the bullets stopped. But Donny continued on, checking the seriousness of his wounds as he ran. He knew distance and cover was his friend at this point. If he was to survive, he'd have to put as much distance between himself and the shooter as possible.

Robbie smiled as he quickly ejected the empty magazine and shoved in another full one. By the time he'd reloaded, the target was nowhere to be seen. He was certain he'd hit the man at least once, and he struggled to maintain control as he felt his pulse quicken with anticipation. He spoke softly to himself out loud. "Don't blunder down there quickly. Stay calm. Focus. Take your time. Be smart."

He forced himself to wait thirty minutes before going down to check for blood, giving the other sniper time to bleed out. He knew instinctively that a mortally wounded man with no chance of flight was even more dangerous than one unharmed.

Finally, he slowly picked his way down the hill to the spot where Donny had been lying in wait. He saw the empty 3.08 caliber brass cartridges, and frantically searched the ground.

A broad smile invaded his face when he saw the blood glistening on the leaves below. He kneeled down and looked off in the trees just to make sure he was still alone. Robbie picked up the leaf and looked at the blood from close up. He let loose with a torrent of swear words under his breath. *No bubbles. No bone!*

He hated tracking wounded game. The sniper looked down at his mediocre rifle and spit on the ground off to one side. If only his rifle was the worst of it. He could deal with that, but, more crucial, was his lack of premium match-grade ammo. All Manny's people could give him had been NATO green tip rounds, and they just zipped on through flesh without causing massive tissue damage and blood loss.

He looked at the blood trail winding off toward the woods. It was ample blood, and, if his opponent kept bleeding like that, he'd be able to track him down within a few hours. But … there was a danger. The wounded sniper had a long-range rifle, had already proven his deadly accuracy, and would be able to set up an ambush or booby traps or a series of both.

He was beginning to wish he'd taken Manny up on his offer of men and quads. Robbie could let them blunder ahead and take the first few bullets for him, while he maneuvered into position for a good, killing shot. Unfortunately, he had no radio and no time even if he did.

It was man against man, and Robbie knew he was the best.

CHAPTER 9

The Hunter becomes the Hunted

GENERAL **B**RANCH PUT THE RADIO microphone down, and walked out of his secure, private room, through the kitchen and out onto the front porch. Dan and Jeremy were already there, sitting in the rockers.

"The trick is keeping a consistent angle while you move the stone across the blade."

Jeremy watched with interest as his father showed him how to sharpen a knife.

"It would be better if we had a beveled block to fasten the stone to, but we can do it this way too. Just takes longer."

Jeremy nodded, and they both looked up when Rodney walked onto the porch. Moses raised his head, but only for a moment before plopping it back down on his paws. Dan saw right away that something was wrong, but he knew better than to pry. Jeremy didn't.

"What's wrong, Uncle Rodney?"

The old general said nothing, just looked off into the woods as if they weren't there. Jeremy looked over at his father with curious eyes. Dan discreetly furled his brow and shook his head no. He carefully put the knife back into its sheath and handed it back to his son with the sharpening stone.

"Why don't you take this inside where you can work in the kitchen on a flat, stable surface? When you can wet your forearm and shave hair with it, then come on back out here and show me."

His son nodded and looked over his shoulder as he walked back into the house. As Jeremy was walking away, Dan called out after him. "And be careful! Don't cut yourself!"

Jeremy knew he was being left out of something interesting, and he didn't much like it. Once they were alone, Dan got up from his rocking chair and walked to the railing to stand next to his uncle.

"Is it something I need to know about?"

Rodney's eyes looked over at his nephew. Dan met his gaze and thought to himself, *He looks older than he did a few hours ago.* Rodney looked back out into the trees.

"Maybe. Not sure we can do anything about it though."

"Is it Donny?"

Uncle Rodney turned toward him. "How did you know?"

Dan shrugged. "Just a feeling. I've had it ever since he left. A bad feeling. Like something isn't going right for him."

The General nodded his head. "Me too. He's really good, but not the luckiest man in the world. This mission needed some luck. It's unpredictable, tough to control. Too many unknowns."

Dan frowned. "How bad is it?"

"Bad. He's hit multiple times. Not life-threatening with proper treatment. But he's being hunted."

Dan looked at him quizzically. "Hunted? By a gang?"

The old man's shoulders sagged as he leaned onto the railing. "They got them a sniper."

Dan turned away from the woods and leaned the middle of his back against the wooden porch railing. He hadn't shaved in a week, so he stroked the stubble on his cheeks thoughtfully.

"We have to go get him."

Rodney shook his head from side to side.

"Can't. Too risky in the daylight to fly the choppers down

there. We need to keep a low profile. And if we drive down it'll take hours and be too late, assuming we make it at all."

He leaned his elbows up on the railing and sighed.

"No, Donny knew the risks going in."

Dan couldn't believe what he was hearing. He moved off the railing and assumed a stiff posture.

"What the hell are you talking about? That man saved my life and the lives of my family when we were dying in the snow in the Upper Peninsula!"

Uncle Rodney didn't answer right away. He turned to face his nephew, and was surprised at the determination he saw in Dan's eyes. He shrugged.

"There are larger considerations. Things more important than one man's life to worry about."

Dan had always been stocky and strong, but the hard life after The Day had strengthened and hardened him even further, on the inside as well as the outside.

"I don't care about that. He saved my life. I owe him mine. He's a Marine. I'm a Marine. There's a million reasons to go after him, and you can't give me one good reason not to, other than some obscure, unnamed story about jeopardizing the entire Midwest. I don't care about all that stuff. We got a man out there bleeding and dying while we sit back here safe and sound. That don't wash with me."

Inside Rodney smiled. *Yes, his boy was a Branch and a true leader. He had the right stuff for the times.* The old man was reminded of all those years after his brother's death when he'd been trying to raise Dan on his own. He'd always wondered if the boy was internalizing any of the lessons he'd tried to teach him. Now he knew that Dan had learned it all and then some. Parenting took faith, but standing before him now was the final product of his hard work and belief.

"Well, there might be one way we can help him …"

Dan unfolded his arms from his chest. "Okay, I'm all ears."

Running on Empty

Sergeant Donny Brewster put the radio back inside one of the many pockets of his backpack. When he'd first called, the General had been vague on whether he could get him out, but then he'd called back only fifteen minutes later with a plan. If he could elude or defeat his pursuer for the rest of the day, they could extract him by nightfall. It was an offer he was in no position to refuse.

Donny rolled over onto his side to finish cleaning out the bullet wound in his back side. Fortunately for him, the round had gone in the thick of his muscle and come out cleanly with no ripping or tearing. He shoved more alcohol-soaked gauze into the entry and exit wounds in an attempt to stem the bleeding, but the gauze was quickly saturated with blood.

Thankfully, the wound on his upper arm was more super-ficial than he'd first thought, and the bleeding had stopped. Donny could even use the arm so long as he was willing to endure the pain associated with movement. The hole in his ear had already clotted over for the most part, and was just a slow drip every ten seconds or so. He quickly shoved two more Tampons into the holes in his backside and taped over them.

He had to keep moving, but he also had to form a plan. Donny thought about the attack on him, and formed a quick opinion on his adversary. He was definitely ex-military, maybe even Special Forces, and not just some gang banger who'd cross-trained into marksmanship. Donny wondered to himself, *Why is this guy shooting target rounds instead of ammo that will do more damage? It doesn't make sense. He obviously knows his tactics, since he's already ambushed me so skillfully, and evaded disclosure long enough to execute the attack. His positioning was textbook perfect.*

Donny opened up a plastic bag and swallowed two more wide-spectrum antibiotic pills. No need to take chances on infection out here in the boonies, especially with wounds as serious as his own. And then Donny thought again, *His at-tacker's positioning had been textbook perfect.* The wounded sniper thought about that for a few seconds as he quickly packed up and moved out again. *Maybe he could exploit that?*

As he limped along through the heavy woods, Donny wondered how soon General Branch would arrive, wondered if he would arrive at all. He quickly shook his doubt away like nasty swamp water running down into his eyes. The General would come. Of course he would come. He wouldn't abandon him, wouldn't leave one of his own behind. The Shadow Militia was a brotherhood. Donny pressed on, ignoring the pain.

The Pursuer Closes in

Robbie looked up ahead and saw the empty plastic bag resting lightly on top of the dead, brown bracken fern leaves. He moved back instinctively into the shadow of the oak tree beside him. He thought to himself, *It's almost as if he placed it there so I could find it on purpose.* Like a paranoid cat, Robbie moved out slowly, turning his neck from side to side in slow motion, scanning the forest for any sign of his prey.

When he reached the plastic bag, he plainly saw the twelve-inch wide circle of blood on the dead leaf floor. A quick scan saw the leaves had been misplaced all around the area. Robbie thought to himself, *So this is where the enemy sniper had stopped to bandage his wounds and tried to halt the bleeding.* His eyes followed the trail of misplaced leaves another twenty feet through the woods, but he saw no more blood. Then his eyes rested upon the empty round cardboard tubes on the ground beside the blood. *Tampon tubes? To stop the bleeding?* Robbie remembered his battlefield first aid training and smiled. There would be less of a blood trail now, but … still … there would be a trail.

Robbie forced himself to move slowly through the woods, making as little noise as possible. It was very difficult to be silent while walking through the thick layer of dead, brown leaves. They were so thick and old they felt spongy beneath his feet. It had been an hour since his last respectable spot of blood, but the wounded man's movement through the early spring north woods was obvious. His prey appeared to be dragging one foot behind him as he struggled across the terrain. There were more hills now, not big ones, just small, gradual rises, but, nonetheless, they seemed to be taking their toll on the wounded sniper somewhere out in front of him. It was only a matter of time now.

Donny stopped for a moment to rest. The weight of the pack on his back, and the Crusader Broadsword rifle attached to the sling on his chest were beginning to take their toll on his stamina. He looked behind him at the trail he'd left, then he reached up and squeezed his left ear lobe to make it start bleeding again. A few drops came down onto the dried leaves.

Two hours ago, when his bleeding had halted, it had occurred to him he should simply fade noiselessly off into the woods and disappear. The General would pick him up after dark, and this episode of his life would be over. But ... there was a part of Donny that just didn't like that idea. It was the sniper part, the part of him that loved the thrill of the hunt, the part of him that had killed strangers in and out of combat, had stalked and hunted and preyed. No, there was a big part of Donny Brewster that wanted to prove he was the better man, the better soldier, and the better sniper. Something told him, something instinctive, that he *needed* to kill this person in order to stay the man he'd worked so hard to become.

Yes, fading away would be the smart, safe thing to do. Donny squeezed his earlobe again and watched the blood drip down to the leaf-covered floor. But, if Donny wanted a safe life, he could have married that pretty cheerleader, had babies and lived in the suburbs. No, Sergeant Donny Brewster didn't want to be safe. He wanted to be dangerous, indeed, thrived on it.

Sometimes he caught himself wondering what General Branch felt like, being so old, being, well, not in his prime anymore. He was reminded of that Toby Keith song, "I'm not as good as I once was, but I'm as good once as I ever was." Donny shook his head from side to side. This was as good as he would ever be, and he'd milk his abilities for all they were worth or die trying. Right now, all Donny could think of was fighting the man who'd shot him. If the man hunting him turned out to be better than him, then, so be it. Donny would die in a hail of gunfire. Better that than sitting alone in a rocking chair.

This was Donny's day, and he would prevail. He reached into his pocket and took out another 1200 milligrams of aspirin and popped them into his mouth. He quickly chewed them up and swallowed. Aspirin was a blood thinner, and he desperately needed to bleed more if his plan was going to work. He reached into his pocket and pulled out another blood-soaked gauze pad. Donny threw it onto the ground and then moved on up the hill. It was a big one. The last one.

General Branch gunned the engine of his quad and took off in a burst of speed over the field stretching out before him. Daniel was close on his heels pulling a small trailer behind his own quad. They had chosen an isolated stretch of national forest as their route down to rescue Donny Brewster. The roads were undoubtedly faster, but there was no sense in taking any chances on being spotted. Besides, once they left Iroquois County, their friends would be few and far between. In general, people had grown mighty leery of strangers in the past six months, and were more likely than not to shoot first and ask questions later.

Rodney looked down at the screen of the locator hanging from a rope around his neck. As long as Donny was still moving, they knew he was okay. All Shadow Militia, even Rodney, had a surgically implanted transponder in their back which allowed anyone with the know-how and technology to track them to within a few yards. And Donny was definitely on the move.

The old man pushed his quad even faster. The sun was well past noon, and they still had many miles to turn.

Robbie looked down at the bloody gauze pad, then up the hill. It was a steep and steady slope. He wondered how the man was still even on his feet, much less heading up that hill.

Something inside Robbie caused him to shudder. Something wasn't quite right. He looked up the hill again. The trail was clear. It was more than clear. It was obvious. That bothered him.

What if ... Robbie let the thought trail on off into the setting sun. He'd been tracking this man for most of the day now. The initial blood had been profuse, but then had dried up within five hundred yards of the ambush. And it had all been dark red muscle blood. No bubbles and no bone. The drag marks were getting more serious and pronounced now, indicative of someone on their last leg, someone beginning to weaken and stiffen up, someone who had gone as far as they possibly could on the sheer strength of a powerful will. But still ... *What if ...*

Robbie looked up the hill and saw the pile of brush just before the peak. He stared closely, thought he saw the slightest of movement, then brought his rifle scope up to his right eye. It was confirmed. There was something moving inside that brush pile. He quickly dropped down to the woods floor and thought. Either the man was too weak to continue and was either dying or making his last stand here, or, this was a trap. Either way, the wounded man was in the brush, and Robbie had to somehow confirm his death or move in to finish him off should he still be alive and dangerous. He didn't dare go back to Manny without a confirmed kill. He knew better. Slowly, Robbie raised up his rifle and looked through the scope again.

After five minutes of patient spotting, he thought he saw the bill of a baseball cap. He watched for fifteen more minutes, then he thought he made out a single dark eye socket.

Donny was in place now, lying silently, waiting, noiseless, in perfect calm, for the storm to follow. What would the other man do? Would he come up the hill? Would he shoot from there. Would he try to flank the brush pile by traversing the hill from the left or right? Donny didn't know. But … still … he waited. Why? Because that's what snipers do. They wait … and they kill.

"We have to hump the rest of the way in."

Both quads were silent now. Rodney moved off a few yards and started collecting brush to cover up his ride. Dan followed his lead and started covering up his own quad and trailer.

"How far away is he?"

Rodney answered without halting his work. "Just a few miles."

Dan nodded. "Good. We should have him safe and sound by daybreak." He placed another branch on his quad. They had to collect a lot, since the trees were still void of leaves. Dan continued. "So which way is he heading now?"

Rodney looked down at the locator hanging from his neck. Dan thought he saw a slight stutter in his uncle's movements. It wasn't pronounced, just subtle, something one would expect from anyone other than Rodney Branch. Then his movements continued as quickly as they'd halted.

"He's not moving anywhere."

"What?" Dan held the bare branch over his quad trailer as his uncle kept moving.

"You heard me. He's not moving anymore."

Dan let the branch drop, then walked over closer to his uncle. "Is he dead?"

As if in answer to Dan's question, ten shots rattled off in

quick succession a few miles away. There was a pause, and then another ten shots rang out.

Dan and Rodney's eyes locked for just a moment. They both gathered up their packs and their rifles. Rodney moved into the lead, and then marched quickly down the hill with Dan close behind.

Robbie ejected his empty magazine and quickly moved to reload, but, before he could do so, he heard the gentle sound of a man laughing behind him. Robbie froze.

Rodney looked down at the locator and adjusted his course slightly to the left. They were going up a hill now, trying to be quiet, but failing miserably. Rodney cursed the dead leaves with each step. The sun was low in the sky now, causing shadows to lengthen and spread out across the woods floor, lending an eerie gloom to the panic. There had been no more gunshots, but they were almost there. According to the transponder, Donny still had not moved.

When they reached the top of the hill, Rodney held up his right hand and both men halted and dropped to the ground as if they were one person. Rodney pointed to the ground about twenty feet ahead. Dan's eyes popped open wide in disbelief. There, dangling from a rope about twelve inches off the ground was a rabbit hanging by its back legs. The rope which held him fast was draped over a tree branch. Dan's eyes followed the rope over twenty feet closer to the hill peak to a pile of brush. Every time the rabbit struggled, the brush moved.

Dan looked over at his Uncle Rodney and saw the wide smile on his face. Both men crawled up to the peak and then looked down to the bottom. They saw two men. One was on the ground on his stomach with his hands zip-tied behind his back. The other, was standing over him. Dan watched through his rifle scope as the man unzipped his fly and urinated on the helpless man's back.

Rodney laughed out loud when he heard the unmistakable voice of Sergeant Donny Brewster. "And that's for shooting me in the ass!"

CHAPTER 10

Final Preparations

SOMETIMES FRIENDSHIP CAME from the most unlikely places. Jackie smiled inside as she securely strapped baby Donna into the olive drab, military-style backpack. Such had been the case with her and Uncle Rodney. After their initial friction, he had warmed to her, at least in private, and he'd even taken a liking to her baby, bouncing the little girl on his knee, and holding her. Once, she'd even caught him making silly baby voices to her child when he thought no one was listening. He even fulfilled his promise of teaching her rifle marksmanship, and they practiced almost every day.

She crossed her arms in front of her the way Uncle Rodney had taught her, and quickly hoisted the pack up and onto her back. She adjusted the waist strap and walked over to the waiting quad. No one was allowed to use the quads without special permission from the General, but Jackie had one allocated for her private use. Why? Because she was on special assignment, by order of General Branch. And no one, not even Dan, was allowed to know what she was doing. She'd been working at it for over a week now, and it was driving her husband crazy. But that was okay. Jackie believed one of the keys to keeping a man happy was keeping him guessing. Never let him figure you out lest he take you for granted, and, above all else, every once in a while throw your man a curve ball.

But that's not why Jackie was doing this. She just wanted to help, and her personality wouldn't allow her to be shoved off onto the sidelines while the men had all the fun planning and preparing and fighting. Jackie Branch was a woman of action!

Jackie slowly mounted the quad and started it up. She reached down and massaged her mending leg. Back before The Day, she'd undoubtedly still be in a cast and on crutches. But times were different now; the need was urgent. Everyone had to pull their own weight regardless of personal sacrifice. For the first time in her life, Jackie felt beholden to the community around her, and an obligation to serve something greater than herself. Jackie had never been in the military, so she didn't realize what she was feeling was a sense of duty and honor. But even though she didn't know the right words, she knew it made her feel good.

She dropped off baby Donna at Marge Leif's house, and was quickly on her way again. Within five minutes she reached her destination. Sergeant Harold Steffens was waiting for her in his pole barn behind his house with the garage door open. She drove the quad in and turned off the engine. It took all their strength for her and the old man to pull the rope and close the door, shutting out the world to the secrets they were doing inside.

The Interrogation

"I've been trained in interrogation techniques. I should be the one who questions him."

Robbie Mankowski was now strapped to a chair in a barred cell at the county jail. On the outside, he remained defiant, but on the inside, he was trembling. He knew there would be no cavalry for him. Manny wouldn't be riding in on a white horse, and there was no hope of rescue. He was at their mercy. He looked into the eyes of Sheriff Joe Leif and saw compassion and civilization. Then he looked over at the cold, stone stare of General Branch. He didn't dare say it, but he wanted

77

to be questioned by Joe Leif, the civilized one.

Rodney Branch walked out of the cell, and Joe Leif followed him into the outer office out of ear shot. When the General spoke, his voice was devoid of emotion. "How long will it take you?"

"Just a few days."

"That's too long. We need to know all we can about their new leader, about how they operate, about what they plan to do and how they plan to do it."

Sheriff Leif was almost pleading. He wasn't stupid. Rodney was an old friend, but he wasn't the friend he'd known all these years. For the first time in his life he wondered, *Who is Rodney Branch? What is he capable of?*

"Listen, Rodney, let's be blunt. I know darn well what will happen to this man if you question him. I know all about military style enhanced interrogation techniques, and I won't let it happen in my county on my watch."

General Branch remained stoic.

"Rodney, you told me you are here simply to advise and assist, that you respect the Constitution and my authority as the chief law enforcement officer of this county. If that's true, then you have no choice but to do it my way."

Rodney turned his eyes toward the Sheriff and smiled. "Of course, Joe. The prisoner is yours. Please call me on the radio with any information you get, so I can incorporate the intel into our defense plan."

Joe suddenly felt relieved.

"Really?"

Rodney laughed out loud.

"Of course, Joe. I'm not a barbarian. You've known me your whole life."

He paused. "The prisoner is yours. Just let me get my satchel. I left it in the cell. Then you can get busy. Please hurry though. We need to know what he knows as quickly as possible."

Rodney started to walk back to the cell. "I'll be back at my place for the rest of the day."

General Branch disappeared from view, leaving the Sheriff alone with his thoughts. *Wow! He really does respect my authority.* And then he felt guilty about doubting his friend's fidelity, his character, and his sense of right and wrong. Joe Leif bowed his head in his hands and wiped the sweat off his brow, he hadn't even realized was there. After wiping his hands on his pants, he sat down at his desk and started writing down questions. He'd interviewed dozens of criminals in his career, and he knew just how to do it. Two days tops and he'd have this man broken.

"BAM!"

Joe Leif jumped in his chair at the sound of the gun shot. It was loud, like the 45 caliber that Rodney always carried. Quickly, adrenaline shot into his bloodstream, paralyzing him in his chair for several seconds. Then he heard a scream. Not a yell, not a shout, but a primitive animal sound that caused Joe's hands to turn to ice. He jumped up and fell down onto the floor as he scrambled around his desk. The scream came again and again and again.

Finally, Joe rounded the corner and raced down the hallway to the cell. He fumbled with his sidearm, not really thinking ahead about what he might do with it. Rodney was just holstering his pistol as Joe arrived. There was sheer terror etched all over Joe's face, but General Branch radiated an eerie calm. He smiled.

"Like I said, Joe. The prisoner is all yours."

And then he walked away. Joe didn't try to stop him. He didn't dare. He looked over at the prisoner, still fastened to the chair. Robbie Mankowski was crying now, weeping like a small child. His left foot was bleeding from a large hole, the blood seeping out of his boot, forming a pool beneath him. The hilt of a three-inch folding jack knife stuck straight up from his right thigh. The blood had soaked into his pants and was now dripping onto the floor.

Joe was stunned and suddenly felt very weak. Robbie lifted up his head and began to plead with the Sheriff. And there, the worst horror revealed itself. Carved into the man's forehead was the letter "M". Blood seeped down into the man's eyes and down to his mouth as he tried to talk without sputtering.

"Please, I, have to … talk."

Joe didn't know what to do.

"I have to get you to the doctor. Quickly or you'll bleed to death."

"NO!"

The force of the man's voice startled Joe into stasis.

"But why?"

The pain in Robbie's eyes held Joe steady like a vice.

"Please … ask me anything. He's coming back."

And Robbie Mankowski talked for hours, even while being treated by the doctor. The Sheriff, feeling terrified, angry and a little grateful at Rodney, wrote it all down.

Making Soldiers

Dan Branch walked up and down the firing line like a sentry, barking out orders, making adjustments and suggestions on how to tighten a bullet group or operate the action of a particular weapon more efficiently. There was nothing typical about these people or their weapons. Their arsenal was more like something you'd see at a pawn shop instead of an army base. Of the twenty or so people on the line, there was a variety of AK-47 types in 7.62 millimeter and AR-15s in 223 caliber. Several people didn't own rifles or carbines, so they were shooting their deer hunting shotguns. As shotgun slugs and most other ammo types were at a premium these days, most of their practice was restricted to dry fire and lecture. He looked down on the end and saw a father and son practicing with .50 caliber muzzle loaders. Under General Branch's orders, no person was turned away regardless of training, race, gender or physical handicap. The best prepared mentally and physically would be placed on the front lines, while the rest would be held in reserve and in support positions. The latest reports now numbered the advancing horde at fifteen-hundred strong and still growing.

The horde was now in the Grayling area getting ready to make their westward turn to Traverse City. According to Donny Brewster, and the info extracted from Robbie Mankowski, the new leader of the horde was planning to set up permanent house in the rich and trendy Lake Michigan port city. Unfortunately for Dan, Iroquois was on a direct line between Grayling and Traverse City. The big port town had everything an unruly mob of cut-throats and villains could ever ask for: rich tourists with expensive toys and plush houses. Most of TC's summer residents had fled Chicago shortly after The Day in their sailboats and yachts, thinking they would be safe and comfortable in their second homes on Michigan's golden coast. This was not a good day to be wrong. They were a soft target, an isolated plum just waiting to be picked. Uncle Rodney estimated they had just one more week to train, and then their troops would have to be deployed throughout the county in accordance with the General Branch defense plan.

Dan continued with his standard lecture on firearms accuracy.

"And the sixth and most important element of marksmanship is trigger press. Indeed, according to the great Masaad Ayoob, the trigger is the heart of the beast. Master that and your group will stay small and inside the bulls-eye. The trick is to maintain a soft and gentle touch while pressing the trigger slowly and steadily directly to the rear."

The people on the line were on the ground in the prone position, dry-firing as he spoke. The intermittent sound of clicking firing pins filled the afternoon air. A mild spell in the weather had set upon them, much to Dan's delight, with temperatures nearing sixty. It wouldn't last long, but he'd take it while he could get it for sure.

"If you can squeeze the trigger without moving the front sight, while maintaining perfect sight alignment and sight picture, then you'll be inside the bull every time."

Dan looked at the plethora of people he had before him, wondering, *A week from now, which of you will still be alive?* Of course, if they failed to stop the advancing horde, then only the lucky ones would be dead. His thoughts drifted momentarily to Jackie and Jeremy and little baby Donna. What would happen to them if ... he let the thought trail off into the sinking sun. He wouldn't let that happen. Marine Corps. The mission. Whatever it takes.

Dan renewed his speech with heightened vigor. Whatever happened, these people wouldn't die because he'd taught them to shoot incorrectly.

An Old Man Prepares

Harold Steffen's back was bent with age. Some mornings he could barely walk, while on others he didn't bother getting out of bed at all. After Myra's death, he'd contemplated following her quickly, indeed, had even held the revolver to his right temple and teased the trigger with a little pressure. But since he'd joined the Shadow Militia, he'd been up every morning at dawn.

The mid-morning sun streaked into the pole barn as he worked, slowly, ever so slowly. There were times when, if anyone by chance had been watching, he could have been mistaken for a store-front manikin. Harold moved the wrench slowly, tightening the bolt down as much as he could. He sighed and whispered softly to no one in particular. "The woman can finish it."

Jackie was with him almost every day now. Harold was the brains. He knew how to fix it, but he no longer had the strength. But Jackie was a strong woman, and easy to work with. She rarely talked, and Harold found that comforting. He'd never liked a woman who talked a lot. Myra had talked out of control, but his love for her had been such that he'd tolerated it for sixty-five years. Sixty-seven if you counted the courtship.

In a few days they could fire up the engine, and a few days after that would be the test flight. It was cutting it close. The horde was almost here, and Harold hadn't flown a plane in almost twelve years. Undoubtedly he would die on the runway, but ... if he could ... if it flew ...

Harold smiled.

CHAPTER 11

The Horde Approaches

MANNY GOT OUT OF HIS BIG Hummer and strode confidently up to the front gate of the Grayling National Guard base. There were olive-drab-clad bodies strewn all over the tarmac, rotting in the cool northern Michigan breeze. In a few more days the smell would be overwhelming.

Major Danskill was waiting for him at the position of parade rest with his body stiff and his arms behind him, hands clasped in a military manner one over the other. There were several HumVees strategically located around the guard shack with their fifty caliber machine guns lowered, manned and ready to shoot at the first sign of betrayal.

Manny looked around at all the military hardware and drooled inside. He estimated they had about one hundred men, all heavily armed with M-16s, Squad Automatic Weapons (SAWs), frag grenades, and rocket launchers. And this was the light stuff.

If he played his cards right, he'd walk out of here armed to the teeth as the mother of all warlords. If he screwed up, well, he'd be carried out in pieces. *Note to self. Don't screw up.*

Manny was aware of the general story of what had happened here just a few days ago. Mostly because he'd been in on it from the start. Major Danskill had been a Chief of Police back before The Day and the commander of a Military Police unit here at Graying. He was a weekend warrior with two deployments in Iraq and another to Afghanistan. He'd been the unwavering servant of the United States Army for twenty years, but Manny knew something the army did not. Major Danskill had a secret vice. Well, two vices, actually. The soldier was addicted to heroin, and he had a taste for small boys, which was hardly regulation. Both hungers were insatiable and becoming increasingly difficult to feed.

Manny was here to fill that need.

☆ ☆ ☆ ☆

Corporal Mike Stanton was perched near the top of the tall Norway Pine in his Ghillie suit peering through his spotting scope at the front gate of the Grayling National Guard base. Colonel MacPherson had sent him here over a week ago to observe and report. A few days ago he'd witnessed a fire-fight, more like a massacre, as one group of National Guardsmen had slaughtered about fifty of their unsuspecting comrades. After that, it had been fairly quiet until a few minutes ago when the yellow Hummer had arrived with an entourage of Suburbans and well-armed bodyguards.

Mike watched as the leader stepped out of the Hummer and approached the gate. He spoke to the Major briefly, then was let inside. His bodyguards remained outside the gate. Corporal Stanton took as many pictures as he could with the camera attached to his spotting scope.

There was silence for thirty minutes, then three deuce and a halves pulled up to the gate and quickly drove out. A few minutes later three Bradley fighting vehicles approached the gate and were let out as well. Mike kept snapping pictures. He would send them via satellite link to the Colonel as soon as this was over.

Then he heard a rumble.

The sound got closer, then, finally, the Abrams tank came into view. The horde now had heavy armor.

Donny Brewster - Intolerable Patient

Even though she was a Registered Nurse, Lisa Vanderboeg didn't appreciate being relegated to nurse maid duties, but she did so out of loyalty to General Branch. And ... well, she had to admit ... out of curiosity as well.

The sniper man was in bed now resting, but he'd fought her all the way, wanting to get up and move around. He'd demanded to know where his rifles were, until, finally, the General had visited and calmed him down. It had been almost two weeks now, and while the other women were training, she was cleaning his wounds while watching her daughter. Although the duty was tolerable, and, some would say, even choice, Lisa didn't like waiting by idly as the horde advanced on her daughter.

She looked over into the corner where Sam was playing. Samantha was a miniature copy of herself, or so people told her, with her long, flowing blonde hair, but sporting the curls of her father. The thought of Lisa's husband caused her to wince. Jim had died shortly after The Day at their home in Grand Rapids. But prior to that Jim had been forced to watch as the men had raped his wife. But, for Lisa, the rape had been nothing compared to the pain in her husband's eyes as he was forced to look on helplessly while two men violated her. At least Sam had been spared.

That same night, after her rape, while the two fiends slept in the other room, Lisa was able to loosen the rope around her wrists. She'd quickly untied Jim, who went into the next room with a busted chair leg. The first man was beaten to a pulp, and Jim had just started in on the second intruder when a shot rang out. The bullet hit him in the hip, breaking the pelvic bone. Jim had gone down instantly. He tried desperately to get up, but couldn't. The man raised his gun to fire again, but Lisa had picked up the chair leg and slammed it into his head. The lag bolt, still fastened to the wood, had pierced the man's eye and driven itself into his brain. He'd died quickly. Jim, on the other hand, had taken three days to pass on, forcing Lisa to watch helplessly. None of her medical training could be brought to bear, simply for lack of supplies and equipment. Lisa and Samantha had cried over his dead body, then held a funeral in their back yard. Sam had taken a lock of her father's hair. They'd left the next day, trying to make it out of Grand Rapids to the north where Jim had relatives.

If not for Jason Little and his family, they would have died for sure. They'd never made it to Jim's relatives, but now, thanks to General Branch, Iroquois was now their home. General Branch had given them sanctuary and a place for her to raise her daughter. Lisa was beholden, and she would pay her debt, whatever the cost, so long as her child could have a shot at a happy future.

"So what's on your pretty mind today, ma'am?"

Lisa came out of her thoughts and looked over at Donny Brewster's perpetual grin. She just wanted to slap him. In another life she might have found him attractive, perhaps even welcomed his flirting, but not today.

"How are you feeling?"

Samantha heard his voice and came over to the bed.

"We've been waiting for you to wake up Mr. Donny."

Donny smiled at five-year old little Samantha. She'd become his special friend and near-constant companion over the past few weeks, much to the displeasure of her mother.

"Well, I'm feeling pretty good today, especially now that you're here."

Samantha smiled. "Are you ready to fight bad guys again?"

Donny laughed and reached back to rub his wound. Then he nodded. "I think I'm getting pretty close. If it's okay with your mommy I'd like to move around a bit and maybe even try to walk." Donny looked out of the corner of his eye to Lisa, but she was stone-cold sober as ever. Donny thought to himself, *If I could just get her to smile ... she would be so attractive. I wonder what happened to her?* Donny hadn't admitted it yet, but he was indeed truly smitten by his young nurse. Despite her melancholy demeanor, Lisa Vanderboeg was a sharp woman, and putting Donny in the same room with her for two weeks was a recipe for romance.

But she didn't seem interested. In fact, she'd rebuffed every subtle advance he'd made. "Nurse Lisa? What do you think? Can I try walking today?"

Lisa thought to herself, *Sure, go ahead. Let's start with a long walk off a short pier.* But out loud she said, "Sure. I think you're ready." In truth, Lisa wanted him up and around as quickly as possible for two reasons: the first being she wanted him to fight the horde to help save her child. Whatever else Donny might be, she knew he was a great warrior. She'd heard from the other girls that he'd killed over fifty men on his latest mission. That intrigued the warrior part of her that had taken root and grown steadily over the past few weeks. Lisa had been changing. The rape of herself, and the murder of her husband had fractured her, and she felt like two people. There was the warrior Lisa, and there was the mother Lisa. She didn't like feeling diametrically opposed to herself.

So, with Samantha's help, Donny sat up and swung his feet out onto the floor. Lisa watched the initial pain ebb across the man's face. Then, as if he had the power to turn it off, the look of pain went away. Donny smiled. "It feels great." Little Sam placed her tiny hand in his own as Sergeant Brewster raised himself up, placing his full weight on his legs. Lisa thought she saw the look of pain again, but it went away as quickly as it had come. The perpetual smile stayed there.

Donny slowly walked around the room with the five-year-old girl leading him. Then he stopped and looked down at Samantha. "Would you like to dance, Miss Sam?"

The little girl's eyes lit up like sparkling blue water. She politely nodded and gave a little curtsy. "Why yes, Sergeant Brewster. May I lead?"

Donny laughed and extended both his hands downward. "Of course. After you, my lady."

Lisa watched in awe as her little daughter danced around the room with a deadly sniper. Both of them laughed as they danced. Suddenly, Lisa smiled, and then she cried. Donny looked over and saw the tears streaming down the woman's face. He quickly bent down to his dance partner. "My lady, I've enjoyed the dance, but I'm afraid I have to rest now. Would you mind if I spoke with your mother alone about my medical condition. Just for a few minutes."

Samantha took a step back and curtsied. She looked over at her mother, saw the tears and ran to her arms. "What's wrong Mommy?" The two girls embraced and held each other for several seconds. Donny watched on, feeling like he was invading their personal space.

"I'm fine, honey. Why don't you go downstairs and play with the Legos. Build me something good, and I'll be down in a few minutes to check it out."

Sam kissed her mother, then ran to Donny and kissed him on the cheek as well. "You are a splendid dancer Mr. Donny."

Donny laughed out loud. "As are you, my lady."

The little girl backed away and pranced out of the room leaving the two adults to talk about things she neither understood nor cared about. When she was gone, Lisa wiped the tears away and looked coldly at Sergeant Brewster.

"I want you to stay away from my daughter."

Donny's smile quickly faded.

"Excuse me?"

Lisa turned her head toward the window. "You heard me. I don't want her getting close to you."

Donny's shoulders sagged, and he moved back over to the bed. The look of pain returned to his face, and this time it stayed.

"Why are you saying this? I like your daughter. She's a wonderful person, and you could be too, if you let yourself."

Lisa stared out at the bare branches on the oak tree in her new front yard. They were swaying mildly in the breeze.

"She's been through enough already. I don't want her bonding to a man who will probably be dead inside a week. She doesn't need that."

Another smile slowly reached his lips, then like the tide, it pushed in until it conquered his face. "You don't want *her* to bond with me, or you're afraid *you* will bond with me?"

Donny got up off the bed again and walked over to Lisa. He was wearing grey, cotton sweatpants and a blue T-shirt. On the front it said, "If God wanted us to be vegetarians, broccoli would be more fun to shoot." Donny stopped a mere twelve inches away from her face. *She has the most beautiful, blue eyes.*

"You know you like me."

Lisa turned back, but now her blue eyes had turned to fire and rage. Her hand flashed out and slapped him across the face, leaving the red imprint of her fingertips on his cheek.

"I want you out of here as quickly as possible. You obviously are feeling much better. Just get out there and kill people. It's obviously what you enjoy most. It's who you are!"

The pain in Donny's eyes was apparent. Even while she was saying the words, Lisa regretted it. But she couldn't stop herself. Nonetheless, she felt guilty and softened just a bit. "Will you just get out there and save us from the horde?"

Donny's smile suddenly returned, as if it had never left. He slowly got down on one knee, reached up and took her hand in his own. Lisa stiffened as Donny gently kissed the hand that had struck him.

"As you wish, my lady."

Then Donny stood. He backed away, never taking his eyes off Lisa's face. He reached the bed and sat down while putting on his shoes. When he was done, he stood back up and walked out of the room.

As the door closed behind him, and she heard his footsteps fade down the hall, Lisa cried in front of the window. Suddenly, she felt very fragile and very much alone.

CHAPTER 12

Battle Plans

T HEY WERE BACK AT THE COURT-
house conference room, and Colonel
MacPherson stood ramrod straight as he clicked
the remote, advancing the PowerPoint presentation one more
slide. The electric cord came down off the projector into a
power inverter which in turn ran cables to a car battery on
the tile floor. The Colonel was wearing heavily starched,
olive-drab fatigues. A Colt forty-five caliber 1911 pistol was
snapped securely in his strong-side retention holster.

"The Horde is advancing now from Grayling at an alarm-
ing pace. If nothing is done to slow the march, they'll reach
the outskirts of Iroquois City in two days time."

The picture of a long convoy was being projected onto
the wall in front of them. Someone had pinned a sheet over
the conference room window to darken the room. The convoy stretched out over a mile. It contained military HumVees,
deuce and a half trucks, civilian semi-trailers, U-haul trailers, a couple of gas tankers, and Dan thought he even saw a
Toyota Prius near the back.

Colonel MacPherson advanced the slide and Dan could
hear the audible rush as everyone in the room caught their
breath. Further back in the column were three Bradley Fighting
vehicles and an Abrams M1 tank weighing over sixty tons.

"But that's not the biggest problem."

The Colonel paused for effect. "The Horde now has heavy armor as well as three Bradley Fighting Vehicles. The forward armor on an M1 of this kind is 600 millimeters thick. It has a laser-guided targeting system, accurate out to 8,000 meters. It's only real vulnerability is from the air, but that involves capabilities that Iroquois County forces do not currently possess."

He looked around at all present, but no one spoke. They appeared to be stunned into silence.

"Now the Bradleys are a different matter. They have sufficient armor to ward off any attack by small arms, and their strength lies in their speed. They can traverse open terrain at a speed of well over forty miles per hour. They could be used as cavalry to outflank any traditional attack or defense, followed up quickly by more infantry to mop up."

General Branch looked around the table, quickly assessing their mood. Dan appeared stone-faced. Sergeant Brewster was smiling. Sheriff Leif looked like a deer in the headlights of a Peterbilt. Rodney smiled in satisfaction. He already knew they could do it, but he wanted Joe to squirm a bit after all the crap he'd been given for torturing his prisoner.

Rodney put on his poker face and looked over at Sheriff Leif. "What do you think we should do, Joe?"

Sheriff Leif looked surprised. He glanced down at the Formica table top in front of him. "I still say we should use your helicopter gunships to take them all out. That would be so much easier."

General Branch nodded. "Yes, it would be easier. We could complete the operation in a few hours time and neutralize The Horde forever."

Joe's brow tightened. "But you're not going to do that, are you, Rodney."

Uncle Rodney shook his head from side to side. "I already told you, Joe. We can't do it. And even if I could, there are down sides. This is an excellent opportunity for Iroquois

County to cut her teeth in battle."

The Sheriff scoffed out loud. "Cut our teeth! Are you crazy? That's an M1 tank! We can't stand up to that thing! It'll drive straight into town and tear us apart!"

Rodney leaned back in his chair. He let out a heavy sigh. Sometimes Joe discouraged him beyond repair.

"Joe, it's only one tank. Now if there were two squadrons of them, then maybe you'd have reason to gripe. But I can teach Jeremy how to take out one lone tank."

Colonel MacPherson nodded. "Absolutely. One tank is nothing. Sure, we'll have to deal with it, but we can give you a plan and the know-how. You just need the courage to execute it. I'm more concerned with the Bradleys than I am the tank."

General Branch stood up and stretched the muscles in his back. Every once in a while, out of habit, he still reached into his breast pocket for a cigarette. He guessed he'd be doing that for the rest of his life, however long or short that might be.

"The way I see it, Joe, we have three phases in our defense to plan. The first two are strictly offensive in nature. One, take out the tank and the Bradleys. Two, wound as many of their infantry as possible. And three, prepare the city for attack."

The Sheriff's head came up in a questioning glance. "Wound them? Why are we wounding them? Shouldn't we be killing them?"

Colonel MacPherson cut in. "Negative, sheriff. Wounding is desirable in this situation. Our tactic is to slow their advance. If we kill a man, he drops and is left behind. If he's wounded, the others are forced to stop and deal with him. Our strategy has always been one of attrition. Buy time, harass their column, depress their morale, make them nervous as hell. All these things when put into a coordinated action will seriously degrade the ability of The Horde."

Dan had been intent on every word from the others in the room. Now he looked up. "But these guys are ruthless. What makes you think they'll stop to render medical attention to their fallen comrades?"

General Branch answered his question. "They won't help them, Dan. They'll shoot them and leave them behind. But that's one more bullet they can't use against us."

The Colonel smiled. "And when done over the course of two days, shooting their own people will degrade morale. That's what we want; to lessen their capability as a fighting unit. They're already a rabble of undisciplined men, and that's a good thing for us. But if we can strike fear and cause desertions, that helps us even more."

Uncle Rodney sat back down again. "I won't blow pretty colored smoke up your ass, Joe. This is going to be tough, and if even a few hundred of The Horde gets through ... well, it won't be pretty on the population of the town."

Dan broke in. "So, basically, we have to stop them all. We have to kill almost two thousand cut-throats and murderers in order to save our women and children."

Rodney looked over at Colonel MacPherson, who then looked over at Sheriff Leif. Joe Leif hung his head.

"I don't know if we can do it." His fear hung in the air like the stench of infection.

Donny Brewster had been silent until now. He'd been thinking about Lisa and little Samantha, and Jackie and baby Donna. Finally, he stood to his feet.

"Permission to speak candidly, General?"

Rodney nodded his consent. "I expect no less from you, Sergeant."

Donny pointed at the tank on the screen. "I'll take out the tank and the Bradleys sometime in the next twenty-four hours. I'll just need a lightly armed fire team and a few more goodies."

Colonel MacPherson looked over at General Branch. Dan could tell they were doing their military mind-meld thing again. Finally, the Colonel nodded his consent. "Very well,

Sergeant Brewster. Have the plan written out for me in four hours, and I'll see you have the men and materiel you need for the mission."

Donny laughed out loud. "Begging the Colonel's pardon, sir. I don't need men. I need women."

This comment raised even the General's eyebrow. Joe Leif opened his mouth to speak, but quickly shut it again. He knew better than to call Donny Brewster, their sniper messiah, into question. If it hadn't been for Donny Brewster, The Horde would have reached them weeks ago.

The Colonel smiled too. "This should be interesting."

Sheriff Leif broke the silence. "That leaves the second phase, wounding as many of The Horde as possible." He hesitated. "I want to do it."

Dan looked up with surprise in his eyes. He hadn't expected that one. But General Branch was not caught off guard. He immediately countered.

"You can't, Joe. We need you here to coordinate and lead the defense of the town, phase three. People here know you and respect you. I'm afraid they still see me as a bit of a lunatic. You are the man they feel comfortable with. They'll follow you. You have to rise to the occasion and inspire them to fight."

Joe looked over, not knowing exactly what to say. He thought to himself, *Am I being insulted or praised?* Dan rescued him from his internal dilemma.

"I want to lead phase two. Donny can help me set up a plan. But I've been helping to train most of the recruits, and I know their abilities. I can pick the right people for the right job."

Colonel MacPherson looked over at the General, who let out a heavy sigh and looked down at the table top. He'd had every intention of leaving Dan behind to help coordinate the town's defense. But the moment Dan had spoken the words, he'd known it was the right thing to do. Dan had the training.

He had the courage and he'd already proven himself in battle. Donny Brewster was undoubtedly the best qualified to handle it, but he'd have his hands full taking out the armor. Rodney looked over and met the Colonel's gaze. The General nodded and only then did the Colonel speak.

"It's decided then. In four hours time we'll meet back here. The three of you will have written plans describing your intentions in every detail. I want logistical needs, manpower requirements, time schedules, the whole shebang."

The Colonel stood to his feet. He cast an imposing shadow across the dimly lit room.

"Any questions?"

The men looked at each other, realizing they now stood on the cusp of history. They would either live or die tomorrow based on decisions they made today. It was a sobering thought.

Donny Brewster was the only one smiling.

☆ ☆ ☆ ☆

Four hours later they all met again. Rodney and the Colonel went over the plans privately, then met with each one individually. They asked questions, pointed out flaws, and played devil's advocate. The end result was the initial battle plans became much stronger.

Joe's plan needed the most help as he had no military experience. In the end, General Branch assigned Colonel MacPherson to work with Joe one on one to hone the plan and make it better. They worked well into the wee hours of the morning. But in the end, even the Colonel was happy with Joe's plan.

While everyone else scattered about to prepare for their phases of the operation, Rodney went back to his house and talked to Jackie. They left baby Donna in Jeremy's care and both hopped on quads. Jeremy looked after them, listening to the sounds of their fading engines, jealous, almost angry at being left out of the action.

When they both reached Harold Steffen's pole barn, Uncle Rodney shook his head in disappointment.

"It's not ready yet?"

Harold looked tired. He'd been working twelve hours a day on the plane, and it was taking its toll on his eighty-some year-old body. Jackie stood nervously off to one side.

"I'm not the man I used to be, General. I just can't move fast enough."

General Branch smiled while standing stiff and proud beside him. He would never let on his disappointment. He thought for a moment.

"You just need an experienced mechanic to help finish the delivery system? Someone with youth and strength?"

Harold smiled. "Well, I suppose so. But youth and strength is a lot when you don't have much of either."

The General forced himself to laugh out loud. "No worries, Sergeant Steffens. Colonel MacPherson's helicopter pilot is still here. I'll send him over right away. He's a captain, but I'm giving you tactical command of this mission. It's all going to rest on your shoulders, Sergeant."

Harold smiled. Then he nodded. "Yes, sir. You can count on me, sir."

Rodney made a call on his radio, then he left Jackie and Harold behind to finish their work. If they failed, there was still a chance to defeat The Horde. But if they succeeded? So many lives would be saved.

CHAPTER 13

__Donny's Crazy Plan__

SERGEANT **D**ONNY **B**REWSTER stood at the head of the courthouse conference room as he gave his briefing. Eight women were seated around the table, while Sheriff Leif and General Branch were seated against the wall behind them as observers.

"The Bradley Fighting Vehicle's main armament is a 25 mm cannon. It fires up to 200 rounds per minute and is accurate up to 2500 meters. To compliment that are twin missiles capable of destroying tanks at a range of over two miles. The Bradley also has a 7.62 mm machine gun, just to the right of the M242 25 mm chain gun."

Donny pressed the remote button and the PowerPoint slide advanced to show a different view of the Bradley Fighting Vehicle. He pressed the button again and again, each time showing close-ups of the equipment he was describing.

"The Bradley is also equipped with a TOW missile system for use against tanks and other armored vehicles."

One of the girls raised her hand, so Donny stopped talking and pointed to her.

"What exactly does TOW mean?"

"TOW stands for Tube-launched, Optically-tracked, Wire command data link, guided missile, not that it matters."

The girl shrugged and added sheepishly, "I'm so glad I asked."

Donny continued without further interruption.

"The Bradley weighs approximately 30 tons and is protected with explosive reactive armor, which means anything we have to shoot at it will bounce off like eggs on brick."

He looked around the table and smiled.

"And those are the easy targets. The real challenge is going to be destroying an M1 Abrams tank. It's long been the main battle tank of the United States for good reason. Here are the specs."

Donny pushed the remote button again and another slide came up showing all the details of the Abrams.

"The Abrams weighs just over sixty tons, give or take a few. In combat it has a four-man crew, though I expect The Horde is still trying to figure out how to train enough men to operate it. The hull and turret armor is about six hundred millimeters thick, too tough for anything we have."

Lisa was sitting near the front. Her initial reunion with Donny had been clumsy, but professional. Much to her surprise, he had requested her for this mission.

"The primary armament is a 105 mm rifled cannon. For support it has three machine guns, one in fifty cal and two in 7.62 millimeter. So, as you can see, it's pretty tough to take out while operating in battle mode.

"The M1 is powered by a Honeywell AGT1500C multi fuel turbine engine with fifteen hundred horsepower. The tank can travel at a maximum speed of thirty-five miles per hour on tarmac and twenty-five off road."

Sergeant Brewster looked around the room. No one spoke. Several women had their heads down. One had tears in her eyes. Lisa broke the silence.

"So how are we going to kill these things? They sound indestructible."

Donny smiled, showing all his bright, white teeth.

"And that's the million-dollar question isn't it? How do we defeat an enemy with heavy armor when all we have are small arms and a few grenades?"

Donny advanced to the next slide. It showed a four-man tank crew in full battle dress standing atop the Abrams.

"The answer to your question is simple. We hit them in their weakest spot, which, for a man, is located directly below the waist."

Donny used the red dot of the laser pointer until it rested on the groin area. He moved it slowly from one man to the next. When he looked up, Lisa was staring at him in horror. When she spoke her anger was obvious.

"You are using us as sex objects? You want us to have sex with these animals to give you long enough to disable these things?"

Donny's smile faded.

"Well, it sounds unreasonable when you word it like that. I just want you to create a diversion. I need only ten minutes. The sex is optional."

Lisa ground her teeth together. General Branch looked on from the back, trying to gauge the wisest response. Sheriff Leif squirmed uncomfortably in his chair beside Rodney. He'd voted against the mission altogether. Rodney decided now was the time to intervene. He stood up and strode confidently to the front.

"Sit down, Sergeant Brewster."

Donny was more than happy to comply. Rodney took a deep breath and then launched into his speech.

"Listen, Ladies, I know this isn't what you were expecting, and none of you have to go through with this. I realize we're asking a lot. If things go bad all of you could be raped or tortured or killed outright. I understand that. But we're desperate here and we need to use all weapons at our disposal, even if that weapon happens to be sexist, dangerous or politically incorrect." He paused. "You've all heard the phrase, 'All's fair in love and war?' Well, sometimes love and war intersect, and that's where you beautiful ladies come in. If I could use men I would, but … I just don't think it'll work as well."

He stopped talking, not knowing what more to say. Like so many other battle plans of his past, it had all made so much sense on paper. But then you add the human element, and things break down.

A slender, well-built brunette was the first to speak. "So, are these guys cute or are they dogs?"

The question caught General Branch off guard. "I'm not sure. We don't have that level of intelligence on the tank crew."

Lisa looked at him and shook her head from side to side. Finally, she spoke up again. "I hate to admit it, but it's a good plan, all things considered."

Another girl, this one a redhead sounded appalled when she responded. "What? Are you crazy? Lisa, they want us to have sex with these lunatics!"

The good-looking blonde laughed out loud. "Get off your self-righteous high horse, Emma. I know darn well you've had plenty of sex before, probably even the rough stuff."

The redhead seemed offended, but clamped her mouth shut without responding. The General continued.

"Ladies, we've been giving you special training for a reason. All those hand-to-hand moves we've been teaching you, and the knife-fighting techniques; they were for this purpose. Each of you is uniquely qualified to accomplish this mission. And if it works, you'll have saved thousands of lives. Men, women, children. All innocent people will live because you did this." He hesitated. "But it's strictly voluntary. Any one or all of you can say no, and none of us will think the lesser of you. We won't tell a soul."

Another woman, middle-aged, attractive, a little on the chubby side asked one last question. "What happens if we don't do this?"

General Branch hesitated, as if finding the words to use, but then he just blurted it out. "If you say no, then we send thirty men to take the armor crews out by force. It will be bloody on both sides, and the chances for success go down exponentially. Plus, there will be no way to get the men out after the armor is destroyed."

"So they'll all die?"

Rodney met Lisa's gaze. He nodded silently. Lisa swallowed the lump in her throat. It went down hard. The General spoke again.

"We're going to leave the room now. You ladies go ahead and talk it over amongst yourselves. We'll be waiting outside when you're ready to give us your answer."

With that, the three men got up and walked out the door. It closed behind them with an echo that pierced Lisa to her core.

☆ ☆ ☆ ☆

"So why did you choose me? Why am I part of the Bradley crew?" Lisa added sarcastically. "Aren't I attractive enough to make the cheerleading squad?"

Sergeant Brewster ignored her question. "Please focus, Miss Vanderboeg. You have just a few hours to learn to operate an M242 Chain gun and an M240C 7.62 millimeter machine gun. It's not easy."

She snapped back at him. "Don't ever call me 'Miss'! It's Mrs. Vanderboeg to you!" She paused, but Donny said nothing. "Now tell me, why did you choose me for this? I want to know."

Donny turned back toward her and placed the remote on the table beside him. He wanted to get through this. He wanted her to learn and prepare for the mission. Yeah, sure, he had some hormones ablaze for her, but this was a mission where people were going to die, and many more would die if they failed. He calmly began his explanation.

"*Mrs* Vanderboeg, you were chosen because the testing we gave you revealed you best qualified to serve as crew for the Bradley Fighting vehicle we're going to use in the attack. You have the night vision of an owl, and your eyes adjust quickly to night flash. Both are good characteristics in a night-time firefight, especially with a high-caliber machine gun."

Donny wondered if he should tell her the rest. She settled the question for him.

"What else. That's not all. I can tell you're holding something back."

Donny smiled impatiently. Then he nodded. "Sure. There are two other things: First, you have a little girl and she needs you. The other girls are single and never been married, so if they die, they won't be leaving anyone behind. I'm not saying being on the Bradley crew ensures your safety, quite to the contrary. This is a very dangerous mission with a high chance of failure. However, you will stand a better chance if you're on the Bradley. Second, we know of your history. You've already been raped once before, and I doubt your psyche could handle it again."

Lisa sat stunned into silence. She squirmed back and forth in her chair. Finally, she spewed her next sentence haltingly. "So … the other girls are … going to… die?"

Sergeant Brewster looked down at the ground and said nothing. What could he possibly say to make her feel better? He felt like they were using these women, and that went against the grain of manhood for him. They should be protecting the women, not sending them into battle. He'd only mentioned the idea to General Branch because he believed for sure it would be thrown out. But the General had latched onto it enthusiastically. "No free rides," he'd said. "The women have to pull their weight, and this plan is tactically sound. They'll never see it coming. It will save lives."

Lisa's eyes started to mist over, but then Donny watched as something else happened to her. Within a few seconds her face turned to granite, and the mist was instantly gone. He watched her grit her teeth with a mighty resolve.

"Show me the training film again. I want to watch it a hundred times if I have to."

Donny nodded and suddenly felt a new respect for her. Lisa watched the film over and over and over again, until, finally, operating the gun, loading it and clearing a jam became almost second nature to her.

After two hours straight, Donny was starting to believe his plan had a chance for success.

CHAPTER 14

Dan Readies his Team

"DAN I WANT YOU TO BE EXTRA CARE-
ful. You're going to be very vulnerable out there for a
few days or even more, depending on how successful
you are. And you're going to be all alone. We won't be able
to get help to you, at least not very quickly."

Dan smiled and flashed his uncle a snappy Marine Corps
salute. His Uncle Rodney scoffed at him. "I told you, son,
we're in a war zone! Stop saluting me!"

Dan and the hundred men behind him were all dressed in
various brands and patterns of hunting camo. They all carried different weapons ranging from high-powered sniper
rifles to primitive bows and arrows. The newly commissioned
Major Branch had organized them into fire teams, squads and
platoons. They were a hodge-podge group to be sure, poorly
armed, and not quite ready for prime time battle, but Dan
didn't question their resolve. He'd picked them not for their
age and fitness, but for their skills and their fighting spirit.
Dan wanted people he knew wouldn't turn tail and run, and
he didn't much care about their gender or their age. Many
of them, and he didn't know exactly how many, would fight
bravely and die.

He'd said goodbye to his family a few hours ago,and it
hadn't gone well. Jackie had been furious that he'd volunteered, and Jeremy had been angry that he was being left
behind. In the end, Dan knew the only way to improve his

relationship with his wife was to come home alive, and he fully intended to make his wife happy.

"Godspeed, Daniel. You'd better come back here in one piece. Don't you dare leave me at home with all that youth and estrogen, because I just can't handle that."

Major Branch smiled and gave his uncle and commanding general a manly embrace.

"Roger that, general. I'll try not to disappoint you."

With that, Dan turned and addressed his soldiers.

"All right, let's head on out. We've got clicks to turn and Horde to kill."

They force-marched down the road at a furious pace. The lead platoon carried a Gadsden flag with the words "Live free or die" at the bottom. It blew in the slight breeze, rippling as the force went on their way, with nothing but the dissonant sound of boots on gravel taking the place of a professional cadence.

☆ ☆ ☆ ☆

That night, after taking a full day to get his fire team in place, Sergeant Brewster peered down at The Horde's encampment. The sun was setting low and they were already settling in for the night. Donny couldn't help but notice the differences in the opposing force. Somehow, they'd become more disciplined, more regimented and effective. He couldn't help but wonder if Manny, this new leader, was even more dangerous than the one he'd killed weeks before.

He brushed the worry aside. It didn't matter. He was a Marine, and all that concerned him was the mission. He looked over at Lisa lying on the ground beside him, while the other three women provided flank security. She was a beautiful woman in a lot of different ways. He chastised himself for thinking about it. *I'm on a mission. Focus! The mission! Focus!*

"What does it look like?"

Donny said nothing. He simply handed her the binoculars and pointed five hundred yards down the hill at their objective. Lisa sucked in her breath. "Wow! That's a big tank."

Donny chuckled to himself. "No kidding. And the Bradleys aren't small either."

Lisa lowered the binoculars. She had camo grease all over her face. So did Donny, and when he smiled, all she could see was white in the fading light. They talked as they waited for the sun to go down.

"So, are you scared?"

Donny couldn't help but think to himself, *I love a beautiful woman in camo and face paint. It doesn't get any sexier than that.* Lisa thought for a moment before answering him.

"I don't know. Guess I just feel kind of numb inside right now. The only real fear I have is not making it back to Sam."

Donny nodded, and a slight sadness moved over his face. She sensed the change. "What's wrong?"

Donny pasted the grin back onto his face, but Lisa saw right through it. "Tell me what's wrong. I want to know."

The smile faded like the setting sun. Finally, Donny let his head drop down. "I don't know. I guess I envy you."

Lisa cocked her head to one side. "Excuse me?"

Donny nodded. "Yeah. I've been on so many missions, been shot at so many times, that I never stop to think about what I have waiting for me at home."

Lisa raised the binoculars again. She scanned the encampment, then lowered them again. "So, who do you have waiting for you at home. And where exactly is home?"

Donny raised his head up again and took the binoculars from her. "No one's ever waiting for me. And home is where my rifle is."

Lisa tried to look into his eyes, but he turned away. "That is so sad, Donny."

"Call me Sergeant Brewster."

Lisa laughed a little bit too loud.

"A little comic relief. I like that in a man."

For the next half hour they watched the camp set up. Donny took note where the sentries were posted outside the camp. He'd already taught the girls how to crawl quietly, and he knew from his last visit that a mixture of rock and country music would be playing loud enough to drown out the sound of their movements. And, if that wasn't enough, the gas and diesel generators were sure to help.

Finally, the sun was down, and they formed up and began the long, slow crawl into position. Donny couldn't help but wonder, *Are we crazy? Is there any real possibility this plan will work?* He didn't know it, but Lisa was thinking the same thing.

✸ ✸ ✸ ✸

Two miles further west, Major Branch and his three platoons of Iroquois County militia had just reached their ambush site. He set his men to work digging in. A man walked up to Dan, started to salute, but quickly recovered.

"Sorry, Dan. Force of habit, I guess."

It was completely dark now, but they'd gathered on the edge of a swamp, surrounded on three sides by high ground where they could use small amounts of artificial light without being seen.

"Did you get them all planted, Larry?"

Captain Larry Jackson was an old man by Dan's standards, but he was knowledgeable on the ways and skills of battle, more specifically, demolitions and guerilla warfare.

"You got that right, Danny boy. They come through here after us and they'll be in for one helluva surprise!"

Dan nodded. "Good. What about the roads?"

Larry nodded, but Dan couldn't see him in the darkness.

"All covered. They'll get through it, but they'll do so slowly, and we'll take a few out in the process."

Dan nodded up the hill. "Larry, you oversee the defenses

while I head up that hill to get a gander."

Larry nodded. "Yes sir, Major Branch."

Dan chuckled at the way his old friend said it. When Dan had grown up, Larry had already been an adult. Now, Dan was leading him into battle as his superior. But Dan wasn't the kind to let it go to his head.

"Hey, Dan. You'd better take someone with you for flank security. We shouldn't take any chances tonight."

Dan smiled in the darkness. Then he thought to himself, *Yes, I'm the Major, but this guy has more experience. A wise man would do well to listen to him.*

"Roger that. Send me two quiet men."

A few minutes later the three soldiers moved as quietly up the hill as possible. Dan was amazed at how hard it was to move through the brush without making noise. Even after seven months without civilization, most of them still hadn't rediscovered the primitive art of moving through the woods.

When they reached the top, Dan dropped down onto his belly and looked out at the bonfires and lights. His two guards spread out to his left and right. He could faintly hear the generators and what appeared to be the sound of ZZ Top singing *Sharp-dressed Man*. It seemed so out of place to him. Then he realized how long it had been since he'd heard music. It had been that night on his way to Eagle River in Wisconsin. He sang the song softly, just barely audible now. "Bye, bye Miss American Pie, drove my Chevy to the levy but the levy was dry. Them good ole boys was drinkin' whiskey and rye, singin' this'll be the day that I die. This'll be the day that I die."

He'd almost died that night. It seemed so long ago and far away. The wind changed directions and picked up speed, carrying the song to him on the wings of the night. "Every girl's crazy 'bout a sharp-dressed man."

Suddenly, the old world seemed so shallow to him. Dan looked off to his right where the paved road led up the hill. To the right of that is where Donny and his girls would be coming, assuming any of them lived through the battle.

Major Branch closed his eyes for a moment and imagined himself snuggling in bed with his wife. He always liked to press his stomach up to Jackie's back and drape his right arm over her side until his hand rested on her stomach. *He couldn't help but wonder, Will I ever do that again?*

He heard someone issue a command down below. He watched for a few more minutes, then gathered his guards and moved down the hill to quiet them down. It was going to be a very long night.

✯ ✯ ✯ ✯

Back at Iroquois City, Sheriff Joe Leif and General Branch sat at the county jail monitoring the radio, hoping for information on how the mission was progressing. But the radio was silent.

"Why aren't they talking to us, Rodney? Don't they know we're sitting back here wanting to know what's going on?"

Rodney involuntarily reached for his left breast pocket for the cigarettes that were no longer there. He hated the waiting.

"They were ordered to maintain radio silence. We have to assume The Horde is monitoring radio traffic now that they have sophisticated comm gear inside the Bradleys and the Abrams. It's not worth the risk just to make the commanders feel good."

The Sheriff nodded his understanding, but he didn't much like it. Joe was staring down at the floor, then he got that eerie feeling that comes only when one feels he's being watched. He looked up quickly and saw Rodney's eyes fixed on him with a grimness that made him shudder. Joe squirmed.

"What?"

Rodney shrugged it off and turned away.

"It's nothing."

Joe cocked his head to one side.

"It is too, something. Now what are you thinking about?"

The General sat up straight in the cheap folding chair and crossed one leg over the other.

"I was just thinking about Robbie, the sniper we interrogated."

The Sheriff nodded. "And?"

Rodney dropped his crossed leg down onto the floor again before speaking. "And, I was just wondering why you didn't give me more grief about it. I expected you to try to arrest me or something. But you did your best at chewing me out, and then you let it go."

Sheriff Leif smiled. "Why is it always the same with you military guys born for greatness?"

Rodney cocked his left eyebrow in curiosity. "Excuse me?"

"You know what I mean, Rodney, so don't be faking humility on me now. I've known you my whole life, and deep down inside, even though you lived right here in this podunk little town, I knew you were different than the rest of us. I knew darn well you were going to do something great or crazy. I didn't know what, and, quite frankly, just between you and me I expected it to be against the law."

Joe shook his head from side to side. "And I guess, according to the old rules, it is against the law, but …" He let the sentence trail off.

"Are you telling me you thought I was a madman? A lunatic?"

Sheriff Leif laughed to himself. "Hell, Rodney, I still think you're a lunatic. After you shot that guy and cut him and stabbed him? I think you removed all doubt on that one. Right about now crazy and reckless is your defining characteristic."

Rodney didn't say anything. He just waited for Joe to finish speaking his mind.

"But I gotta tell ya, Rodney, even though the things you do are against everything I was trained for, and everything I'm emotionally prepared for …"

Joe looked down at the floor. "You get results." He hesitated, almost ashamed of himself. "You're the man who should be leading this county, not me. You're the man who can make the tough decisions under stress. I can't do it, but it's like you do it without even blinking."

The General sat unmoving, listening, gathering intel, wanting his friend to go on.

"The way you took charge at the campsite a while back, throwing that flash bang into the crowd, then coming back with supplies and recruiting them. It fixed everything." He paused long enough to make eye contact. "And when you stabbed that guy in my own jail, I was furious. But not at you - at myself."

The General locked eyes with the Sheriff.

"But after I slept on it that night, I realized I wasn't mad at you. I was mad at me, for not having the guts to do what needed doing. I had to rely on you. My way, my inability to act decisively would have ended up killing more civilians, the ones I'm sworn to protect." The Sheriff lowered his head. "I'm ashamed of myself."

For a few seconds, General Branch remained silent, assessing what his friend *wanted* to hear as opposed to what he *needed* to hear. In the end, he did what he always did. Rodney spoke his mind.

"Listen, Sheriff, I hear what you're saying, and I agree with it all, so far as you went. I've always known that good peacetime leaders seldom make good wartime leaders. But the opposite is also true. During peacetime I feel like a fish out of water. Maybe that's why I've spent my whole life either fighting or preparing for a fight. But the truth is this war won't last forever, and when it's done and the smoke clears, Iroquois is going to need someone like you to help them rebuild. That's where you shine."

The Sheriff looked up hopefully. Then he smiled. "So, you make the mess and I'm stuck cleaning it up?"

Rodney laughed out loud. "You got that right, Joe!"

The two men laughed together for a bit, then somehow got on the subject of fishing before The Day. Fishing had changed after the lights went out. Sport fishing was nonexistent, but instead, people now fished for survival.

The radio stayed silent, but Rodney and Joe just kept talking into the night, waiting, reacquainting, reassuring each other they were both the same friends they'd been before The Day.

CHAPTER 15

Night time Assault

"SO IS IT TRUE?"

Lisa was huddled on the ground beside Donny, listening to the music and voices coming out of the camp. They were only twenty yards away now, hiding in the shadows being thrown by the lights of the camp, waiting for the moment when they would attack and most assuredly be killed.

"Is what true?"

Donny looked over at her, and the light from the camp hit him in the side of the cheek. "You know. Is every girl crazy about a sharp-dressed man?"

Lisa was amazed at Donny's ability to stay calm and even make jokes in a deadly force situation. She moved closer to his ear before whispering. "Will you please shut up? Aren't you the least bit afraid we might die tonight?" Lisa couldn't see his face, but she assumed he was grinning.

"Only if it enhances my chance of survival."

Donny looked over at the other three members of his fire team: Tara, Brenda and Lynne. All three were dressed in *Victoria's Secret* negligees. The women had taken the time to fix their hair, make-up, even their nails before moving into this jump-off position. Donny watched them, and could tell they were nervous. If he told the truth, he was nervous too. Donny didn't want them to die, but he saw little chance for them. He'd gotten to know them better the past few days, and he was starting to hate himself for coming up with this plan.

"Stay here until the men are busy with the girls. Then sneak up to the troop compartment door and join me inside the Bradley. It's the one farthest from the bonfire. It's the only one with the troop door in the DOWN position."

Lisa followed Donny's gaze and nodded. She looked over at the other girls, and swallowed the lump in her throat. She was feeling guilty about her comparatively safe role in this plan. While the other three girls were being repeatedly raped, she'd be deep inside the safety of an armored fighting vehicle. Lisa thought about returning to her daughter, Samantha, fighting the ambivalence of feeling good about her role and bad about her guilt. She'd heard Donny use the term "survivor's guilt", and she knew she was feeling it now, well before the mission's end. She shook her head and told herself, *Don't count your chickens before they hatch, girl. First you have to survive long enough to feel guilty.*

She looked over at Donny, but he was already gone, now kneeling beside the other girls. She couldn't make out what he was saying, but she did hear Tara reply, "Can't we just get this thing over with. I'm freezing in this skimpy little outfit."

Lisa watched from her vantage point as her comrades moved into position on the far side of the camp. She lost them from view, and the next time she saw them they had left the safety of the bushes and were marching up to one of the Bradley Fighting Vehicles.

"Hey guys. Manny sent me over here with these three girls. Said it's a special treat to celebrate the addition of armor to our group."

The three women were trailing in his wake, strung together with a rope with wrists tied up. All eight of them saw the girls and stood up in unison, as if they all had the same thought. At first, The Horde members didn't say anything. Finally, one of them spoke.

"Manny said that? These women are for us?"

Just as Donny had predicted, the men were so excited about the girls they didn't even ask who he was. He played along with the ruse as best he could.

Donny nodded. "Yeah, that's what he said. He said to let the armor guys get first crack at these girls. Said you could have them all the way till morning."

The men crowded around the girls, moving in like wolves ready to attack. Donny remembered his last time inside The Horde's camp as the lifeless body of the woman had been thrown out of the semi trailer. She'd been raped to death. He prayed the girls would catch a break.

The dominant male of the pack reached out and grabbed Tara by the wrist. "I want this one first!" Then he cut the rope tethering her to the others and drug her to the back of the closest Bradley. Tara resisted but didn't scream and was no match for his strength. Donny listened to the whirring of the electric motor as the troop compartment door came down. Finally, the man stepped inside and dragged Tara behind him. Three more men grabbed Brenda and took her to the second Bradley. "You two can hold her while I go. Then we can trade off until we're done." Lynne was hauled away by three more men and ended up in the Bradley closest to the woods, the one Lisa and Donny were going to use to complete the mission.

That left Donny standing alone beside the bonfire with the remaining Horde soldier. The man turned toward him, and Donny's heart caught in his throat as the man called him by name. "Hello Donny."

Lisa was just about to sneak closer to her assigned Bradley when she saw Donny begin to talk excitedly to The Horde member beside the fire. The man was big, much bigger than Donny, and held himself straight and proud. His hair was cut short, but he had a good week's growth on his face. Lisa got a

117

sinking feeling in her stomach when she saw The Horde soldier pull a bayonet out of its sheath from his belt. She wanted
to cry out, *Donny, watch out! He's got a knife!* But there just
wasn't time and she was too far away. She raised her M4 instinctively and was about to aim in when both men separated.
Donny went to the Bradley closest to Lisa, and the other man
hurried over to where Tara had disappeared.

Lisa's heart was pounding now, wondering what was going on and what she should do. Then Donny's words came
back to her, *Just follow the plan*. But even that confused her,
because even Donny wasn't following the plan, and the plan
belonged to him!

In the end, she made her way over to the back of the
Bradley and peered in just in time to watch Donny holster the
suppressed nine millimeter pistol. Three men were crumpled
on the floor, and Lynne was retrieving her negligee from the
bench seat.

Donny barked to Lisa in a low voice. "Get her some
clothes. Then man the twenty-five millimeter chain gun." He
walked out the back and into the night.

Adam Cervantes came in low behind the big man, and
raised up with his bayonet ready to strike. He plunged the
big knife into the man's back between the vertebrae, sever-
ing his spinal column. The man dropped to the floor like a
bag of wheat, banging his head on a stowage compartment on
the way down. Tara looked up at him with terror in her eyes.
Adam smiled as he raised one forefinger to his lips and made
a shushing sound.

"Hurry up and get your clothes on, then go to Donny's
vehicle. I'll meet you there."

Then he turned and strode out the Bradley where Donny
was waiting. Together, they moved quietly to the remaining
Bradley. They were surprised to see the compartment door
was still up, and Brenda was pinned to the dirt while the other

man came down on top of her. Donny shot the man on the left with his suppressed Glock in the back of the head while Adam came in unannounced on the right slashing the other man's throat as he moved.

The man on top of Brenda gave out a surprised cry just before Donny's knife slit his windpipe. The dying man fell down on top of Brenda, gurgling blood into her face and on the ground around her. Brenda turned her head to one side and wretched out the contents of her stomach, all the while trying to wipe the blood from her eyes.

Adam looked over at Donny. "It's good to work with you again, brother."

Donny looked at him grim-faced. "Let's get out of this place while we still can."

Adam Cervantes smiled. "Fine, but I get to drive."

Dan Branch watched from two miles away as Donny and Lisa opened up with the armaments of the Bradley. Lisa targeted the other two Bradley's with the twenty-five millimeter chain gun while Donny loaded up the TOW and sent a rocket into the Abrams Tank across the field. Lisa had expected an explosion and a column of flames reaching up to the sky, but the death of the tank was less dramatic than she'd anticipated.

Adam already had the six hundred horsepower engine running, and, as he began to drive away, Donny targeted the two shot-up Bradleys just to make sure they never moved again. Once they were away, Donny manned the 7.62 M240 machine gun and took out as many of The Horde as he could. He focused his efforts on the bonfires, while Lisa lit up as many vehicles as she could with the chain gun.

As they drove away into the night, The Horde's camp site was alive and burning. Dan Branch lowered his binoculars and nodded his head as he smiled. "Impressive."

Larry Jackson stood beside him laughing. "We'd best get

in place, Major. This night isn't over by a long shot."

Dan nodded and both men moved off into the darkness, barking out orders as they went.

"Over there! Up that hill! I see the flare." Adam Cervantes pointed up at the flare now on its downward plunge to the earth below. His head was jutting up out of the Driver's Vision Port. Lisa was still manning the chain gun while Dan reloaded the machine gun to her right. The rest of his female fire team was in the troop compartment getting back in their camo, preparing to engage anyone who pursued.

Lisa looked back at The Horde encampment, amazed at the burning and chaos they'd caused. At present, there was nothing for her to do, so she focused on listening through her helmet as Adam and Donny talked back and forth.

"We need to get off this road, Donny. They'll be coming for us soon. We're only going thirty miles per hour and they'll catch us in no time."

She heard Sergeant Brewster laughing in her ears.

"All we have to do is make it over that hill and we'll be safe. We just have to make sure they catch us on the downhill side."

Adam didn't answer right away. "What do you have cooking, Donny? What's going on?'

Donny laughed again. "You'll see. It'll be fun."

Lisa was now convinced that Donny Brewster was crazy. But still … she found him interesting. She saw lights moving now, coming out of the camp, more than she could easily count.

"Donny, we have lights coming toward us from the camp. Lots of them, maybe twenty or more."

"Thanks, Lisa. I see them. Start shooting at them."

Lisa thought for a moment. *That didn't make any sense.*

"Dan, I can barely aim this thing, much less hit a moving target while bouncing up and down on this road."

Once again, the laugh came that was starting to grate on her nerves. "Just start shooting. I want them to know where we are. They have to follow us."

Lisa fired away, aiming as best she could at the light down the hill. They heard and saw the big twenty-five millimeter gun, and all the lights began to focus on their location. They steadily came closer.

Lisa kept thinking to herself, even as she fired with little effect down the hill. *He's crazy. We're going to die. I know he's crazy. Please, God, let him be sane.*

They crested the hill just before the quads caught up with them. There were over twenty of the little vehicles, lit up in the night like fireflies, closing on them, cresting the hill, then swarming around them. They began to spout fire. Lisa heard the bullets helplessly clanking against the Bradley's armor and she cringed at the sound.

"Stop it right here, Adam. This is where we make our stand."

Lisa couldn't believe what she was hearing. Apparently Adam had a problem with it as well.

"Donny Brewster have you gone mad!? We should be heading off through the boonies right now before those HumVees catch up with us. They've got TOWs mounted to a few of their vehicles. If they can figure out how to use them, we're dead if we stay here for very long."

Donny laughed again, this time almost hysterically. That's when the first quad ran into the trench that Dan Branch and his men had dug. The driver flew over the handlebars and landed in a heap. Another quad met the same fate, then another and another. The quads slowed but didn't stop.

"That's impressive, Donny, but how are we going to stop the TOW missiles? They're almost up the hill."

Donny's answer confused him.

"Viper Actual this is Viper Mobile, do you copy, over?"

There was silence. No response. Donny repeated the transmission. "Viper actual this is Viper Mobile, come in, over?"

There was another pause. The HumVees were almost up the hill. "Viper Actual this is Viper Mobile, if you can hear me, 'Fire for effect!' I say again fire the FPF!"

Parachute flares began falling from the sky, and Lisa cringed down into the gunner's seat as the night lit up all around her. She watched as tracer bullets streaked through the darkness, seeking out the quads. And wherever the tracers landed, the lesser guns focused. There was such a massive hail of gunfire she was happy to be inside the Bradley where it was safe. She watched as one of the HumVees lit up in flames. She thought she saw a lone soldier running away from it and jumping down into a hole. Then, just as quickly, another militia man jumped up and ran to the burning vehicle adding another Mason jar of gasoline to the fire.

As Lisa watched, a dozen men jumped out of the trench to throw Molotov cocktails against the sides of the three remaining HumVees. Six of the men were cut down instantly by fifty caliber machine guns mounted on top of the vehicles, but the rest got through and two more HumVees started burning in the night. Lisa heard screams as men on fire ran out into the darkness before falling to the ground as the life burned from them.

The remaining HumVee turned around and vanished over the hill and into the night. As quickly as it had started, the battle was over. The troop compartment door came down slowly and all of Donny's team exited the back. Lisa looked around at the carnage illuminated by the three burning vehicles. As she watched, almost a hundred men rose up out of the trenches and walked toward her.

Two men approached the Bradley and Donny Brewster snapped to attention, saluting crisply.

"Darn it, Donny, will you please stop that. You're twice the soldier I am."

Donny laughed. "Doesn't matter, Dan, cuz you're the Major and I'm just the sergeant."

Major Branch paced forward and threw his arms in a bear hug around his friend. He looked over and nodded to Adam Cervantes. "And you must be Adam."

Army National Guard Staff Sergeant Cervantes stiffened and gave Dan a salute. Dan hesitated, then straightened and returned Adam's salute. "Guess I'm going to have to get used to that."

Then he lowered his right hand and extended it to Adam. "Thanks for your help, Adam."

Staff Sergeant Cervantes clasped his handshake.

"It was my pleasure, Major." He then nodded at the dead bodies all around. "Nice ambush. You do good work."

A grim look overcame Dan. "Not good enough. We lost some men."

The Major nodded and then turned away. As he walked off, Donny turned and smiled back at the four women behind him. "Nice work, girls. You did great!"

But none of the women were smiling back. To the contrary, they wore the faces of women scorned.

Lisa turned to Brenda. "I say we shoot him for keeping us in the dark like that."

Brenda nodded. "Yeah, and then we castrate him for allowing us to think we'd be raped and murdered."

Donny started to back away. "Now girls, let's not overreact. Don't get all emotional on me. You did great!" Donny kept backing away, but the four women kept converging.

"Hey Dan! I need to talk to you about our plans." Donny ran off after the Major, leaving the women alone with Staff Sergeant Cervantes. The girls turned their attention to him.

Tara came forward, her short, blonde hair shining in the firelight. "I want to thank you for saving my life." She moved to him and wrapped her petite arms around the big soldier. Adam bristled, not knowing how to respond. Brenda and Lynne followed suit, followed by Lisa.

Donny Brewster had reached Dan thirty yards away and

they both watched through the firelight.

"Dan, I don't get it. I saved their lives, and look how they repay me. They threatened to castrate me and Adam gets a group hug? I don't get it!"

Dan chuckled and shook his head. "I told you to tell them the whole truth, but you wouldn't listen to me."

Dan turned away, leaving Donny to catch up. Both men walked off into the night, surrounded by carnage, heading off to plan the next round of death.

CHAPTER 16

DONNY **B**REWSTER WAS LYING face down on the deck in the back of the Bradley Fighting Vehicle with his pants pulled down to his ankles when General Branch marched up and looked in.

"Sergeant Brewster, I hope I'm not interrupting anything."

Lisa maintained her focus on Donny's bare behind as she poured on more rubbing alcohol and cleaned out the wound. Donny screamed in pain. "Why are you rubbing it so hard!?"

The General chuckled to himself. "Now, Sergeant, we all told you it was best to tell your fire team the full details of the mission. Maybe next time you'll obey the orders of your commanding officer." General Branch nodded to Lisa.

"Thanks for your service, Miss Vanderboeg. I hear you did great back there in combat last night."

Lisa smiled up at him. "You're welcome, General Branch. I'm just anxious to get home to my little girl."

The General nodded. "You can take one of the quads to your home. I'll send someone by to pick it up later."

Donny turned his head and tried to look behind him. "Don't call her 'Miss' or she'll bite your head off, general."

General Branch looked over at the woman with a question in his eyes. She looked back with a mischievous smile on her face. "The General can call me Miss Vanderboeg anytime he likes. And do you know why?" Lisa poured more rubbing alcohol into the wound where Donny's stitches had ripped. He screamed in pain.

"General, you have to save me from this woman! She's going to kill me."

The General ignored him and so did Lisa. "I'll tell you why, Sergeant Brewster, because, unlike you, the General is a gentleman. He tells a lady when she'll be in danger and when she's safe. Not like a scoundrel who lets her unnecessarily worry about being raped and murdered."

She stuffed a gauze pad into the once-healing bullet wound and twisted it. "Now hold still! I have to get out all the infection or we'll have to amputate your buttock."

It took all Rodney's self control to hold in his laughter. He winked at Lisa. "Nurse Vanderboeg, I think I see more infection down deeper. Make sure you get it all out. The Sergeant is important, and we'll need him to fight on the front lines very soon."

Donny's forehead hit the floor with a thunk. "It's too late, general. I'll be dead long before The Horde arrives." Donny screamed again.

"Shut up, soldier! I haven't even touched you yet!"

The General regained his composure before speaking again, this time in his command voice.

"Nurse Vanderboeg, when your patient regains consciousness, please tell him we have a meeting at my command post in fifteen minutes. It's mandatory."

Lisa nodded and smiled before returning to Donny's bare behind. There were some days when she just loved being a nurse.

☆ ☆ ☆ ☆

Colonel Roger "Ranger" MacPherson stood before the gathering of officers and noncoms inside the CP tent. He was ramrod straight, muscular and taut with military bearing.

Every fiber of his body screamed out the command, *Obey me! I'm in charge here!* He looked out at the thirty or so leaders within the Iroquois County Militia seated in front of him. He studied them now, just as he had studied men for decades of his Army career. Some of them were terrified and others were eager; while the remainder occupied every spot in between along the continuum.

"Sergeant Brewster of The Shadow Militia will now give you a briefing on last night's engagement."

The Colonel watched as Sergeant Brewster walked slowly up to the front. He couldn't tell for sure, but the Colonel thought he detected a slight limp in the Sergeant's gait. He noted it for future reference as he walked to his seat in front and took his place at the right hand of General Branch.

The sides of the tent were rolled down, and a small pot-bellied stove was burning in the center. A storm had moved in this morning, bringing a mass of arctic air down from the Upper Peninsula. Even though it was early April, a blizzard was expected that night.

"Last night we attacked The Horde encampment with a four-woman fire team, effectively destroying one Abrams tank and two Bradley Fighting Vehicles." Donny paused for effect. He noticed the men looking around at each other at his mention of four women attacking The Horde. He thought to himself, *Perhaps that will shame them into bravery.* "The third Bradley was captured and is now in our possession, and will be used for defense of Iroquois County."

Sheriff Leif stood near the back of the tent, just listening, soaking it all in. He was the acting commander of the Home Guard, and it was his plan they'd be putting into effect when The Horde finally rolled into Iroquois City. He was amazed at what The Shadow Militia had done the past month to train the county militia. He looked at Donny Brewster and recalled how he'd first mocked Rodney for sending just one man to hold off The Horde for an additional three weeks. He would never ridicule The Shadow Militia again. They were a force to be reckoned with. They'd trained the county, equipped them, and imbued his people with hope and courage. His only reservation was of his own character. His own self doubt nagged at the corners of his mind with every waking moment.

Am I good enough? Will I fight or will I freeze?

Donny Brewster continued speaking.

"In our escape, we attacked The Horde, killing dozens as we fled. Major Branch and his militia company were entrenched in a pre-arranged ambush site. They attacked and destroyed three HumVees and twenty-two quads. Total enemy casualties is estimated at ninety-seven dead and twenty-eight wounded." He paused for a moment as the militia soldiers smiled and looked around at one another. A happy murmur rose up from the crowd. "Unfortunately, it was not without a cost. Eight militia were killed and seven more wounded."

Donny looked over at Colonel MacPherson, signifying he was done. Then he walked stiffly back to his seat.

The Colonel stood and walked back up to the front of the room.

"And now, General Branch will address the meeting."

As he walked back to his seat, Rodney got up and placed himself where Colonel MacPherson had been standing just a few moments before. He looked out at the crowd and smiled grimly. Just a few weeks ago some of these people had been homeless in the state game area, others had been living lives of quiet discontent, just fighting to put food on the table for their families. Today, it all had changed. Now, they were fighters. They were reluctant warriors. He looked into the third row back at eighty-some year-old Harold Steffens. Jackie Branch, his own daughter-in-law, sat beside the old soldier. He wondered if their role would change the outcome. It was still a secret what they planned to do.

"Aerial reconnaissance supplied to us by Sergeant Harold Steffens has given us the following intelligence." He looked over at Harold and smiled slightly in thanks. "After last night's attack, The Horde is now bogged down and regrouping fifty miles east of Iroquois City. Major Branch and his company of Militia Rangers have been hampering their movements using guerilla tactics all morning and afternoon. So far they report another fifty-three enemy dead and one-hundred and twenty-five wounded. That's an estimate, but I have confidence in the numbers."

He paused and tried to read the crowd.

"The Rangers will continue to harass and slow The Horde as long as they can, thereby giving Sheriff Leif enough time to prepare and harden Iroquois City defenses. Major Branch has already lost ten more men since last night."

A grumble went up from the crowd.

"All men who fall will be returned to Iroquois. They will receive a funeral with full military honors, with their families present. They are forever to be considered heroes. All who fall in defense of the weak will be celebrated in song and reverence for decades to come. Their families will be taken care of, and they will not be forgotten."

The grumbling lessened, but did not stop completely.

"Sheriff Leif will be coordinating the defense of the town. He will now outline his plan and give final assignments and logistical orders for preparation."

The General stepped back to his seat. While Sheriff Leif walked up, he did so slowly, wondering all the while, *Will I be brave? Will I run? Will I freeze? Or will I fight with honor?* But, through all the thinking, the most obvious possibility, that he would die, never crossed his mind.

The Militia Rangers

Dan Branch pulled out his satellite phone and let it hover in his hand in front of him. He waited for the lead truck to reach the Improvised Explosive Device (IED) before pressing the button. The small explosion rocked the truck as the engine block was compromised with armor piercing rounds shooting

129

up from below. The long line of trucks and cars stopped, forming a bottleneck and a perfect ambush site. The militia opened fire from heavy cover as The Horde scrambled to leave their vehicles one hundred yards down the hill. Dan had planned his ambush well. The Horde would have to charge up the hill through a hail of gunfire to counterattack and drive them off. But by then, Dan and his militia would be miles away.

Major Branch let his men fire several rounds each until all the easy targets had been wounded. Men of The Horde screamed below in agony from shots to the groin and legs. They would eventually die, but not until slowing the advance and striking fear into the hearts of their comrades.

It was over in thirty seconds. Dan gave the order to fall back, and all twenty-five of his soldiers quietly withdrew. An hour later they would be set up a few miles down the road for another attack.

Manny Takes Charge

Down below, Manny cursed at the ineptitude of his soldiers as they cowered behind the engine blocks of their vehicles. The shooting had been silent for two minutes now, but still no one was moving to counterattack. Fueled by anger, Manny broke from cover and raced to the front of the column.

"Get up you fools! They're gone already! How many times do they have to do this before you figure it out?"

Manny stood out in the middle of the road, totally exposed. "See! Look at me! Grow some balls and push this truck off the road so we can get going again. None of this will end until we reach Traverse City."

Manny had been analyzing the militia's tactics all morning. It was a battle of attrition and he was losing it. Manny had studied military history, and it reminded him of the April 19th, 1775 battle of Lexington Concord. The British with a far superior force were followed and hounded all the way back to Boston by peasants and farmers shooting from behind rock walls and trees.

A man was screaming on the ground off to his left as he lay in agony clutching his now-shattered and bleeding private parts. Manny regained his sense of calm as he walked up to the screaming man, unholstered his pistol and shot the man in the head. The screaming stopped. One by one, The Horde stood up, more afraid of Manny than the militia. One of them organized a clean-up, and soon the truck was pushed off the road.

During the process, three more people were wounded by toe poppers. Manny shot two of them, but the last man quickly stood up and limped off to bandage his wound. Manny let him go. He'd already examined this new technique of the militia. The booby trap was planted in the ground along the side of the road at every ambush site. It was simply a short piece of PVC pipe affixed to a small square of board with a nail jutting up into the pipe. The militia placed a .223 caliber round into the pipe with the primer resting lightly on the nail. When stepped on, the bullet was pushed against the primer, exploding the primer which fired off the round. The bullet went through the man's shoe, sometimes exiting and hitting him in other places as well. Manny remembered reading about this as he'd studied the Vietnam War.

As he stood thinking, waiting for the truck to be removed, another man screamed to his left and fell down into a small hole in the ditch. Manny walked over to confirm what he already knew. The man clutched at his foot in pain. A penny spike pounded through a board was sticking out the bottom of his boot. "Shut up or I'll shoot you!"

The man instantly quieted. Manny reached down and yanked the board and nail off the man's boot. The man screamed once but quickly regained his composure. Lifting the nail to his nose, Manny smelled the distinct odor of feces. He tossed the nail back into the hole and walked away.

These people were very good at their jobs, and Manny wanted to know why. More importantly, he was going to need help. At this rate he'd never make it to Iroquois City, much less his final destination.

Manny yelled out to his assistant. "Buster! Get me my radio!" Within a few minutes he was arguing with someone. Buster sat by listening, all the while thinking to himself, *Things aren't going as planned.* Already several people had snuck off into the woods, and more would follow if something wasn't done. Worst of all, Buster would have to tell Manny the bad news.

Finally, Manny dropped the radio handset and smiled. The alliance had been formed.

Many miles away, back at the Grayling National Guard base, Major Danskill put down the radio and yelled at the Sergeant. "Send in Captain Foster. Now!"

While the Sergeant carried out his orders, Major Danskill opened the wall safe and took out the Sat Phone. It was only to be used when talking to his superior.

As he waited for his boss to answer the phone, he smiled and shook his head in amusement. How long had it taken? Just a few days for Manny to lose his tank and his Bradleys? As a military leader, the man was incompetent. And now he wanted more. More tanks, more men, more ammunition. Major Danskill laughed at Manny's insatiable thirst for power. Every man had his vice, his weakness, his own personal lust to be either conquered or fed.

"Yes, sir. This is Major Danskill with a situation report."

The man on the other end simply said, "Go ahead."

"As you suspected, we have movement in northwest Michigan. It's organized in a military fashion."

Danskill listened to the response before replying. "Yes, sir. Right away, sir. We'll leave within the hour."

A thousand miles away, deep inside a fortified bunker, the man disconnected from the Sat Phone. The call disturbed him.

Civilians organized into military units, making coordinated and military-style attacks. That could be a problem as he preferred unorganized and terrified resistance. Who could be leading these people? He wondered.

He set the Sat Phone on the coffee table beside him. It was a special coffee table, stolen from the estate of a Columbian drug lord, hand-carved out of some rare jungle tree. He didn't know the name of it. Most importantly, the drug lord and his entire family was dead now. He'd seen to that personally, and he viewed the table as just a souvenir from another exotic country. His life was full of souvenirs, and they were ornately displayed about him in his sprawling bungalow: lamps, couches, paintings, even a few statues. He liked the finer things in life, and his living area looked more like a Manhattan penthouse than a huge complex of underground bunkers.

The man glanced over at his assistant, who stood there almost at the position of attention. "I like military officers. They're so competent, so efficient, so meticulous in planning and detail." He paused, "But, most importantly … they're polite."

Sammy Thurmond nodded, his blank eyes staring out at the wall on the far side of the room.

CHAPTER 17

MAJOR **D**ANSKILL FOCUSED ON the GPS screen intently. His XO, Captain Foster, stood beside him like an obedient pitbull eager to serve his master. After receiving the urgent distress call from Manny, he'd left Grayling ASAP. Manny was an incompetent. Danskill had always known that, and he planned on exploiting that trait when the time was right. But for now he'd just play along like a good little rent-a-soldier.

"Captain, we should hit them here. They'll be expecting the same counter-attack from Manny and his men, so it should be a rout. We want to capture a few alive for intel, but the rest need to die. Understood?"

Captain Foster smiled. "I'll draw up the plans immediately, sir."

✮ ✮ ✮ ✮

Dan Branch looked down at the advancing column of vehicles coming toward him and his men. They were now just inside Iroquois County only thirty miles from his family. Most of his seventy remaining militia rangers were feeling the same sense of urgency as Dan was. They'd killed a few hundred of the Horde, but they kept coming, gaining in strength, and every time they passed through a town they picked up more recruits. Dan had learned from a refugee how the Horde was able to enlist the service of so many men. Upon reaching a town, they would line up all the residents, then separate the men from their families. Through a bullhorn, the Horde leader would issue the ultimatum: either enlist and serve in his army, or watch your wives and children be raped and killed. Most men complied to save their families. And that's how the Horde continued to grow despite the losses inflicted by Dan Branch and his Militia Rangers. It also explained why some of the Horde soldiers were deserting.

"On my command, Captain Jackson." Dan lifted his binoculars and peered down at the center of the enemy column. He didn't want them getting used to the same old tactics and refining their counterattack, so he was hitting them in the rear this time just to mix it up and keep them guessing. Dan had noticed the Horde was getting better at reacting to his ambushes.

"Blow it, Larry."

Captain Larry Jackson pressed the button and a second later there was a huge explosion down on the road. A deuce and a half truck was thrown up twenty feet in the air; it traveled backwards as it flew and landed on a Toyota Prius two vehicles to the rear. Two other SUVs were blown off to the side, leaving a huge crater where the road had once been.

"Holy ... Larry, what was in that one?"

Larry Jackson smiled. "I told you these fertilizer bombs worked."

"Fire!"

In accordance with the plan, all his men picked out targets of opportunity. They shot men in the groin. They shot vehicle tires. Most importantly, anyone down below who looked like they were taking command, those people were given top priority. This time Dan let them shoot a bit longer than before. He figured the size of the blast would leave the Horde more disoriented than usual, and he knew from past experience the enemy quads would all be massed in the center front of the column waiting to react to their attack.

"Cease fire! Move! Move! Move!"

All seventy of Dan's men moved as one unit to the rear of the enemy column. They made their way down the hill and crossed the road to their prearranged rally point. They'd never done this before, and the Horde wouldn't expect it. Once on the other side, Dan and his men moved a mile off the road and formed a group. Off in the distance they could hear the quads buzzing angrily up the hill where they'd launched their ambush. There was a muffled explosion and Larry Jackson smiled at the success of his booby trap. *One more quad bites the dust.*

"Okay men, third platoon set up perimeter security. All the staff NCOs come with me to debrief and plan the next attack. We move out again in twenty mikes!"

Third platoon followed orders while the rest of the rangers sat down to take a break. Most of them were military veterans of one sort or another, but the average age was forty-five years old. Dan had been amazed how quickly these old men had hardened in the past few days of battle. They were old, but they were tough and grizzly north woods men, and, most importantly, they were fighting for their homes and their families. So far they'd made a very good accounting of themselves, and Dan had grown proud to lead them.

He huddled off to one side of the left flank now with his leaders and pulled out the plastic laminated topographical map of Iroquois County. Captain Jackson was still smiling. But then, without warning, Dan raised his hand, and a look of concern spread across his face like a malignant infection.

"Can you hear that?"

The small group of staff noncoms froze in place, none wanting to admit what they all knew was true. "Everyone, get down behind cover! Incoming!"

And while the Militia Rangers hid in the brush, the steady womp, womp, womp of turning rotors came closer.

✯ ✯ ✯ ✯

"Eagle Leader, this is Sparrowhawk. I have infrared confirmation of company size unit one click east of your location. What are your orders?"

There was a moment of silence as the Apache attack helicopter circled the Militia Rangers from above.

"Sparrowhawk, this is Eagle Leader. Engage and destroy enemy ground units, over."

The Apache helicopter pilot hadn't always been evil; it was just something that had happened to him a little bit at a time. A bad decision here, a mean action there, and then, finally, the day when he'd made the move to follow Major Danskill. His wife and family were probably dead, so nothing else really mattered. What he'd discovered, is once he'd started down the road … there was no turning back. One sin just seemed to lead to another, and another, and another. Until, finally, opening fire on seventy men defending their home just didn't seem like that big a deal anymore.

The pilot looked though the Integrated Helmet and Display Sighting System which was already slaved to the aircraft's 30 mm automatic M230 Chain Gun. Wherever he looked with his helmet, the chain gun followed. In the first pass, he lit up the woods and tore the rangers to shreds. Then he started to bank around for his second pass.

Down on the ground, third platoon was firing frantically at the Apache but with no effect. Major Branch looked on helplessly from forty yards away. In five seconds thirty-five soldiers were torn apart, and the helicopter was banking for a second pass. Dan heard Captain Jackson yelling beside him, then realized he was being shaken violently.

"Dan! They've got infrared! We've got to retreat!"

The Apache had completed his bank now, and Dan finally reacted and took command.

"Retreat to rally point! Retreat to rally point! Retreat!

Retreat!"

And with that Larry Jackson threw Dan behind a large oak tree as the Apache made his second pass. More body parts, dirt and wood chips flew up and out through the brush. The noise of the gun was deafening and the small arms fire died down as people fell to the ground and as others scattered through the woods.

Dan looked down at his feet and saw he was running now. Captain Jackson was pushing him along from the rear yelling at him to run faster. Four hundred yards down the embankment they came to a river. By now Dan had recovered his composure and dived head first into the water. The icy cold closed over him and shocked his system to its core. Larry Jackson dived in after him as did several of his other non coms. The current was strong and moved them quickly downstream. They swam for the far bank, but all their gear and clothing weighed them down. Just when they were about to drown, Dan's feet hit the surface of a sand bar and he wearily brought his feet underneath him and raised up to a standing position.

Off in the distance, the sound of the chain gun ceased, leaving an eerie calm to the woods. Then they heard the Bradley fighting vehicles moving in to mop up whatever resistance was left. Dan's head was swimming in a frozen fog. *My men are dead. The Horde is advancing. They have attack helicopters. They now own the sky.*

"Larry, see if your radio still works. We need to get this intel to General Branch and Iroquois City."

They trudged on over to the far bank of the river where Captain Jackson fired up his radio and relayed the information back to base.

☆ ☆ ☆ ☆

Major Danskill stepped out the back of the Bradley and looked at the ground, littered with blood and flesh and bone. He smiled.

138

"Captain Foster! Bring the survivors to me for interrogation."

His Executive Officer looked over with a frown on his face. "I'm sorry, sir. There are no survivors."

Danskill looked over at him perplexed and raised his right eyebrow in question. "Really?"

"Yes, sir. They refused to be captured. They fought to the last man."

The Major raised his left hand up to his chin and continued to peruse the carnage. He felt ambivalent about this. The soldier part of him was impressed. They fought to the last man. That was praiseworthy. But without prisoners there was no intel, and they'd be going into Iroquois City blind. And he wondered, what kind of force am I up against? These aren't just farmers. He shrugged. It didn't matter. Whoever they were they'd be killed - to the last man if need be. He had Bradleys and tanks and Apache helicopters. Whoever they were; they didn't have a prayer. He walked over and kicked a dead body just to make sure.

☆ ☆ ☆ ☆

General Branch set down the radio and plopped himself heavily in the folding chair beside him. His eyes looked off in the distance, seeing nothing but a blur. Finally, Sheriff Leif spoke to him.

"What does that mean, Rodney? Are all of them dead?"

General Branch looked up and met Joe's gaze. He shook his head from side to side, wearily, as if it took every last ounce of energy he had left. Suddenly, Joe saw a tiny glimpse of Rodney for what he was deep inside: weak, old, just an ancient old man who'd outlived his prime and wanted nothing more than to die and sleep through the ages. "No, Sheriff, there are seven of them left, maybe a few others, but they're all scattered or dead."

"But the Horde has more Bradleys and now an attack helicopter?" Joe paused. "How did that happen?"

Uncle Rodney looked down at the floor. "They must have come from Grayling. I pulled the surveillance too soon. I guess that was a mistake. I'm sorry."

Sheriff Leif moved over to the cement block wall and leaned heavily against it. Then he looked back over at the General, and his next words were more of an indictment than a statement of fact. "But you have attack helicopters. You have equipment we don't even know about yet. You could have stopped this!"

Rodney Branch slumped his shoulders and looked down at the floor. Inside, he knew it was true. Yes, he could have stopped them. He could have supported them, but … at what future price … at what unintended consequences?

"Don't just sit there! Say something! We trusted you! We followed you!" The Sheriff, all six and a half feet of him walked over and grabbed Rodney Branch by the shoulders and shook him hard. "Now what are you going to do about this?"

Something inside the General snapped loose like an iron lock, and he jumped up, grabbed Joe's hand and rotated it behind the man's back with the quickness of a cat. In less than a second big Joe Leif was on his knees with a 45 pistol placed on the back of his head.

"Just shut up. I have a plan. Of course I have a plan. But don't touch me! I don't like it!" Rodney holstered his firearm and walked away. "Now come on, Joe. We've got work to do."

The Sheriff, still stunned and on his knees, looked after the old man as the door opened and closed behind him. *How had he done that?* He kneeled a few seconds longer, and then got up and followed.

CHAPTER 18

THE YOUNG BOY STUMBLED UP THE concrete steps of the courthouse, opened the door and fell inside. He'd been beaten and slashed with knives across his face, chest and back. The boy crawled to the conference room leaving a bloody trail in his wake. He reached up his broken hand and scratched on the wooden door.

From inside, Sheriff Leif heard the scratching and opened the door. He gasped when he saw the bloody boy at his feet. Colonel MacPherson rushed over and scooped the twelve-year-old boy up and placed him on the conference table in the center of the room. The boy was mumbling the same thing over and over again. "They're here! They're here! They're here."

Joe's face hardened and he stepped over and placed his hand in the boy's open palm. "Joshua, is that you?" The boy's face was cut so badly it was hard to tell. "Is that you, Joshua?"

The boy went silent. Colonel MacPherson reached up to the boy's throat but could find no pulse. "He's gone, Sheriff." Joe Leif threw his head down on the boy and cried on his dead body. Colonel MacPherson stood ramrod stiff. He waited a few seconds, then grabbed Joe by the shoulders and lifted him up straight. He rotated the Sheriff around until they looked eye to eye. "Where did this boy live, Joe? I need to know how close they are." Joe didn't answer, so the Colonel shook him. "Where are they Joe?"

Joe Leif looked up with terror and despair in his eyes. "His family lives right here in town."

2 Hours later - Iroquois City Courthouse

"We sent a squad to the boy's house. His father was murdered along with their little girl and a newborn baby." Colonel MacPherson's voice broke as if the saying of it was too much to bear. "Looks like the mother was abducted. The two Home Guard who were stationed in front of the courthouse for security appear to have deserted. We don't know if they were in on it or not."

Joe Leif sat at the conference table with his head in his hands near despair. General Branch listened from the head of the table. His eyes were stone-cold when he spoke. "We have to assume The Horde knows all about our defenses." He looked over to the Sheriff. "You'll have to make some changes Joe, some big changes." Then he looked over to Sergeant Harold Steffens. The old man looked tired, but very much alive. "What did you see from the air, Sergeant?"

The ancient man locked eyes with the General and smiled. "They've made camp seven miles east of town in the state forest. Looked like about two thousand strong with hundreds of vehicles of all types. They weren't making any attempt to hide themselves. I think they feel indestructible right about now."

The General nodded. "I agree. They're pretty confident. But what about the Bradley fighting vehicles and the Apache helicopters?"

"I saw none of them, Not even tracks in the snow. And if I'd seen an Apache they would have blown my little crop duster out of the sky. I can't out fly them and I have no armaments."

Sheriff Leif moved his hands away from his face and looked over at General Branch like a wounded animal about to die. "We have to evacuate the city, Rodney. It's our only

142

hope of survival."

Rodney Branch said nothing. He simply shook his head signifying disagreement. Joe Leif stood up at the table towering over the shorter man in a last-ditch attempt to posture him into submission, but General Branch would have none of it. He glanced over at Colonel MacPherson. "Take charge of the city's defenses and make the necessary changes. Try not to embarrass the Sheriff in how you do it. Invoke his name as if he's still in charge."

Sheriff Leif's face turned red. He tried to speak, but nothing came out. Finally, without saying a word, he stormed out the door. General Branch watched the man leave, then looked over to Sergeant Steffens. "When can you fly again?"

The Sergeant answered calmly. Rodney noticed the old man looked ten years younger since the day they'd met. "I can be up again in two hours."

The General nodded. "Thanks Harold. I need to know where they are at nightfall. I don't think they'll attack until tomorrow. They've covered a long distance and they'll need time to rest and regroup. And they are cocky, so they'll feel no need to hurry. In the meantime they'll be stripping the countryside of food and supplies. I expect they'll be partying tonight. Then they'll sleep in and be moving against us about noon tomorrow. In the meantime we'll bring as many people as we can inside the city and arm all who will fight." He looked over at Colonel MacPherson. "Colonel? Are you seeing anything I'm not?"

Colonel MacPherson shook his head. "No, I don't think so. But I would like some more intel. Permission to send in Sergeant Brewster?'

"Good idea, Colonel." He looked down at the map spread out on the table before them. "So where is the Sergeant right now? How long will it take to get him in play?"

The Colonel smiled. "He's been observing The Horde all day sir. All I have to do is make the call."

General Branch returned his smile. There were times when he depended on Ranger MacPherson more than anyone knew. Sometimes it got lonely at the top.

"Then this meeting is adjourned. We'll meet back at night-fall to make final plans to defend the city."

As General Branch walked out, Colonel MacPherson and Sergeant Steffens looked after him.

"Where do you think he's going, Colonel?"

The grizzled, old army ranger stared at the still-closing door. "Beats the hell out of me. But wherever he's going, it can't be good for The Horde."

Sergeant Steffens almost laughed out loud. He was amazed at the confidence these two men inspired in him. Here he was eighty-six years old and flying into battle. He thought to himself, *Are you watching me from up there, Myra? Are you proud of this old man?*

He smiled to himself, confident that he'd soon be joining his wife. The thought gave him a great measure of courage and peace.

Dan Branch comes home

Jackie Branch saw her husband coming and ran out to meet him at the end of the drive. Dan killed the quad's engine and braked before he ran over her. She tackled him just as he stepped off the vehicle, and both of them almost fell to the ground. Dan looked over and saw Jeremy looking out from the porch.

"Don't you ever leave me again!"

Dan hadn't had time to clean up, and he was still wet and muddy from the all-night trek back to Iroquois City. Her husband was smiling, but it was a weary look, one filled with internal suffering and shame. Jackie saw the look on his face and frowned. "Aren't you happy to see me?"

Dan nodded. "Of course I am, honey. It's just been a long week," Then he hesitated, wondering how much to hold back. "I've killed a lot of men. And most of my rangers are dead."

His wife held him close. She reached up with her clean, soft hands and stroked his face. "It's okay, baby. Uncle Rodney filled me in. It wasn't your fault. There was no way you could have known. Not even your uncle knew."

In his mind, Dan knew she was right, but in his heart, he wasn't so quick to dismiss his responsibility. He knew it was a burden he would carry for the rest of his life. Dan held her quietly for several seconds, soaking in the reassuring smell of her long, black hair. The snow was a few inches deep and there was a chill in the air. With all his adrenaline used up, Dan began to shiver.

"Oh, honey. Please come inside by the fire and get warm. I'll get you out of those wet clothes and give you a bath."

The two of them walked to the house, leaving the quad where it was. Dan hugged his son blankly. He felt all used up, like a dirty dish rag all wrung out and lying draped over the sink.

After a bath, fresh clothes and a hot meal, Dan, Jeremy and Jackie were seated around the table as baby Donna played on the floor.

"What was it like, Dad?"

The stern look on Jackie's face gave her son a voiceless rebuke. Dan didn't answer at first. Jackie thought he looked lost inside himself, and she wondered if she would ever get him back again. Finally he answered his son.

"We killed them for several days, as many as we could. And then they attacked with an Apache and killed most of my company. Only seven of us survived that I know of."

"Oh." That's all Jeremy could muster. His romantic, boyhood picture of war had just been shattered. Jackie broke the silence.

"Is Larry Jackson okay?"

Dan nodded. "Yes, he made it plus most of my noncoms. We were off to the side when the attack happened. That's the only reason we survived."

Jackie hesitated before asking the next question. "What's going to happen now, Dan? What does it look like?"

Her husband looked down at the baby smiling on the floor and chewing on a rubber spatula. He seemed to be gaining strength from the little girl's innocence. "I have to be back in an hour. Colonel MacPherson is leading the Home Guard now."

Jackie looked perplexed. "I thought Joe Leif was doing that?"

Dan shook his head. He seemed to be recovering as he talked to his family. "No, not anymore. I guess he had a bit of a falling out with Uncle Rodney. We don't know where he is right now. The Horde is about seven miles east of town in the state forest. They're getting ready to attack tomorrow. I'm supposed to gather up all the refugees and arm them as best I can and organize a new company by morning."

Surprisingly, he got off his chair and sat down on the floor beside baby Donna. He began to play with her as if no one else was in the room and The Horde was a million miles away. Jackie looked over at Jeremy, but saw he was already looking at her. Their eyes met and she nodded to him.

"Dad, I think I should be part of your new company. I want to fight."

Dan stopped playing and lay down onto his back. The baby crawled up and rested on his chest. After a few seconds, she closed her eyes and quickly fell asleep. Jackie looked down, and, in better times would have been the happiest woman in the world. But not today. She got up and took the baby off his chest and moved her to their bedroom. When she came back out Dan was seated at the table again. He looked different, somehow rejuvenated back to the old Dan, but also a little bit like his Uncle Rodney.

"I think that's a good idea, son. I don't want you to have to fight, but quite frankly you have the training and the experience. And if The Horde breaks through, well … I think the lucky ones will be dead."

Jackie was surprised at her husband's candor, but certainly saw his reasoning. "And what about me, Dan? Do I fight?"

Dan shook his head. "Not this time, honey. Uncle Rodney has something special you can do that will keep you and the baby safe while still helping the cause. He said he'll stop by tonight and brief you on it. He didn't tell me the details. He said I didn't need to know."

Jackie chewed on that for a bit. A month ago she would have disbelieved it, but not now. Since their talk in the woods and her special assignment with Sergeant Steffens, she'd gained a great measure of respect and trust for Uncle Rodney's abilities and his intentions.

She nodded her head silently and helped Dan and Jeremy get ready to go. Within a half hour they were packed and loaded on the quad to head back into town. Jackie stood on the porch and waved as the quad fired up and raced away. She watched until the quad was completely out of sight and she could no longer hear the engine. Then she walked back inside to watch her baby sleep.

CHAPTER 19

The Horde Encampment

MANNY STOOD IN FRONT OF THE big, log cabin lodge at the state forest campgrounds and surveyed the expanse of his domain. He was reminded of the words about Alexander the Great: *"And when Alexander looked out over the breadth of his domain, he wept for there were no more worlds left to conquer."*

Manny hoped that someday he would be able to weep just as Alexander had before him. He'd studied all the great military leaders, Genghis Khan, Atilla the Hun, and Adolf Hitler, and what he lacked in practical experience, he made up for with ruthlessness and focused study. But he didn't like this campground, and he couldn't wait to move out tomorrow morning for the final attack on Iroquois City. This campground had them hemmed in by woods, and it would be just too easy for someone to sneak in close and attack or infiltrate. And then his mind turned to more serious matters.

Major Danskill, *What was he going to do with him once he'd served Manny's purpose?* More importantly, what would Danskill do once Manny had outlived his usefulness? He was smart enough to know it was a marriage of convenience, and the divorce rate among scoundrels was one-hundred percent.

Once Traverse City was taken, Major Danskill would have to die. That was a given. But how to achieve it; that was the only remaining question. He'd have to be careful as the

Major had proved himself a worthy adversary with plenty of resources.

Beyond that, Manny was already planning out the invasion of Grand Rapids. He hadn't liked being tossed out of the city, but he'd had no choice, and he fully intended to return as the conquering hero just like General Mac Arthur to the Philippines. Could he launch a two-pronged invasion by attacking with a land force from the north and an amphibious assault from Lake Michigan? He suspected there were hundreds of sailboats at TC he could use for just such a purpose. How many new recruits would he gain in Traverse City? Probably thousands more. It was a big town.

A group of six men walked up to Manny and stood before him. Manny's three bodyguards made no move to stop them, though they remained vigilant with M4s at the ready.

"You sent for us, Manny?"

Manny smiled. He liked Albert, the way he obeyed so readily. He hated the name though. "Albert" was just too nerdy. "Yes, Al. Sit down please."

Albert looked around for chairs, but finally just plopped himself on the cold concrete. The five men with him looked around reluctantly before following suit. Manny remained standing, all five-feet, eight inches towering over them.

"I need some more intel."

Albert cursed Manny but only on the inside. They'd already been up half the night taking prisoners from inside the city, and he'd been hoping for a rest before the attack. If not for the drugs in his bloodstream he'd be dead on his feet. Manny was a slave driver to say the least.

"I need you to scout an area to the north of the city at these grid coordinates." Manny pulled a piece of paper out of his pocket and handed it down to his lieutenant. Albert looked at it and nodded his head.

"Is there anything special you want us to look for?"

Manny smiled. Albert's name may be nerdy, but he was

undoubtedly perceptive. "Yes, I want you to spy on Major Danskill. Just watch for a few hours, then take a prisoner, as high a rank as you can safely get, and bring him back to me for interrogation." Manny also pulled a stack of cards out of his pocket and handed them down to Albert. "These are non-picture documents that identify you as citizens of Iroquois City, just in case you get caught. I don't want you traced back to me."

Albert looked at the top document. It was an Iroquois County library card for a man named Lenny Switzer. He didn't like this job. It sounded dangerous. But the million-dollar question was: What is more dangerous? This mission or defying Manny?

"Yes, Manny. We'll get right on it."

Manny smiled and nodded. "I need it done before day-break, so hurry." Manny turned to walk away but stopped and turned back abruptly. "Oh, and … you and your men will be richly rewarded." The other men smiled, but Albert just nod-ded as Manny turned and walked away. It was going to be a very long night.

☆ ☆ ☆ ☆

Donny Brewster watched through high-powered binocu-lars from underneath the snow-covered brush pile as Manny walked back inside the lodge. As near as he could tell these six men had just been given a job to do, and Donny planned on be-ing there to supervise while they carried it out. He watched as the six men got up and followed their leader back through the camp and into one of the smaller cabins. Fifteen minutes later they emerged carrying M-16s and full backpacks. Wherever it was they were going, they were humping it at least part of the way. The six men walked over to quads and threw their gear into a trailer before mounting up and driving away. As the little caravan snaked their way through the campsite, Donny slowly and carefully left the cover of the brush and faded back into the woods. As he headed back to his own quad a half mile away, he pulled out his radio and talked as he ran.

"Tango two this is Tango one, over."

The response was almost immediate.

"This is Tango two, go ahead, over."

"Do you have a visual on the midget caravan heading out of camp?"

"Roger that, Tango one. They are nearing the entrance."

"Please maintain surveillance as long as possible. Let me know which way they go. I'm shadowing them on quadback."

"Roger that, Tango two."

Donny didn't bother to sign out. He broke into a full sprint and was soon on his quad heading to cut them off.

Ten Miles North of Iroquois City

Major Danskill put the radio back down on the elegant, oak dining room table and called for his second in command.

"Captain Foster!"

Within seconds the Captain entered the room and stood at attention. "Yes, sir."

"I just received word that Manny is sending six men to our location to take a prisoner for interrogation. They should arrive on quads from the east. Please double the guard tonight and extend the listening posts out to a mile."

Captain Foster saluted and strode out of the room. Major Danskill looked down at the map on the table. Manny was no problem. He could handle the gangbanger turned General Wannabe, but there was something else bothering him. He studied the map and the layout of the Iroquois City defenses. They were just too perfect, too precise, too … military.

He couldn't help but ask himself, _Who is their leader?_ The question vexed him to his military bearing core. He had to find out. Danskill had long studied military science, and the words of Sun Tzu called out to him now. "_If you know the enemy and know yourself, you need not fear the result of a hundred battles. If you know yourself but not the enemy, for every vic-_

tory gained you will also suffer a defeat. If you know neither the enemy nor yourself, you will succumb in every battle"

The ancient warning bothered him. Know the enemy or succumb. He knew they weren't mere farmers, but … *who are you?* The ambushes and heavy losses inflicted on Manny's column was not just text book perfect; it was also peppered with creativity and improvisation. Without the Apache helicopter and its infrared sensors and chain gun, he never would have found the attacking force to destroy it.

Manny had over two-thousand soldiers, but, however well-supplied, they were undisciplined and untrained. The thought hit the Major like a sledge hammer. *They might be beaten.*

Major Danskill looked down at the map again. He would use Manny to draw them out, and if Manny was destroyed, so much the better. But Manny could weaken them, making it easier for his own force to take the town. But first, he needed a plan. He needed to find their weakness. He looked to the west and smiled.

Five Miles East of The Horde

Donny Brewster let out half his breath and pulled the trigger slowly and gently to the rear. He felt the recoil and then looked through the scope to see the quad pull to the left and lurch to a stop. The quads behind them stopped as if on command. All six of the men got off their quads and stood near the flat tire, just staring down at it helplessly.

Donny keyed his radio, "Tango two this is Tango one. Fire for effect." Then he raised his own rifle scope to his right eye and began firing again.

Albert was looking straight at his second in command when his head seemed to explode before his eyes. He hesitated, paralyzed in shock, as two more of his men went down almost in unison. As Albert ran to his quad, the remaining two men in his command slumped to the ground. One of them, shot in the pelvis, continued to scream and writhe on the ground in agony. A merciful follow-up shot to the head silenced him.

Albert jumped on the quad and reached down to turn the key. The next shot went into his quad's engine block. Then he heard an engine roar to life and watched as someone raced toward him. He jumped down behind the engine and unslung his M16 off his back as he moved. Just as he raised it to fire, a bullet hit him in the left ear, tearing it completely off. Albert dropped the rifle and fell to the ground, clutching at the bloody mess. A few seconds later he was looking up at the muzzle of a 9mm Glock pistol.

Adam Cervantes spoke in a hushed, almost soothing tone. "Hello Albert. Do you have a few minutes? We need to talk."

CHAPTER 20

The Defense of Iroquois City

MAJOR **B**RANCH **LOOKED OUT**
over the eighty-seven people huddled in a
mass in front of the courthouse steps. They
were an odd bunch, some were just kids no more than twelve
years old while others were in their seventies. Almost a quar-
ter of them were women. On the inside, he sighed, knowing
he'd been given an impossible task. On the outside, his face
beamed with pride at his new command. And when he spoke,
his voice was loud and steady, exuding the permanence of
bedrock, imbuing his new troops with his own strength.

"The Horde is camped seven miles east of town. They have
two-thousand men and will attack the city in the morning. If
they succeed, then most of us will be dead. Refugees tell us
The Horde always rape the women and children before killing
them. Then they devour the town and all its resources like
locusts before moving on." Dan studied the haggard faces in
front of him. They'd already been through so much. It seemed
unfair to ask more of them. But these were desperate times.

"But this is our town. We live here. Most of you were born
here, and we're not going to let that happen to our families.
Let there be no mistake: we are fighting for our homes and
our very existence. The Horde wants your wives and children,
to devour them, to torture them, to take from them their very
souls." Dan hesitated as he looked out across the crowd, won-

dering if his words were having any impact. "But here's what I say. I was born here. I was raised here. I was in Wisconsin hundreds of miles away when all this happened, but I didn't stay there. I fought my way back. I came home. And now I'll fight to protect that home. I have a wife and two kids, and if The Horde wants them, then I have only one thing to say to The Horde. Molon Labe." Dan pronounced the ancient Greek phrase 'Ma-lown Lah-vey'.

"My Uncle Rodney taught that to me as a kid. It means 'Come and get them'. It was first uttered by the Spartans at the Battle of Thermopylae in 480 BC when King Xerxes of Persia asked them to lay down their arms and surrender their freedom."

Out of the corner of his eye Dan saw a middle-aged man reach his arm around a fourteen-year-old boy and squeeze. "But now, almost twenty-five-hundred years after the Spartans refused to surrender, I stand here before my friends and my home town, and I ask you to fight. And I would never ask you to do anything I wouldn't do myself." Dan placed his hand on Jeremy's shoulder and squeezed. "My own son will be fighting beside me. If we fail - we die. But if we win - our children live on."

Dan looked down and saw a determined look on his son's face. "But we will never surrender! We will never give up! We will never yield! We will fight until our very last breath so that our children and their children can live on. But I need to know … who will fight beside me?"

And then there was silence. It was deafening. And Dan couldn't help but wonder, *Are they going to leave, or will they stand and fight?*

Finally, an old man and his wife in the front row stepped forward. The man was carrying a double-barreled shotgun in his left hand. Without warning he raised it up over his head and screamed in a grizzled and throaty voice "Molon Labe!" His wife repeated his words. There was more silence, and then another man near the back cried out as well. "Molon Labe." Dan raised his own AR15 above his head and answered their cries "Molon Labe"! Then Jeremy did the same beside him. Like the ripple on a quiescent calm, just waiting for the wind to disturb it, the crowd rose up and lifted their weapons above their heads and cried out in one voice "Molon Labe"! Over and over the crowd chanted the battle cry "Molon Labe! Molon Labe! Molon Labe!"

Almost a block away Sheriff Leif heard the war cries of his own people and huddled in shame behind a dumpster.

Five Miles East of The Horde

Donny Brewster and Adam Cervantes stood outside the small pole barn with their prisoner tied up inside propped up against a bale of hay. As it turned out, Albert had allergies and they could hear him sneezing incessantly like a machine gun.

"I say we torture him until he tells us everything."

Sergeant Brewster shook his head at his friend and laughed. "Are you kidding me? He's already soiled himself and he's dying of allergies. All we have to do is ask him straight out and he'll sing like a canary."

Adam turned away. "Yeah, I know. I've never tortured anyone though, and I was hoping to expand my resume."

Donny reached over and put his right hand on Adam's left shoulder. "Well, at least your heart is in the right place. You're dedicated. I like that." Inside there was a pause in the sneezing, and they heard Albert yelling as loud as he could. "There are grid coordinates in my pocket written on a piece of paper!" He sneezed several more times. "Major Danskill and all his forces are there. He's got six Bradleys and three tanks. The attack helicopters are there too!"

Donny looked over at Adam and cocked his head to one side. "This man's loyalty to The Horde is truly awe-inspiring. Should we let him live?"

Adam smiled and looked out across the field and into the woods. "So we're not going to torture him? I've always wanted to water-board someone."

Donny reared back his head and laughed. "I like you, Adam. You're pretty cool for a National Guard guy. I was water-boarded once, just for fun. It takes a lot of water. We don't have any."

Adam's eyes sparkled in the light of fading day. "Hey! I could've been a Special Forces guy too." He paused. "I just lacked the physical stamina, mental acuity, and the advanced training."

Donny smiled again and turned to walk back into the pole barn. "Let's go get some more intel."

Adam opened the door and let Donny go first. "So are we going to torture him or not?"

Two-thousand Feet Above The Horde

Harold Steffens had been an infantry soldier during World War II with the Third Armored Division, but after the war he'd learned to fly bi-planes. After the excitement and trauma of world war, he'd been anxious to get home and marry his childhood sweetheart, Myra. He'd gotten a stable job at a nearby factory and they'd started a family, bought a house outside Iroquois and had lived there all their lives. Flying his bi-plane had supplied the thrill he'd needed to escape the boredom of small-town life. World War II had changed him forever.

Then in 1964 he'd quit his job at the factory and bought a Grumman Super Ag-Cat. For decades he dusted the fields of Iroquois with fertilizers, weed killer and seeds, whatever the farmers wanted. Even though his Super Ag-Cat was old, it still responded well, and that was more than he could say about his own, tired, old body. Nonetheless, today he felt up to the task of saving the world.

The basic Grumman Ag Cat had been the first airplane specifically built and produced by a major aircraft company for agricultural aviation. The first Ag-Cat flew its maiden flight on May 27, 1957, and had been in the air ever since.

Harold's Super Ag-Cat had a 600 horsepower engine, a length of 23 feet and a wing span of 35 feet. But the most important aspect of Harold's plane was the 300-gallon spray tank and all the supporting nozzles. But for Harold's final mission, 300 gallons wouldn't be enough. That's why he'd been working so hard the past weeks retrofitting it with a 500-gallon tank. If he was honest with himself, he didn't even know if it would get off the ground fully loaded. But the stakes were high, so he was willing to take the chance. It wasn't that big a deal since he planned on dying tomorrow anyway. He made a mental note to have someone cut down the trees at the end of his runway; it would do no one any good if he crashed and burned on take-off.

Harold flew over The Horde encampment taking pictures with the digital camera the way General Branch had instructed him. As long as he stayed up high he'd be safe from small-arms fire. After ten minutes he had all the pictures he needed, banked the plane and headed home.

Ten Miles North of Iroquois City

The sun had already set, and Adam and Donny surveyed the old farmhouse two-hundred yards away through Night Vision binoculars. On the outside it looked like any other farm, with the exception of the Abrams tanks, Bradley Fighting Vehicles and Apache helicopters. They tried to count the tents and soldiers, but there were just too many of them. Donny finally settled with an estimate of two-hundred.

"Should we try to get closer?"

Donny shook his head. "Why? You got a death wish?"

Adam smiled in the darkness. "No, just wanted to add recon to my resume." Donny lowered his binoculars.

"Does it look like they're getting ready to move out to you?"

Adam nodded. "Yup. Tents are starting to come up. Stuff being stowed into the Bradleys and the trucks."

Just then one of the Abrams tanks started their engine.

The sound dominated the night and drowned out the voices of the soldiers. "Looks like they're running through the Abrams start-up checklist to me. That JP8 hybrid diesel fuel has to warm up for 20 minutes, according to the book that is."

Donny nodded in agreement. "Let's fall back to the quads and get this called in. The General needs to know about this."

They quietly withdrew and made their way back to the quads over a mile away.

In The Bunker

General Branch had just left the house with his squad of Shadow Militia security detail. They were an impressive bunch of soldiers. Baby Donna was asleep now beside Jackie in a wooden crate filled with blankets. Uncle Rodney had taken her and the baby into his bedroom. She'd been shocked at the austerity of the little room. It was barren except for a wooden footlocker, a cot, a pot-bellied stove and a metal, olive-drab wall locker. But Rodney hadn't stopped there. He'd also taken her through another locked door and down a manhole using a ladder leading below the house. It was like a fallout shelter, only much more advanced.

She looked around her now in awe at the stacks of crates and boxes. Now she knew why they had so much food. But it was more than that. On a wooden box beside her was written "TOW 2A/B". The box she was using as a chair said "M72A2". Jackie had no idea what that meant, but Uncle Rodney had left explicit orders not to touch anything.

He'd given her a sleeping bag, a cot, a portable bucket latrine, and there were several pallets of MREs and bottles of distilled water off to her left. She could probably survive down here for months if she had to.

But the main reason she was here was the fancy radio in front of her. She didn't know what it was or how it worked, but Uncle Rodney had given her written instructions on how to monitor the broadcasts and what to listen for. She'd taped the list of frequencies to the desk she was sitting at. Some were for aviation; some for armor; and others for ground troops. She surmised the aviation frequency was for talking to the Apache helicopters, wherever they were. But to her knowledge not even Uncle Rodney had any tanks.

Out of curiosity she opened the file drawer on the left side of the desk to see what was inside. She reached down and picked up the hand grenade. It seemed heavy for its size, and it was shaped wrong. In the movies she'd seen grenades were always shaped like pineapples, but this one was round. She saw the pin and was careful not to touch it.

Baby Donna started to cry, so she picked her up and rocked her back and forth. Under no circumstances was she to leave the bunker. In fact, even if she wanted to she couldn't, since Uncle Rodney has locked it from the outside.

Her instructions were clear and simple. Monitor all three of the radio frequencies and listen for one phrase: "Fire the Golden FPF ." If she heard that phrase, she was to relay the message over a different radio that was off to the right. It was bigger and more complicated, but it was already set up for her. She just had to turn it on, depress the handset and transmit.

Just then she heard someone talking; it was on the ground forces frequency. She recognized the voice as Donny Brewster. "Tango Actual, this is Tango one, over."

Uncle Rodney's voice came back almost immediately. "Tango one this is Tango Actual, go ahead, over."

"This is Tango one, we have confirmed sighting of the following: two-hundred enemy soldiers, four Abrams tanks, two Apache attack helicopters and four Bradley fighting Vehicles. Please confirm receipt of transmission, over."

"Roger that, Tango One. Message is received. Please send coordinates, over."

"This is Tango One with figures to follow:" There was a slight pause. "4 - 4 - 1 - 1 - 7 -5 - 0 - 5. I say again 4 - 4 - 1 - 1 - 7 -5 - 0 - 5. Please confirm, over."

"This is Tango Actual, I confirm as follows, 4 - 4 - 1 - 1 - 7

-5 - 0 - 5, over."

Donny's voice came back right away. "This is Tango one, the enemy force appears to be bugging out. What are your orders?"

There were several seconds of silence before Uncle Rodney came back. "Tango One this is Tango Actual, your orders are to observe and report. Do not engage without authorization."

"Roger that, Tango Actual. Out."

Jackie looked down and spoke to baby Donna. "Wow! We're listening to the whole war in the comfort of our own home! This might be cool!"

CHAPTER 21

COLONEL MACPHERSON SAT down at the table across from his commanding general. Rodney was impressed with the man. For the decades he'd known Ranger MacPherson, he'd always seemed unflappable. He never got tired, never got discouraged, never wavered in his duties or made poor judgments. The two of them were alone now for the first time in days.

"Why the hell do you continue to follow me after all these years, Mac?"

The Colonel smiled slightly. "It's because I have no life of my own to speak of, sir. No wife, no kids. My prostate's the size of Texas, so sex hasn't been an option for over ten years now."

Rodney laughed out loud and then took a sip of his coffee. He liked it thick and black, especially the night before battle. When the laughter died down the Colonel spoke again. "Actually, sir, if I may be so candid, the reason I follow you is because you're one of the few men who are worthy of my service."

General Branch cocked his head off to one side but remained smiling. "I'm not even sure how to take that, Mac. Care to expand?"

The grizzled, old soldier across from him locked eyes with his general. "I follow you because when I served under you in combat you exemplified what it means to be an Army Ranger. Honor, duty, integrity, courage. They're not just words to me. I would die for those words, and so would you. I follow you because you've earned my service through your personal sacrifice and bravery, and because you were the first to see the need for The Shadow Militia."

Colonel MacPherson paused and turned away to look at the wall. "I follow you because no one else leads me where I want to go the way you do. You've got more brains and balls than anyone else out there. And then ..." He paused again and smiled just a tad. "There is the matter of my prostate."

Rodney Branch reared back in his chair and laughed as hard as he could until the whole table shook. About a minute later the room was quiet again. The General stood up from his chair and walked over to the window. He looked out into the darkness. Neither man said anything for a time.

Slowly, the General turned and spoke. "We have four Bradleys, four Abrams tanks and two Apache attack helicopters moving quickly to our rear flank. They're supported by two-hundred professional infantry."

The Colonel nodded. "Yes, I know. I heard Sergeant Brewster's transmission"

Rodney looked over at his second in command to meet his gaze. "That doesn't concern you?"

"Of course it concerns me. And we have to deal with it. The big question is how?"

The General nodded and moved back to the table where a plastic-laminated map was spread out before them.

"Sergeant Brewster has them here and moving in this direction. They'll be in position to attack within a few hours. But I don't think they'll attack until The Horde has done its worst damage. And that won't be until tomorrow, maybe later if I have anything to say about it. But when they do attack; it's going to be tough. The citizens of Iroquois have no weapons capable of taking out an Abrams."

Colonel MacPherson interrupted his thoughts. "You know we can't help them beyond our charter?"

Rodney nodded with genuine sadness. "I know, but there must be something we can do to help, to give them a fighting chance. They've been brave and they deserve that much."

The other soldier looked down at the floor. "I know, sir. But I have to remind you of our rules of engagement. We can't tip our hand. If we do, well, then it's not just Iroquois that will suffer. Let's face it, sir, we're only here because this is your home town. There are cities like this all over the country being raped and pillaged. This is but one, small town among thousands."

Rodney turned his back on the Colonel and stared out the window again. "Are you saying it was a mistake for me to intervene here?"

The Colonel smiled to himself. "Of course not, sir. You and I both know generals don't make mistakes. Let's just call it a calculated risk with avenues for both success as well as failure."

Colonel MacPherson was watching the General's reflection in the window and thought he saw the hint of a smile.

"Colonel, you said one of the reasons you follow me was my sense of honor. My honor tells me we can't give these people hope and then abandon them. We have to find a way to help them within the bounds of our charter."

He turned back around and a smile spread across his face as he spoke. We are fighting a battle with a militia army of farmers and factory workers." He paused for effect. "So tell me, Colonel, what do farmers and factory workers have that can take out an Abrams tank?"

At first the Colonel seemed confused, but then, little by little, a smile of his own took root and bloomed across his military face. "You're a genius, sir. A military genius!"

Rodney Branch scoffed at his friend. "Yeah, right. But you and I both know we're just two old men on the downhill side of life with nothing to lose and nothing left to live for. The General smiled. "And then there's the matter of your prostate. I'm going to requisition you a new one after this battle is over."

The Army Ranger snapped to attention and gave the General a crisp, military salute. General Branch snapped to attention and returned the salute.

"I'll make it happen, sir."

And with that the Colonel rushed out the door in search of the right materials in the proper proportions.

Restoring the Sheriff

"How did you find me?"

Colonel MacPherson remained stoic in front of Sheriff Leif. "Your wife told us you might be here at the church. I think it's a good place to be right now. I've always been a praying man myself, especially on the night before battle."

The Sheriff was sitting all slumped down in a wooden pew near the front of the auditorium. A large wooden cross filled the center of the podium up against the wall. "You must think I'm a real coward to walk out the way I did, to leave the fight and demand we retreat in order to survive."

The Colonel stood ram-rod straight before him. As usual, every muscle in his body was taut in readiness. "I don't get paid to think, Sheriff Leif, I get paid to follow orders."

The Sheriff tried unsuccessfully to lighten the atmosphere with his next remark, but failed miserably. "The Shadow Militia gets paid? By who?"

His remark went unanswered.

"I don't pretend to understand civilians, sir. They don't compute to me. I'm a simple man with black and white thinking. My selector switch has only two modes: FIGHT and DIE. Anything beyond that seems irrelevant to me."

The Sheriff stood up and stretched his back, then he ran his right palm through his greasy, unwashed hair. "What do you want with me, colonel?"

165

"The General needs your help with a project."

"A project?"

"Yes, sir. The General would like you to build a series of bombs to help defend the city against an armored attack from our western flank, sir."

"What?"

The Sheriff collapsed back down in the church pew and began praying again while Colonel MacPherson filled him in on the details.

The Horde Encampment

Manny called it making love, but, in reality, it took only about forty-five seconds before it was over. The woman left his bed in silence, and Manny would never see her again. That's the way he liked it, and he never slept with the same woman twice. Relationships were just too time-consuming and complicated. Manny noted that few of the other great conquerors allowed themselves to get tied down or mixed up in constraining female relationships. In Manny's mind, women were good only for cooking and breeding. It was simple, straight forward, and it made sense to him.

Outside his lodge, he could hear the music and voices of the party in full swing. The debauchery would continue until about 2 a.m. when it would begin to subside and eventually fade away altogether by three o'clock. It was predictable.

That bothered him from a security standpoint, but he knew there was little he could do about it. His soldiers weren't really soldiers at all, and therein laid both their greatest strength and their greatest weakness. Manny knew so long as he kept the men fed, laid and drugged, they would follow him to the ends of the earth. But if he wavered on even one of the three, they would turn on him like jackals on a carcass. He had learned the secret to being a great leader; *People will only follow you so long as you're taking them where they already want to go.*

Manny got out of bed and walked over to the log-made table. He loved the smell of pine. He looked down at the map and smiled. It was a good plan. Estimates showed less than five-hundred townspeople in arms against his twenty-five hundred. He knew they'd captured one of his Bradley fighting vehicles, but that would have to be deployed against Major Danskill and his forces as they attacked the town from the western flank. He called it Operation Hammer and Anvil. Danskill was the anvil, cutting off any escape, and The Horde was the giant hammer that would smash down on the farmers and townspeople futiley trying to protect the town. That was assuming they were still there to fight. Some of the towns they had already rolled through, the smart ones, had been abandoned long before their arrival, and all they had to do was collect up the supplies before partying and moving on.

But another thing weighed heavy on his mind. Albert was yet to check in. He'd sent him to spy on Major Danskill and capture a prisoner for interrogation. But Albert had fallen off the face of the earth. Had he been captured? If so, he was surely dead by now. Had he deserted? Not likely, but if so, Manny could get ten more people like him in a matter of hours. Albert was easily replaced.

The music was blaring away outside his window, but he wanted to sleep. Love-making always did that to him. He recognized the song now, and started humming along with the lyrics.

I've paid my dues - Time after time
I've done my sentence - But committed no crime

Yes, *Queen* was a good group.

And bad mistakes - I've made a few
I've had my share of sand kicked in my face
But I've come through

Manny could relate to that. People had kicked him before, but he'd gotten the best of them.

We are the champions - my friends
And we'll keep on fighting - till the end

The song blared on and soon Manny was singing as loud as he could, so loud that he never heard Buster walk up the stairs and into his bedroom.

We are the champions
We are the champions
No time for losers
'Cause we are the champions - of the world

Manny looked up in anger, embarrassed by the situation and that Buster had heard his terrible singing voice.

"Who said you could come up here?"

Buster looked confused. "Ahh, you did."

Manny was naked, so he walked over to the dresser and put his clothes on. Buster waited patiently by the door.

"So are you going to tell me what the hell you want or just stand there all night?"

Buster's face flushed red. He didn't like being yelled at. "Ah, well, I just thought you wanted to know when we're bein' attacked, that's all."

"Attacked!"

Manny jumped on the bed and landed on the other side where his boots lay on the floor. "Well why didn't you say so? Where are they? What's happening? Talk to me!"

Buster seemed confused by all the questions, so it took a moment to sort them out.

"Answer me! Now!"

"A bunch of quads and trucks raced up to the campground entrance and killed our guards. Then they set the ticket booth on fire along with a couple trucks we had up there."

Manny finished lacing up his boots and jumped up, grabbing his M4 as he went. "Let's get down there and find out what the hell's happening."

Manny stormed down the stairs followed closely by his

assistant. Manny heard gunshots, but *Queen* was still playing loudly in the background.

The Horde would not sleep tonight.

CHAPTER 22

Preparing the Iroquois Air Force

IT WAS LATE AND **S**ERGEANT
Steffens was exhausted. But for some reason he just couldn't sleep. The Captain had left two hours ago and everything was as ready as it ever would be. The larger tank was fitted; the spray rack had been modified to increase the flow, and the Super Ag Cat was fueled and ready for its final mission. The big question weighing heavy on his mind was this: Could he even get the thing off the ground? He knew it was too heavy, much heavier than the specs called out, but he felt the added payload was worth the risk in the toll it would take. Harold didn't mind dying tomorrow. He didn't mind going home to Myra. He looked forward to it, actually. In fact, if truth be told, and if by some remote chance he survived, Harold knew he would be disappointed.

He held the flare gun in his hand, and looked down at it now. He seemed amazed at the wrinkles and gnarls that had overtaken both his hands. Old age had a way of sneaking up on a man. One day he was young and strong and handsome, and the next ... well, in the next, his life was almost over now. He recalled a sermon he'd heard from decades ago on the fleeting nature of life. Harold had memorized the verse to keep death from sneaking up on him.

"Yet you do not know what your life will be like tomorrow. You are just a vapor that appears for

a little while and then vanishes."

Harold sat in the wooden chair in his pole barn beside the airplane, moving in closer to the pot-bellied stove. It gave off just enough heat to keep him from freezing to death. He was the entirety of the Iroquois County Air Force. Harold knew the General and his Shadow Militia had more than enough firepower to destroy The Horde and Major Danskill's puny forces, and Harold had always wondered why he didn't just do it and be done with it. Why should so many townspeople have to fight and die without reason? All the death seemed in vain. But the General had revealed to him the secret reason, and Harold had agreed. It was far better for one old man to die, and Harold didn't mind dying to save others. Self sacrifice was how he'd won the Silver Star so many years ago in France, and that's how he'd lived the remainder of his life. To change now would seem to disrespect everything he'd lived to date.

No, Harold Steffens would finish strong. He moved his left hand up to his collar and fingered the silver bar General Branch had pinned on his uniform. He recalled the General's words of just a few hours before.

"Pilots are officers, and you, sir, have exemplified in every fashion that you are an officer and a gentleman."

Harold smiled. He spoke out loud to his plane. "Better late than never." And he wondered if Myra would be impressed. Lieutenant Steffens pulled the green, wool blanket up around his torso and closed his eyes, waiting, just waiting for the dawn, waiting for the final vapor to rise up and fade away.

The Iroquois Welcome Wagon Visits The Horde

Chain saws fired up all across the state forest campgrounds, and trees began to fall everywhere. Twelve oaks fell across the camp's access road, effectively trapping Manny and his men on the wrong side of the camp, thereby rendering them unable to head back in. Manny fumed helplessly as he watched his trucks at the main entrance burn out of control.

Back inside the camp Major Dan Branch and his company of men and women wreaked wholesale havoc in the darkness. Manny had taken all the alert guards to the camp entrance with him, leaving only the drunk and sleeping to protect his encampment. Most of The Horde slept through the devastation that was now ensuing.

General Branch's orders had been clear. "Reduce The Horde's ability to transport soldiers." Major Branch accomplished this by throwing dozens of Molotov cocktails, nothing more than Mason jars filled with gasoline, on most of the vehicles. That gave the militia plenty of light to work by. Meanwhile, sharpshooters hidden in the brush cut down any of The Horde members who were alert enough to pop out of their tents. The fire and confusion allowed Dan's soldiers to work unopposed for almost five minutes. Chain saws felled trees onto the roads and trucks. All of the cabins were set on fire, and most of the occupants died mercifully in their sleep from smoke inhalation. Five dedicated men shot out the tires of any trucks escaping fire or the trees.

By the time The Horde was able to organize any real resistance, Major Branch and his militia faded back into the trees and began the seven-mile walk back to Iroquois City.

Protecting the Iroquois Rear Flank

Colonel MacPherson's original idea had been to place a series of truck bombs beside the road leading into town from the west. But, to his credit, Sheriff Leif had improved the idea. "If we place the bombs in plain sight they may cause suspicion and be easy to evade. Let's make it harder for them."

And so Joe Leif had enlisted the service of Mark Englerth who owned a local excavation company to dig a long trench using two back hoes. They worked through the night, but by 4 a.m. the task was finished. The local farm bureau had donated fifteen-thousand pounds of Ammonium Nitrate fertilizer, while the plating plant across town gave them enough

Nitromethane solvent to create a trench bomb over one-hundred-twenty yards long. They linked it together with a series of blasting caps and wires then covered up the fresh dirt by using the city's snowblower. As if signifying His divine approval, it snowed an inch from 4 a.m. to 6 a.m., and by daybreak the mother of all bombs looked like just another stretch of road.

To give them more options, Colonel MacPherson also had four mobile bombs made. Two old clunkers plus a Yugo and a Toyota Prius. Both of the latter were requisitioned in the dead of night from the local car dealership. All four of them could be detonated remotely. General Branch had personally organized the defenses for the east side of town where The Horde was expected to make a frontal attack. But, just in case, he also stationed one-hundred defenders to the north and also to the south of town, They could be used as a ready reserve and to prevent The Horde from flanking the town. The mobile fertilizer bombs were spread out across the city as part of a rapid reactionary force.

By 6 a.m. General Branch gave final orders to the Home Guard leaders. They were huddled around a large bonfire near the center of town as he spoke.

"You soldiers did a great job. Because of all your hard work this town now has a fighting chance. I want to thank the Sheriff for his leadership and his ingenuity at covering our rear flank." He glanced over at Joe Leif who was now in his Sheriff's uniform. It was clean and sharply pressed thanks to his wife, Marge. The Sheriff just nodded and looked down at the ground sheepishly. He knew the truth, how he'd walked out only hours before, and he was humbled and thankful for this second chance.

"I want to thank Major Branch and his men and women from the newly formed Militia Rangers who attacked The Horde camp just a few hours ago. Because of their bravery

and military creativity, we'll have several more hours to prepare."

He held his hands out in front of him to soak in some
warmth. The snow had stopped now, but it had left a thin blanket of pure whiteness all around them.

"Before I give you your final orders, I'd like to have Father
Fish and Pastor Bowman say a few words to God on our behalf."

Both men came forward and stood side by side in front of
the fire. They were wearing Car-Hart insulated coveralls with
home-made snow camo made from white bed sheets. Father
Fish was holding an over and under twelve gauge trap shotgun
in his left hand with the hand-carved, mahogany stock planted
in the snow. Pastor Bowman wore a holstered Springfield XD
in 9mm but also held a 30.06 hunting rifle with a Bushmaster
scope. Father Fish spoke first.

"Dear God. We come before you with praise that we have
survived for so long. We are deeply grateful for your steadfast
love and mercy. Please be with us in the coming battle. Focus
our minds, embolden our hearts. Fill us with courage and resolve for what we are forced now to do. Amen."

Pastor Bowman stepped forward and took a more direct
approach to God. "Dear God. The Philistines are marching on
our city. We need to kill them. To the last man they need to
die. They are evil and don't believe in you. We must purge the
land of their lust for power. So come to us in the time of our
need. Help us kill them all. Amen"

General Branch smiled. "Now those were mighty fine
prayers, men. Thanks and keep talking to God for us. We need
all the help we can get."

Then he turned to the others as they stood around the
bonfire. They moved in closer to hear their leader's every
word, and to somehow, if it was possible, soak in any leftover
strength he might be giving off.

"Okay, we've got our work cut out for us on this one. I

won't BS you about it. Lots of us are going to die in the next eight hours." He looked around from man to man, meeting eyes whenever he could. "But if we fail, if even a hundred of these butchers make it into town, you can kiss your families goodbye, because they'll leave no survivors. It will be a slow and painful death for the people you love and hold dear."

Then he hesitated. He needed to embolden them, leave them with strength and hope.

"But if you follow my orders; if your hearts remain true and strong, you will prevail and your children will be saved." The General rubbed his hands together in front of the fire.

"Now ... here's what we're going to do."

CHAPTER 23

Meanwhile Back at the Horde

BUSTER STAYED OFF TO ONE SIDE as his boss roamed back and forth like a caged animal. The sun had just come up and the extent of the damage done by the Iroquois Rangers was becoming more and more apparent. Most of The Horde's vehicles had been destroyed or rendered useless, but several of them could be salvaged just by changing the tires.

"Get me a hundred chain saws and start cutting these trees up and get them out of the road! I want to be moving into that town in two hours."

No one moved so Manny unholstered his pistol and fired it three times into the air. "Did you people hear me?" Buster backed away, putting a standing tree between himself and his boss. Others, most of them still hung over from the night before, simply stood and stared blankly at their leader.

"I said move!" And to emphasize his point, Manny walked up to the biggest man around him and fired one shot to the head. The man went down instantly in a heap.

"I said move! Now!"

The encampment instantly fell into a frenzy of people now miraculously sober. They searched out chain saws and began clearing the road. Within the hour, two of the deuce and a half trucks were drivable and began hooking up ropes to the logs and pulling them out as well.

For the next two hours Manny stood by with his body

guards, all with weapons drawn, watching intently to make sure no one slowed down. After that work was completed, Manny called his remaining leaders together for a talk. Many of the others had died the night before, burned to death in the cabins.

"We're going to walk seven miles into Iroquois City. And when we get there, anyone who opposes us is going to die. Anyone who surrenders is going to be raped, tortured and killed. When we catch the leader, I want him taken alive. I have a special brand of pain to inflict on him. Do you all understand?"

The twenty-three men nodded, almost in unison. "And another thing, if any of your men balk, if they hesitate, if they run, you are to shoot them immediately."

Some of the men smiled, others were terrified, while others simply stared back at him blankly. These men were the soulless, the damned, and they had abandoned long ago any shred of human compassion or dignity. They would do as ordered so long as it kept them alive, gave them power and brought them pleasure.

At 11 a.m. The Horde was assembled on the road leading out of the state campgrounds. They were a rabbled-looking bunch, but still numbering almost two-thousand strong. Manny extended his left palm out to Buster who was standing beside him. Immediately Buster handed over the megaphone, and Manny moved it up to his mouth.

"We stand poised on the cusp of our greatest battle." Buster thought to himself, *What's a cusp?* "But we will move ahead and we will crush them like no other enemy we've faced. Last night they attacked in a cowardly fashion, in the dead of night as we slept. But now we are awake and we are not happy! We will attack in force and kill every living creature. We'll kill the men, the women, the children, even their dogs and cats must die."

Manny paused to gauge their response, but no one said anything. "And when we are done, after they've been sufficiently raped, tortured and killed, we will take everything of value and then burn the town to the ground. No stone will remain on top of another." Still no one said anything. There were no cheers as Manny had expected. So he went on.

"And then we march on to Traverse City, the jewel of the Michigan west coast, plush with million-dollar homes, ripe for the picking. We will conquer it and live there like kings, lacking nothing, and all our dreams will come true."

The crowd finally erupted in cheers and Manny smiled and raised up his M16 and fired into the air. The crowd reacted by raising their own firearms and firing as well. A few minutes later the crowd quieted, but not before three of them slumped to the ground dead from accidental gunshot wounds.

They dragged the bodies off the road, and Manny gave the order to move out. The Horde was on its way.

The Final Launch of Lieutenant Steffens

Lieutenant Steffens had already gone through his pre-flight checklist, and the Super Ag Cat was now roaring down the field beside his house. He'd begun his take-off run up in his driveway to allow him extra speed. With the added weight of his new spray tanks, he'd need every ounce of energy just to make it in the air.

Halfway down the runway, Harold got a sinking feeling in the pit of his stomach. He thought to himself, *I'm not going to make it.* But he pushed ahead anyway. He had to make it off the ground. Lives depended on it. Three-quarters of the way to the trees he began to pray. "Please God. Help me get in the air. I have to get in the air." Just as he reached the end of the field his wheels lifted off the ground, but the trees were looming ahead, getting bigger with each passing second. Harold prayed under his breath. *Please God.* Just before he reached the trees a gust of headwind pushed under his wings and lifted him above the woods. Harold started breathing again. "Thank you God."

The plane was sluggish with the extra weight, but Harold built up more airspeed and was soon gaining altitude. He looked back at the home he'd built with Myra, where they'd raised their children, where they'd lived their lives and made their mark, and he couldn't help but think, *It's hard to believe it was all but a vapor.*

He banked the plane and headed for The Horde gaining more altitude as he went.

The Deadly March to Town

Major Dan Branch had organized his new Rangers into four-person fire teams, and they began attacking The Horde five miles outside of town. This time The Horde was without quads and was unable to pursue them, so each fire team lay down in the open fields about one hundred yards north of the road and fired until The Horde had passed them by or until they ran out of ammo. But that wasn't a problem since the ammo was quickly replaced using stockpiles Dan and his Rangers had hidden along the route.

When cover was available they took advantage of it, but it hardly seemed necessary against a mass of two thousand people moving at two miles per hour. The trucks in the back of the column were carrying all the ammo, and they were quickly rendered useless with well-placed shots to the tires. Manny ordered his troops to carry the ammo by hand and this slowed them down even more. Dan had also placed hundreds of booby traps along the road in the early hours of the morning in the form of toe-popping mines, punji sticks and even a few claymore mines his uncle had given him. The claymores were the worst, going off and shredding dozens of people in the tightly packed column. Three miles from town only fifteen hundred Horde remained. As Dan watched from a hill above the road, he ordered his Rangers to intensify their fire. If even five-hundred of the Horde made it to town the city would be over run.

Sergeant Donny Brewster, Lisa Vanderboeg and Staff Sergeant Adam Cervantes were waiting in the Bradley Fighting Vehicle about two miles outside of town. They had it warmed up and ready to roll in defense of Iroquois. Lisa was manning the 25 mm cannon while Donny stood ready on the 7.62 mm machine gun.

Adam had parked the Bradley behind a berm which hid them completely about five hundred yards to the south of the road. Because there were Apache Attack helicopters in the area, behind them they'd dug small trenches to dive into just in case they were attacked from the air. Donny knew their Bradley was capable of killing everyone in the column and halting the advance, but, nonetheless, he felt uneasy. This was just too simple. And Donny Brewster had lived neither a simple nor a lucky life.

"Wait for me to open fire, Lisa."

Lisa nodded. Her stomach felt queasy, and she fought back the urge to vomit. When Donny's machine gun went off it startled her so much that it took several seconds for her to join in. But when her cannon opened up it deafened her ears completely. Donny, more practiced at shooting automatic weapons was dead on almost immediately. His bullets chewed up the column as he raked back and forth. People went down in blood and bone while others dove for nonexistent cover. Once Lisa's 25 mm cannon found the range bodies were blown in half and all hell broke loose. Donny concentrated on the left, while Lisa fired to the right.

Manny was near the front of the column when the machine guns opened up, tearing the center of his march to shreds. He dove for cover as did everyone around him. He immediately reached for his radio and tried calling Major Danskill again. But Danskill hadn't answered him in almost twenty-four hours now. He suspected the Major had captured Albert and his raiding party and was holding it against him.

From one mile east of the road, Major Danskill watched from the safety of the Abrams tank. Immediately he knew what had happened, indeed, had expected it. Because that's what he would do in that situation. Without bringing the Bradley's big guns to bear, Manny's column would undoubtedly roll through the town and remain a viable fighting force. And Danskill just couldn't have that, so he allowed Donny's machine guns a full minute before ordering the Apache to attack the entrenched Bradley. He laughed as Manny's men were torn to pieces.

"Reloading!"

The fire from the 7.62 mm machine gun silenced as Donny took time to arm up. Lisa slowed her rate of fire as targets were now on the ground and harder to find. Adam was atop the vehicle with binoculars searching the air.

Donny had just finished reloading and was about to fire again when Adam yelled. "Cease fire! Cease fire! Air attack!"

Donny swung the machine gun around and began firing on the approaching Apache Attack helicopter, but before it got close enough for accurate hits, Adam saw the Hellfire missile separate from the approaching aircraft.

"Jump! Get out!"

Donny saw Adam spring off the Bradley, so he jumped off himself. Lisa was the last to leave just before the Hellfire exploded into their fighting vehicle.

The helicopter hovered over the smoking Bradley. "Eagle Leader, this is Sparrowhawk. Enemy Bradley is destroyed. There are no survivors, over."

From over a mile away Major Danskill smiled. His plan was falling into place nicely. The lone Bradley Fighting Vehicle was the only weapon the town had capable of destroying an

Abrams tank. Now his armor could roll in through the rear flank unopposed followed up by two-hundred well-trained infantry. He would rout the townspeople, and then kill Manny. Then he'd take command of the remainder of The Horde and march in to Traverse City where he would enjoy some R&R while waiting for further instructions.

"Sparrowhawk, this is Eagle Leader. Good job. Take up aerial recon above the city, over."

"Roger that, Eagle Leader. This is Sparrowhawk, out."

With that the Apache attack helicopter raced away in preparation for the next battle.

CHAPTER 24

Death from Above

THE ENGINE ON HAROLD'S SUPER Ag Cat sputtered a bit, so he quickly adjusted the fuel mix to even out the engine. He could see The Horde column about a mile ahead. They were on the road and marching, but in less force than he'd seen last night on his final recon patrol. He passed the abandoned trucks, sitting there, dead and motionless on the road to town. He let them be. His primary objective was to kill as many people as possible before they reached the town. As the Horde moved away, he saw hundreds of dead bodies in front of him, but almost a thousand strong still marched on toward Iroquois City.

Harold looked down at the flare gun in his lap and smiled. The plan had been his all along, and he was oddly proud of it. He laughed out loud at the irony, but his laughter was lost to the sound of the plane's engine. The plan he'd devised and worked so desperately to bring to fruition would undoubtedly also bring about his own demise. But it was a death he could live with. It had honor, and how many people these days could hope for such an outcome.

Harold lined up on The Horde and began his final approach.

General Branch at HQ

It was the thing Rodney Branch hated the most about being a general; he couldn't stand the waiting while others were out fighting, killing and dying. The map was spread out in front of him on the table, and every time the radio reported a change, he'd reach down and move some of the plastic toys from one place to another. He reached down now and turned the Bradley Fighting Vehicle onto its side. Thank God Donny and his crew were okay. And thank God they'd taken out five hundred of The Horde before being knocked out. But it was a major loss ... one that Rodney had anticipated. The loss of the Bradley's TOW missile launcher was irreplaceable ... unless ... you happened to have several cases of them in your bomb shelter, which of course Rodney did. Several days ago he'd had his Ford F250 truck converted into a mobile TOW launcher. It was parked on the courthouse steps waiting deployment.

Over the decades General Branch had studied his Sun Tzu religiously.

> *"Appear weak when you are strong, and strong when you are weak."*

The latest battle outside town had raised several questions for him. Mainly, why had they taken out the Bradley only after Donny had destroyed half the attacking infantry? Why hadn't the Apaches been flying cover for the ground units? Why were there no strafing runs on Dan's Rangers? Why was there no bombardment of the town by the Abrams tanks? This was not a traditional battle plan, and it led Rodney to believe he was dealing with two separate forces instead of one coordinated unit.

He thought about it and shook his head. He yearned to know the answers to those questions. He needed to know who he was fighting. For Sun Tzu had also said:

> *"If you know the enemy and know yourself, you need not fear the result of a hundred battles. If*

*you know yourself but not the enemy, for every
victory gained you will also suffer a defeat. If
you know neither the enemy nor yourself, you
will succumb in every battle"*

General Branch knew himself, and he knew one of his two enemies but … it would have to do. Besides, he still had some surprises, and he was pretty certain neither of his enemies knew he existed.

Three Miles east of town

Major Danskill put the radio down and thought for a moment. Traditional rules of warfare demanded a softening-up barrage by the Abrams tanks before moving in, but that was unnecessary now that the Bradley was destroyed. If the enemy had mortars or artillery they certainly would have used them by now. Manny's approaching Horde would have definitely flushed them out. Everything the enemy had done so far suggested they were an organized resistance but possessed only small arms. With the best intel he had, Major Danskill concluded he was up against a force of about five-hundred well organized and determined fighters. They were probably all townspeople who were being lead by a combat veteran who just happened to live in this town. It made sense, and there was no reason for him to deviate from his original attack plan, He would send the armor in the back door as soon as Manny's Horde breached the town. Manny would then do most of the fighting and take the lion's share of the casualties. And that suited Major Danskill just fine.

And then he heard the sound of an engine approaching from the east. He turned and looked to the sky.

"What the hell?"

Lieutenant Steffens opened the spray nozzles and hundreds of gallons of one-hundred octane gasoline sprayed down on

185

the advancing Horde below.

Manny looked up at the approaching bi-plane and snarled. "What the hell?" Then he smelled the gas and watched as the deadly mist rained down on the remnant of his army. Manny flew into an uncontrollable rage, raised up his M16 and fired at the crop duster as it flew toward the head of the column. It was the last thing Manny ever did.

Major Danskill looked on in shock and disbelief as the remainder of The Horde was incinerated. His eyes followed the trail of fire as it blossomed in orange fury all the way up into the sky as if chasing the plane.

"Wow. That's impressive."

Then he angrily slammed his fist down on the metal armor of the Abrams and screamed out in pain.

"Who are you?"

Harold Steffens heard the unexpected concussion below him and glanced over his shoulder. Upon seeing the flames racing up through the sky toward his plane, he quickly fumbled to turn off the sprayer. The fire stopped climbing toward him. As he flew into the east side of town, Harold looked down at the useless flare gun on his lap. His original plan had been to make a second pass to ignite the gas, but he hadn't foreseen the fact that enemy small arms fire would do the job for him.

As Manny and his Horde burned all the way to hell, it finally occurred to Lieutenant Steffens that he was still alive. While flying over the old, red, brick courthouse, Harold rocked the bi-plane's wings. He'd always wanted to do that.

That's when he heard the voice of General Branch over his radio. "Great job, Lieutenant! You got them all!"

Harold smiled as he replied to his commanding general. "Roger that, sir. What are your orders?"

There was silence. Then a reply. "Stand by for further orders, Lieutenant."

General Branch put down his radio and smiled. He looked up at the bi-plane as it flew overhead. On the underside of the wings, written in hunter-orange paint were the words "Molon Labe." Rodney snickered to himself and thought, *That's a nice touch.* Then he turned back triumphantly to the task at hand. "One army down and one more to go."

But quickly his face grew stern. Four Bradleys, four Abrams and two Apaches plus two hundred infantry. The math didn't add up. He needed a plan. The General reached down and picked up his radio again. "Ranger One this is Iroquois Leader, come in, over." A few seconds elapsed before his nephew answered.

"This is Ranger One. Go ahead, Iroquois Leader."

"This is Iroquois Leader. All units return to base. Out."

Dan Branch looked down at the radio as if confused by the abruptness of the command. Then he looked out at the long trail of fire and smoke. There was no movement out on the road, but the smell of gas and burning flesh was causing some of his people to vomit. He thought to himself. *Okay, I guess he knows more than I do. Besides, no point in sticking around here.*

"Captain Jackson! Get everyone saddled up. We're heading back to HQ!"

The Captain smiled and yelled for the nearest sergeant. Soon, they were all on their way back into town.

☆ ☆ ☆ ☆

Two miles away Major Danskill looked down at the burning Horde. The flames were starting to die down now, but the smoke and the smell would linger on for some time to come. Captain Foster looked over at him before speaking in a tentative voice.

"What are your orders, sir."

His commanding officer didn't speak for almost a full minute.

"Sir? Your orders?"

Danskill looked up from his thoughts. Then he formed his words with a sneer.

"Tell the Apaches to find that bi-plane and shoot it down." He hesitated. "Tell the Bradleys and the Abrams to proceed to the rally point as planned. The Abrams will bombard the city and then the Bradleys and infantry will move in to mop up."

Captain Foster nodded his approval, confident that his boss was in full control of the situation. He scurried away to carry out his orders.

Several miles away Harold Steffens landed in an open field and taxied to a stop beneath the trees. According to his general's orders he was out of sight from the air.

And now he waited.

CHAPTER 25

The Final Battle

"IT'S THE ONLY HOPE WE HAVE."

General Branch looked across the room at everyone present. Donny Brewster looked excited while Lisa and Adam seemed unsure. His nephew, Major Dan Branch, was wearing his best poker face. Colonel MacPherson was stoic as always. Rodney looked over at Sheriff Leif and was surprised to see him smiling.

General Branch raised one eyebrow before addressing him. "Care to speak your mind, Sheriff?"

Joe Leif looked down at the table and then back up again. Then he glanced around the room at each person present before speaking. "Every single time I've doubted you over the past six months you've proved me wrong, so I think I've learned my lesson. Last night I was arguing for an evacuation of the whole city, because I just didn't have enough faith in you or my fellow citizens. I was still seeing them as Bill the Pharmacist and Jim the factory worker and Louise the stay-at-home mom." He placed his folded hands up on the table top. "Well, I was wrong. I underestimated my town. We're not civilians anymore. We're fighters. We're warriors. I can't believe it, Rodney. I just watched an eighty-four-year-old man use a crop duster to destroy an entire army."

Colonel MacPherson shrugged. "Well, technically it was just a battalion."

Joe kept smiling. "Doesn't matter when it's the only battalion in town, and it's advancing to kill you."

Lisa piped up. "That's a good point." Then she turned to the Sheriff. "Sheriff I've seen things the past few weeks I thought I'd never see. I'm a Registered Nurse and I just killed a few hundred Horde with a 25mm cannon." She grew quiet and her eyes misted over for just a moment before drying up again. "Granted, they all needed killing, but … the point is we've all changed. And if we surrender now, then it's only a temporary fix. There will be other Hordes, other rogue armies that will want to kill us … or worse."

She looked past General Branch to the wall behind him. "I say we fight now while we can. I like the plan, and it has a chance of success."

General Branch looked over at Dan as if asking the question without speaking. Lisa noticed it and was amazed they seemed to know what the other was thinking. Major Branch simply nodded.

The General looked back to the group grimly and began issuing a string of orders. As each person was directed, they got up and left the room to carry out their part of the plan. If it was to succeed; if they were to survive; if the approaching armored units were to be defeated; they would have to work together; they'd have to be brave.

There was no room for error. And a little bit of luck would not go unwelcomed.

☆ ☆ ☆ ☆

By the time the bombardment of Iroquois City began, most of the inhabitants had already been moved into basements and to the outer edges of the town thereby minimizing casualties. Nonetheless, dozens of men, women and children died in the five-minute barrage. Half the buildings were fully or partially destroyed while many of the remaining houses were damaged.

Major Branch and Captain Jackson were in a foxhole on the western edge of town. They could plainly see the lone

Bradley Fighting Vehicle drive down the road and stop just fifty yards from their position. Sheriff Leif was in another foxhole just thirty yards to their left. In his left hand he held the remote detonator. It was charged; it was ready to go, but he waited.

The Bradley's hatches opened up as both the machine gun and the 25mm cannon began firing on the nearest buildings. But no one moved. Everyone maintained their fire discipline.

Up on the ridge, standing beside the row of four Abrams tanks, Major Danskill peered down on the town with binoculars. He saw the foxholes and guessed they were manned. The fact his lone Bradley had not been attacked was suggestive of one of two reasons: they had no arms to destroy a Bradley, or, they were waiting for bigger prey.

Danskill had sent in the lone Bradley to verify the road wasn't mined and to get the defenders to tip their hand. Truth is he could no longer afford to underestimate his adversary. They probably had nothing to counter the Bradleys and certainly had nothing to destroy the Abrams, but there was no hurry. He could afford to feel them out. He looked over at Captain Foster who was standing beside him.

"Send in the other Bradleys but hold back the infantry."

Captain Foster nodded and passed on the order. A few minutes later the three remaining Bradleys moved down the road in standard formation, being careful to maintain a distance of thirty meters from nose to tail.

Back in the foxhole, Sheriff Leif watched as the Bradleys came closer. He waited. He wanted the Abrams. He waited. But the Abrams didn't come. He waited. Eventually all three came to a stop behind the leader. Their hatches popped open and the guns were manned. Joe took one last look down the road to make sure the Abrams weren't coming and pressed the plunger.

The men jutting out the hatches were cut in half instantly. Everyone inside the armored cavalry were crushed like Jello as the concussion turned their insides to mush. Two of the Bradleys flipped over several times before landing off the road. The other two miraculously remained upright, but came to rest in a deep hole where the road used to be. There were no survivors.

Sheriff Leif looked on in awe. Jeremy poked him in the shoulder, but Joe hadn't plugged his ears and couldn't hear what the boy was saying to him.

Major Danskill's face flushed white in horror. He'd never seen a blast like that before. But his horror was quickly replaced with rage. *His Bradleys! They were gone! His cavalry was gone!*

Just then he heard the sound of a small-engine plane coming from west of his position. He looked over and saw the small crop duster coming toward him. It was but a speck in the sky, but it kept growing as it came closer. A queasy feeling grew in the pit of his stomach.

"Prepare for air attack! Where are my Apaches? Where is my air cover! I told them to shoot it down!"

As if in answer to his question, the Apache appeared on the horizon and began to close on the Super Ag Cat.

Lieutenant Steffens had flown the long way around town far to the south and taken up position to the west as General Branch had instructed him. And there he had waited until he received the call just a few minutes ago.

He looked ahead and saw his primary objective, then he saw the huge trench where the highway coming into town used to be. He thought to himself, *Nice job, boys. I'm not the only one fighting today.*

Then he looked to his six and saw the Apache closing in on him. He'd never make it to the ridge and the four Abrams tanks. He had to make a decision. That was when he saw two-hundred soldiers in a ravine to his left waiting to attack the town.

He laid the stick full over to the left and kicked full left rudder. As he turned he switched on the sprayers and dumped the fuel onto the enemy troops below. Harold looked ahead and saw the Stinger missile coming toward him. Harold smiled and dove for the ground, feeling more alive than ever before.

The ensuing fireball lit up the sky and quickly sucked all oxygen from the ravine. Most of the enemy died from collapsed lungs. Some inhaled fire while others were simply incinerated. The luckiest died instantly from the concussion. The remnants of Lieutenant Steffen's plane showered down hundreds of yards away, while the attacking Apache was caught in the blast and lost control. It crashed on the edge of the ravine. The remaining Apache, a mile behind, saw the danger, turned around and raced away to the west.

Major Danskill and Captain Foster looked on from half a mile away. At first they said nothing. Then the XO looked at his Commander. His face was white as a sheet.

"What are your orders, sir?"

But his commanding officer said nothing. The warning of Sun Tzu kept running through Major Danskill's head like a broken record threatening to explode his brain.

> *"If you know the enemy and know yourself, you need not fear the result of a hundred battles. If you know yourself but not the enemy, for every victory gained you will also suffer a defeat. If you know neither the enemy nor yourself, you will succumb in every battle"*

Major Danskill turned and walked up to the nearest Abrams. He hopped on top, but not near as nimbly as he had a few minutes before. The Captain looked after him.

"Are we attacking, sir?"

In answer to the Captain's question, Danskill turned his back on his XO and climbed down into the Commander's hatch. Captain Foster looked around, and suddenly noticed he was the only one outside. The turret moved to the left and then opened fire, the concussion knocking the XO to the ground.

Soon all four Abrams were once again bombarding the town, but this time they wouldn't stop until the town was destroyed.

CHAPTER 26

Kill or Die

❝HE'S GOING TO DESTROY THE TOWN!
We have to get them first!" General Branch ran out of
the red brick courthouse as quickly as he could just as
shards of brick and clumps of mortar rained down all around
him. They were targeting the courthouse with its big clock
tower first.

Rodney reached his pick-up truck and jumped inside. Soon
he was rolling down Main Street headed for the north side of
town. He picked up his radio and began barking out orders.

☆ ☆ ☆ ☆

Down inside the bunker, baby Donna was crying, so
Jackie quickly made a bottle and shoved it into her daughter's mouth. She couldn't believe all that was happening. Five
hundred of The Horde killed by her husband and his Rangers;
another fifteen-hundred killed by an old man with a crop
duster. She felt a sense of pride that she'd been part of that
by helping Sergeant Steffens repair his plane. Four Bradley
Fighting Vehicles killed by fertilizer. And now, another two
hundred infantry and an Apache Attack Helicopter destroyed
by Harold Steffens. Her heart went out to him as she realized
he certainly must have died in the attack.

But her husband and her son were safe so far as she knew.
She looked down at baby Donna and smiled. The town was

saved!

But wait! More radio traffic was coming.

"Mac, I need you to lead the four mobiles up that slope and get them as close to the Abrams as you can. Then park them and get the hell out of there!"

Rodney thought for a moment. "Sergeant Brewster, meet me at the library. I need your help with the TOW." He waited for both men to reply, then continued his orders. "Dan, take charge of all ground units. Converge on the ridge from both left and right flanks. Draw their fire. Keep them as distracted as you can. You have to give Colonel MacPherson enough time to drive the mobiles up that slope."

Major Branch yelled some orders into his radio while Captain Jackson readied the men for attack. Two minutes later one-hundred men jumped out of their foxholes and ran thirty yards to the long trench caused by the fertilizer bomb. They jumped down inside and made their way to the end which brought them over one-hundred-twenty yards closer to the Abrams. On the east side of town two-hundred more of the Home Guard were readying for a similar flanking maneuver.

"Get everybody with a Molotov up near the front. And we have two LAWS. I want them up here too! The rest of you, get ready to move out. As fast as you can, follow me to that ditch line about one-hundred yards further down the road."

He looked over at Captain Jackson. Both men seemed wild-eyed with adrenaline. "Larry, I want you to direct the two LAWS. As soon as they bring their fire to bear on us, I want you to hit them as hard as you can."

Larry Jackson gave him a look of skepticism before speaking. "What if they don't fire, Dan? These things are probably left over from the Vietnam War."

Dan just slapped his friend on the back. "Well, if they don't go off, then we're all dead. Just make them work, Larry."

And with that Major Branch screamed out a command and climbed up the side of the trench. His men followed him like a trail of tireless ants.

Major Danskill laughed inside the tank as he watched the gunners fire the big 120 mm guns into the town. From only five hundred yards away pieces of the town came back at them crashing into the side of the hill. It was a joy to watch the town disintegrate in front of him. He wondered if the Militia Commander was already dead. He hoped not because he wanted the man, whoever he was, to suffer as long as possible.

"Major Danskill! Look at our right flank!" The Major looked through the periscope and saw several dozen men, scurrying like insects up the hill a few hundred yards away. They were currently buttoned down, so he barked out an order to his machine gunner. "Get up there and hit them with the fifty cal!"

A few seconds later he was relieved to hear the barking staccato of the fifty caliber machine gun. He looked into the periscope again just in time to see several of the men fall down in pieces. The others made it to a ditch and were pinned down there. Major Danskill smiled. They weren't going anywhere.

Captain Jackson looked over at Ed Brown, who had been the elementary school janitor prior to The Day. "Have you ever fired one of these before?"

Ed shook his head. "No, but I've read the directions five times. I think I can do it." Jackson let out a nervous laugh. "Okay then. We'll do it by the numbers in unison. Follow my lead!" A few seconds later Captain Jackson fired his LAW, and the 3.5 inch rocket plumed its way up the hill and slammed into the side of the nearest Abrams tank. The machine gunner was thrown backwards and his gun went silent. The janitor's rocket hit low and exploded in the ground below a second tank. The Abrams rocked slightly but remained undamaged. Captain Jackson and the janitor shrieked with glee from inside the trench. They looked up and saw Dan and his men rushing up the hill almost to safety.

"Major Danskill, look to our left flank. We've got about two-hundred infantry coming up the hill."

The Major brought his periscope to bear on the left flank and was surprised at what he saw. He couldn't believe that so many people were stupid enough to charge uphill into the teeth of four Abrams tanks. He thought to himself, *Stupid rednecks.*

"Man the fifties and the 7.62 mm machine guns and cut them down. But I want the big guns to keep chewing up the town." The machine gunners in three of the tanks moved out the hatches and began pouring lead into the advancing Home Guard. Dozens of them went down, but they kept advancing. Major Danskill watched from his periscope in awe of their courage or their stupidity or whatever the hell it was.

"Major! We have a frontal attack!"

Major Danskill couldn't believe his eyes. "Is that a Yugo?"

"Yes sir. And a Toyota Prius. And that one off to the left looks like a Dodge Charger. One of those old *Dukes of Hazard* cars."

As he looked on, another car pulled out of the town behind the others. It could barely run and was throwing black smoke out the back.

"Target them all with the main guns. I don't want them reaching us."

Dan and his twenty men had worked their way to the rear flank of the Abrams and were now only about ten yards away. Dan watched as the machine guns raked into the advancing townspeople. Something inside him snapped as he jumped up and began shooting into the side of the closest tank. His other men stood up as well and threw their Molotovs on the turrets. The gas erupted into flames and two of the machine gunners screamed as they burned. The remaining gunner turned his fifty cal around and two of Dan's men went down immediately. Dan ran forward and emptied his M16 into the machine gunner's body. Most of his rounds hit body armor, but several made it through to flesh. The fifty cal went silent. They threw their remaining Molotovs on the other tanks and rushed back into the brush behind them. All the machine guns remained silent, and the infantry on the left and right flanks advanced unopposed up the hill.

Major Danskill paid no attention to his machine gunner's dying screams. He was too focused on directing the fire of his main guns at the advancing automobiles.

"Get that Prius first!"

It took a few seconds, but the Toyota Prius was targeted and soon flew up in the air landing in fuel-efficient pieces.

"Now get on the Yugo!"

A few seconds later the Yugo was destroyed.

"Sir they're too close now, and they're zig-zagging up the hill. They're right on top of us sir! Sir, we're taking small arms fire from both flanks now. The machine gunners are all down."

Major Danskill swore as loud as he could through clenched teeth before issuing his next command.

"Take us down the hill as fast as you can. I'm going to run right over that hick town."

One of the tanks didn't move; it had been hit with almost a dozen Molotovs, but the other three started off down the hill. The lead tank hadn't gone far when it was rocked by a huge explosion as the Dodge Charger slammed into it. The remaining car bomb was too slow, and Major Danskill's tank raced past it unharmed. Finally, the old junker slowed to a halt unable to travel any farther. The engine sputtered and died.

Both tanks were halfway down the hill now and were firing their 120 mm guns as they raced toward the town. The infantry atop the hill was out of the fight now, and all they could do was watch from a distance as the two tanks destroyed their home.

Without warning, two hundred yards from the town, the aft tank blew up and rolled over on its side.

"What the hell was that?"

"We're the only ones left, sir." The gunner's voice sounded frantic as he struggled to maintain his military discipline. "What are your orders, sir?"

Major Danskill hesitated. *How had they done that? Who was he up against?* Danskill muttered under his breath. "I hate Sun Tzu!"

"Sir, what are your orders?"

The Major was visibly upset. He gritted his teeth in determination, but finally common sense overtook his emotions.

"Retreat! Full speed. Get us the hell out of here as fast as you can!"

On the outskirts of the town in front of the city library, Donny Brewster struggled to reload the TOW. General Branch moved away from the sight and stepped over to help him lift the missile and load it into the back of the tube for a second launch. It took the better part of two minutes to complete the reloading process. By the time the General returned to the sight, Major Danskill was out of range.

Sergeant Brewster threw his boonie hat down on the truck bed and stomped on it. General Branch keyed his radio mic. "All units report in."

"Major Branch reporting in, sir."

"Captain Jackson reporting in, sir."

"Captain Alvarez reporting in, sir."

Then silence. Rodney spoke again. "Colonel MacPherson, report in, over."

There was no answer. "Dan, did you see Mac. Where is he?" There was an uncharacteristic urgency in the General's voice. Dan's answer came back and crushed Rodney like a hammer and anvil.

"I don't know. He was driving one of the car bombs."

There air waves were silent for several seconds.

"Find him!"

CHAPTER 27

The Price of Victory

"LET THE NAMES NOW BE READ. LET the names now be heralded and revered in story and song, passed down from one generation to the next. Let the names of all who fought and died in resistance to evil be remembered forever more."

General Branch, in his army dress uniform, stepped away from the pulpit. All the remaining townspeople were assembled inside the town's largest remaining church. There had been six churches before the attack. Only two had escaped the bombardment without damage.

It had been two days since the battle for Iroquois City, and the smoke had cleared. Most of the bodies had been removed. With the help of Mark Englerth's bulldozers and back hoes, The Horde had been buried in mass graves outside town. The ravine where Harold Steffens had incinerated the remaining two hundred enemy soldiers had been filled in. But every person, man, woman or child who had raised arms in defense of Iroquois County was now being given a funeral with full military honors.

Sheriff Joe Leif stood and walked toward the simple, wooden pulpit. He was also in his dress uniform, freshly shaved and as sharp as Marge could make him. When he reached the pulpit, he put the stack of papers on the wood in front of him. Behind him was a large, wooden cross. The piano was to his left, but it wasn't playing today.

"The following people died in defense of liberty:

Colonel Roger "Ranger" MacPherson - Shadow Militia
Lieutenant Harold Steffens - Honorary Shadow Militia
Lou Dobbins - Home Guard
Celeste Evans - Home Guard
Peter Smith - Militia Rangers
Larry Winkler - Home Guard
Connie Polowski - Militia Rangers
Robert Vanderveen - Home Guard
Richard Dyskstra - Militia Rangers
Henry Overbeek - Militia Rangers
Jonathon Janowski - Militia Rangers
Emily Duran - Militia Rangers
Stephen Frank - Home Guard

Jackie Branch sat in the front row with her husband and her son, holding her baby in her arms. Her family was alive. So many others were dead. So many lives had been shattered. In her heart, she knew - no matter what happened from this point on - life would never be the same again. She looked around to find Sergeant Donny Brewster, but he was strangely absent.

Up on the podium, Sheriff Leif continued to read the names of the fallen. Ten minutes later he finally finished.

Joe Leif looked up from the list he'd been reading and looked out into the church, filled to capacity and overflowing out into the lawn. They'd left the doors open so everyone could hear.

"Friends both old and new, citizens, all people of Iroquois. I am humbled by your spirits, your bravery, your focus and your sacrifice." Joe's voice started to waver, but he cleared his throat and pressed on. "Today we honor those who gave their lives so that we could live. Nothing we can do will ever outshine the way they fought and died in defense of our families and our homes." He cleared his throat again. "But there is one thing we can do to bring honor and give meaning to their sacrifice. We can rebuild." He paused to let the words sink in. "We can make Iroquois County a safe haven to all people in need, to all people who value freedom, who are willing to defend it with their lives as they did our friends on this list. We can and will rebuild our home and make it a bastion of liberty."

The Sheriff turned and faced General Branch. "But first, we continue to honor our fallen heroes." He snapped to attention and crisply saluted as best he could, copying what he'd seen from the Shadow Militia. The General seemed surprised, but he stepped forward, came to attention, and returned the Sheriff's salute.

After the salute, Rodney walked forward and placed his hand on Joe's shoulder. "Sheriff Leif, The Shadow Militia remains at your service. You are the leader of Iroquois County, and we are here in an advisory capacity, at your discretion. We hereby renew our pledge to give our lives, our fortunes, and our sacred honor."

General Branch turned to the citizens and proclaimed in a loud voice. "To all who would take our freedoms, we give warning; we challenge you; we chide you; we dare you with every wisp of our souls, Molon Labe. Come and get them. We wait for you."

The county of Iroquois stood to its feet, crying out in one voice:

"Molon Labe!"

"Molon Labe!"

"Molon Labe!"

"Molon Labe!"

All except one man, remaining small, almost invisible to the citizens. He pulled the hood to his coat down over his forehead and gritted his teeth in anger. Finally, now, only after defeat did he know his enemy. Major Danskill faded to the back of the crowd and then disappeared in the coming Iroquois spring.

As the Major walked away, seven independent blasts reached out into the sunshine of the fading northern winter and echoed into one. A few seconds elapsed and another volley was fired. And then another, as the twenty-one-gun salute was completed.

Behind him, fading as he walked toward the edge of town, the sound of bugles reached his ears. He sang the words to himself as he marched away.

> *Day is done, gone the sun*
> *From the lakes, from the hills, from the sky*
> *All is well, safely rest*
> *God is nigh.*
> *Fading light dims the sight*
> *And a star gems the sky, gleaming bright*
> *From afar, drawing near*
> *Falls the night.*
> *Thanks and praise for our days*
> *Neath the sun, neath the stars, neath the sky*
> *As we go, this we know*
> *God is nigh.*

☆ ☆ ☆ ☆

"What do you think, Colonel. Should we take him now?" Sergeant Donny Brewster looked through binoculars at Major Danskill as he marched out of town. The Colonel shook his head.

"Not yet. Let's see where he's going first. I want more intel."

EPILOGUE

THE BLIND MAN PUT THE SATELLITE phone back down on the ebony coffee table. *The Shadow Militia*. He'd heard the name spoken in whispers, but had never believed it to be real.

Jared Thompson motioned with his right forefinger for his assistant to come closer. Sammy Thurmond obeyed him immediately.

"That was Major Danskill from Michigan. Send someone to bring him in for a meeting. I want to handle this personally. It could be important."

Sammy Thurmond moved out of the room, and the blind man was left to ponder. *A small army destroyed by mere peasants? Not likely.* He needed more information. Jared sat down on the couch and reached over to the coffee table for his glass of wine. It was so difficult to get good, French wine these days. The End of Days had played havoc on his wine cellar.

But now, what to do about the Islamic events now unfolding in Dearborn, just east of Detroit. While other states had already come under his control, Michigan was turning out to be a real pain in the butt. Jared picked up the file folder in front of him and pulled out the photo of Imam Abdul al'Kalwi. He was a ruthless man, a charismatic leader, unifying the huge Islamic population, and threatening to conquer all who stood in his way.

Jared took a small sip and placed the photo and the wine goblet back on the ebony coffee table. Yes, he contemplated the many problems he faced. Rednecks rising up in the South; mountain men holding out in the West; a small army of Muslim fanatics threatening to conquer the north, spreading over the land like a Saracen tide; and now, a new enemy came forth: The Shadow Militia.

The blind man took another sip of his wine, then leaned back on the couch and took a nap. Life was just getting interesting.

Coming soon!

The saga continues in

—The Saracen Tide—

Books by Skip Coryell

We Hold These Truths
Bond of Unseen Blood
Church and State
Blood in the Streets
Laughter and Tears
RKBA: Defending the Right to Keep and Bear Arms
Stalking Natalie
The God Virus
The Shadow Militia

Skip Coryell lives with his wife and children in Michigan. He works full time as a professional writer, and "*The Shadow Militia*" is his ninth published book. He is an avid hunter and sportsman, a Marine Corps veteran, and a graduate of Cornerstone University.

For more details on Skip Coryell, or to contact him personally, go to his website at www.skipcoryell.com

Made in the USA
Charleston, SC
18 September 2016